Are Libraries
Obsolete?

WITHDRAWN

ALSO BY MARK Y. HERRING

Fool's Gold: Why the Internet Is No
Substitute for a Library (McFarland, 2007)

Are Libraries Obsolete?

*An Argument for Relevance
in the Digital Age*

MARK Y. HERRING

McFarland & Company, Inc., Publishers
Jefferson, North Carolina

Nihil obstat quominus imprimatur

LIBRARY OF CONGRESS CATALOGUING-IN-PUBLICATION DATA

Herring, Mark Youngblood, 1952–
     Are libraries obsolete? : an argument for relevance in the
digital age / Mark Y. Herring.
        p.   cm.
     Includes bibliographical references and index.

     ISBN 978-0-7864-7356-4 (softcover : acid free paper) ∞
     ISBN 978-1-4766-1591-2 (ebook)

     1. Libraries and the Internet.   2. Libraries—Forecasting.
3. Library science—Forecasting.   I. Title.
Z674.75.I58H47 2014
020.285'4678—dc23   2013050517

BRITISH LIBRARY CATALOGUING DATA ARE AVAILABLE

Cover images © Fuse/iStock/Thinkstock

Edited and designed by Robert Franklin

Manufactured in the United States of America

*McFarland & Company, Inc., Publishers
     Box 611, Jefferson, North Carolina 28640
     www.mcfarlandpub.com*

For Carol

Quos amor verus tenuit, tenebit. —Seneca

Table of Contents

Table of Contents

Preface and Acknowledgments

The changes that have occurred in librarianship over the last decade and a half are more than all the combined changes that have occurred since Dewey. No, I'm not over one hundred years old, but I became a librarian in 1978, so I think I can say with some assurance that the changes I have witnessed over the last fourteen or fifteen years are far more remarkable and long lasting than those theretofore. The question that is on everyone's mind—and it really is on the minds of many librarians though they are reluctant to admit it—is, Are libraries obsolete? That is what this book is about.

I won't answer that question here (I give a strong hint in the Introduction) but let me say what the book is not. This is not a screed against the Internet, though to raise even an air of criticism about the World Wide Web makes some web aficionados hyperventilate. On the other hand, even to hint to some librarians that libraries may possibly be, one day, in some sort of decline that may end in a tailspin that may make them, well, not as robust as they are now—you can see by the convoluted construction how much I'm hedging to avoid their wrath—is to commit the highest form of heresy. My prayer is that I have not offended either side so much that they both hate the work here.

I am not anti-anything in this book, especially when it comes to the web. Look what happened to the much-beloved Jonathan Franzen, now the much hated, after his "What's Wrong with the Modern World" appeared in September 13, 2013, issue of the *Guardian*. The "wrong" is all our device-mania, and twitterverse blew up in his face for that, calling him a curmudgeon, one of the nicer comments. In order to make the case, however, one has to draw a line in the sand. As Flannery O'Connor once said in another context entirely, you sometimes have to write in all capitals before people will notice.

1

Depending on where a reader stands vis-à-vis my line may make him or her call me a Luddite on the one hand, or a Quisling on the other. I have tried to give both sides a fair hearing but the fact of the matter is that, for librarians, this current age is moving against both us and libraries. For those who love the web and all its glory, however, there are, many, many things that we need to fix before we move forward with the replacement. So, to both groups, this book is a bit like Joan Rivers' famous line, "Can we talk?"

On the one hand, the pressure to make the Internet the be-all and end-all of everything in our lives should be obvious by now to anyone who has ever been online. Misconceptions abound about how we can make this work, but enthusiastic supporters of all things web-based are in a delirium to have it replace everything. Librarians have been whistling in the dark a little about this. Our professional organization, the American Library Association, appears at times schizophrenic on the question, on the one hand urging on libraries all kinds of web-based solutions and urging us to be more Google-like, and on the other, worrying if we are obsolete, but careful not to say so explicitly while encouraging us to be all things to all people. My effort here is to talk about the elephant in the room and try to say something useful about him other than he's large and sometimes gets in the way.

Some will complain that this book is nothing more than a bad réchauffé of my previous book, *Fool's Gold: Why the Internet Is No Substitute for a Library*. Everyone's a critic. I can say that the content of this book is as up-to-date as I could make it, and 90 percent or more of all the references are to materials written in the last four years. All of which is to say that the arguments made in *Fool's Gold* appear to be valid today. When discussing the web's quality, breadth and depth, readers may balk that there is some overlap, or it's a distinction without a difference. I, of course, object to that characterization and contend that in order to discuss these things, some reiteration or duplication is necessary. I ask readers' forbearance.

Why me? I have worked in libraries since 1978. I have seen everything from the OCLC's first "update" "send" to Dialog's phone-receiver modem and blue sheets. I coded a web page the hard way, know some pine, and watched as libraries moved from an exclusive print-based operation to one that is rapidly becoming an entirely electronic one. I have written on the topic a lot, and after I penned a piece for *Against the Grain* revisiting the "10 Reasons" in my regular "Red Herrings" column, Robert Franklin of McFarland saw the article and asked me to write this book. So, if anything, let's blame him, shall we?

This book in in three parts, the first of which is a re-visitation of my "10 Reasons Why the Internet Is No Substitute for a Library" that appeared in 2000 in *American Libraries*. While that article, subsequent poster and eventual book by that title all resonated well with anyone in the library profession, not many outside it liked it. By 2010, however, some in the library profession were wondering if any of the points I made in 2001 still rang true. The first part of the book answers that question.

Part Two focuses on four areas that the web has created new problems for and that I think deserve far more scrutiny than have been given: reading, literacy, privacy and piracy. My contention in this part is that these are very serious concerns and if libraries really are to be replaced by the Internet, these four matters have to be resolved first. My biggest fear is that (a) we won't address these matters or (b) simply dismiss them and still move forward with the replacement.

Finally, Part Three looks at the present and the future. Chapter 13 examines where we are now with an eye to the future. Chapter 14 looks squarely in the eye of the future using an environmental scan (an initialism called TEMPLES). One view says, yes, libraries are obsolete after all. The other says, no, and here's why. I do take a side but will leave it for readers who slog their way to Chapter 14.

I do not pretend that I have all the answers. My attempt here is to give one man's impression of what it might be, relying on thirty-five years of academic library experience as a director or a dean at three different institutions, combined with very wide reading in the area.

Writing books is a very solitary experience. My thanks go to a few folks who helped me along the way. Dot Barber is my administrative executive specialist at Winthrop and has worked at Dacus for more than forty years. She kept the office running and my calendar as free as possible so I could make progress on the book over the last year. Michaela Volkmar and Anne Thomas work in our interlibrary loan department and have been instrumental in getting for me about 100 different items, quickly, easily, and efficiently. Although they were not aware of it at the time, others also helped me here at Winthrop: Nancy White in circulation and Carrie Johnston, in library systems. My management team of David Weeks, who runs our Public Services division, and Dr. Ronnie Faulkner, who runs our Technical Services division, took on more responsibilities, too, so I could meet deadlines. Finally, one of our student workers, Erica Truesdale double checked all the weblinks cited in this book to make sure they still worked before this book went to press. Thanks to all.

I have to say a special work of thanks to add to my boss, our provost and vice-president of academic affairs, Dr. Debra Boyd. Dr. Boyd is every dean's perfect boss. She provides guidance when necessary and support always. Of course none of these individuals is in any way to be held accountable for the contents of this book. If any part deserves praise, it is owing to them; all the blame for mistakes or slips of pen is mine alone. Why did I make them? As Johnson once said, when a female companion pointed out errors in his dictionary, "Ignorance madam, pure ignorance." No, I don't have his track record; still, the quote obtains.

I would be greatly remiss if I did not also thank Robert Franklin, president of McFarland. I have complained in the past about the lack of fact-checking in publishing today, but Mr. Franklin and his team have made me eat my words with respect to this book. Any errors that remain in this book are of course my own. But he and his team have done yeoman's work to make this book better and richer. Words cannot express my deep and abiding appreciation for correcting my blunders, repetitions, and [infernal] tendency to obfuscate, all in an effort to make this book the best it can be. I only hope it measures up to their expectations.

Lastly, I owe a huge debt of thanks to my wife of forty years, Carol Lane, who took on more of this book than she did for any of my other eight. Carol is an English teacher (she's been teaching high school English for more than thirty years) and has her own daily responsibilities. Many readers will doubtless empathize with her drudgery when I tell you that she read through this entire manuscript three times at least, and many parts of it four or five times (and, behold, we are still speaking to one another!). If any part of it reads well, it is owing to her keen eye for detail. Whatever part comes across as ham-handed is my voice as I am a very difficult student. While I have dedicated other books to her, and surely she would prefer something more sparkly, it's only right, after all she had done on this book, to dedicate it to her, too.

PART ONE

When I wrote (in 2001) "10 Reasons Why the Internet Is No Substitute for a Library," I hoped to forestall a tsunami of change I feared coming, change that for the most part I didn't think would be good for libraries. As I retell in the first chapter, the article, then the poster, and finally the book all resonated well with some, not so well with others. Over the intervening years, however, more and more readers began to think that my arguments had not held up well with the many and varied digital changes that have since arrived. So, now nearly a decade and a half since the article appeared, I thought revisiting those ten reasons might be a good idea.

What I discovered, surprisingly, is that many of the reasons do in fact, still hold. In this first part, I look again at all ten reasons and assess which ones do hold water, and which ones have sprung a leak. At least eight of the reasons appear to me to be solid defenses of continuing full service libraries for at least another couple of decades. Too many of those eight reasons strike me as important and substantial enough for us to "just chill" a bit before we burn all those library cards. The two remaining reasons, while not exactly dead, are weak enough to argue that they still have some validity but certainly not as much as before. For a scryer to score 80 percent a decade and half later is not all that bad.

What I did not count on, and which occurred just prior to this book going into typesetting at McFarland, was Judge Denny Chin's decision in favor of Google and its massive book scanning project. The decision itself did not surprise me; I rather suspected it would end that way, given all of Google's power and money to outlast any dissenting parties. What caught me off guard was a decision eight years in the making coming right *now*.

The decision has been greeted with an ecstatic Twitterverse, all atwitter, as one would expect. Many librarians also hail this decision as a great one, and why not? Google's success, its very existence, was largely brought to us by the efforts of librarians at huge research universities that made the books for this project possible. So, yay! We now get our Shakespeare courtesy of Viagra ads, or worse. But do we really? Might we also not have to pay in the end? No one knows for sure.

To pick a cliché, the Google decision is a game changer, if it is upheld on appeal. I cannot imagine that it will not be. The Authors Guild, God bless them, does not have enough money to drag it out for long. Now that everyone may well have access to twenty million volumes literally at their fingertips bodes well for the continued growth of MOOCs (the research library part is now taken care of), online classes, big data companies and not so much bricks and mortar libraries, colleges and universities, authors, publishers (big and small) and intellectual property. If Google's approach was, in fact, "fair use," I cannot imagine another copyright case ever going to court again. If Google is "fair use," everything is fair use.

It remains to be seen where all of this will end up, but the writing is ever clearer on the wall. Ask not for whom the bells toll, dear library, it tolls for thee?

I certainly hope not, but it feels, everyday, a little more and more like I'm whistling past a graveyard.

CHAPTER 1

Introduction

Books come about for a lot of reasons, and some of them good ones. Of course, every writer thinks his or her idea is, if not the best one, then certainly in the top five percent of all great books. I am no exception to that vision of grandeur rule. But honestly, this book has a history that may prove of interest to more than just my immediate family.

BRIEF HISTORY OF THIS BOOK

In 1999, when I came to my current job, the institution I serve had been talking about a new library building for at least a decade. Ida Jane Dacus, the current building (then and now), was more than three decades old (now four and a half), and she showed every line and wrinkle. Since our legislature provided funds for "academic buildings," the solution seemed a no-brainer. But one other matter obtruded: in the early 2000s, some very vocal legislators thought the Internet had made libraries obsolete.

All of a sudden, our legislators were so many Steve Jobs. Another legislator opined that "everything was on the Internet so why did our students need a new, big, library building?" Still another had argued that—I am not kidding—we didn't need a library because you could have a central place, and every student who wanted a book—any book—could have it "zapped" to her or him instantly.

Sigh.

Readers will also note the timing of all this coincided rather well with a push in our own profession to combine Information Technology (IT) services with the library itself. In fact, some institutions of higher education had *already* moved the library in with IT and had the library dean or director reporting, not to the vice president of academic affairs or provost, but to the head or director of IT. This only further complicated any argument to the contrary about the importance of libraries. To make matters worse—if they could be—my own institution had seen that very transformation of folding library services into IT before I arrived. It "worked" so poorly that it was rescinded almost as soon as it was implemented.

One fall afternoon, our president called me, said he had a meeting with legislators, and asked if I could come up with a brief piece, bullet points really, that would argue the need for a new library, while refuting the idea that the Internet had replaced it. I said I could (though at the time I wasn't sure what that refutation would look like). When he told me he needed it right away, my heart sank a little.

I began crafting what I thought was a solid defense of libraries, one that focused both on what has made them great and why the Internet could not replace what libraries had done for society for the past two millennia.[1] I sent the piece over and, hearing nothing negative, thought it must have been a little useful.

Over the next six months, I continued to think about this topic. I knew it was important, and I saw throughout librarianship a great deal of confusion, anxiety and even fear about the Internet and its relationship to libraries. Perhaps I could do something else about all this. It's one thing to send "talking points" but quite another to provide something lasting on a wider scale. Was all I had written localized only for this library, or could some larger principles be extrapolated?

"10 Reasons Why the Internet Is No Substitute for a Library"—Outdated? Wrong?

In 2001, I wrote "10 Reasons Why the Internet Is No Substitute for a Library."[2] Wanting it to reach a large audience, I naturally thought of *American Libraries*. The article resonated with many readers. So well, in fact, that *AL* placed it for a time on its persistent links page of about a half dozen other articles that folks kept asking for. Not long after the article appeared, requests for reprints flooded in. *Education Digest* reprinted it, and a few other magazines did, as well. Before long, it turned up in about seven different languages.

A few people wrote to me after it appeared asking if they could get "the poster." One didn't exist, of course, just the article. Eventually I decided to print a poster myself, hoping I could break even on costs. With the poster created and printed, I stepped back and held my breath.[3]

To date, we have sold more than 3,000 copies, all the proceeds going into the library's faculty and staff development funds (and the reason why I have not given the poster away for free when asked). Even today, the poster still sells, though, of course, not as much the first five years after it and the article appeared.

By now you must be thinking that I feel pretty good about myself, and I must admit it was gratifying to have written something that not just relatives said they liked. I was invited to speak at several different venues, some small, some quite large. More than one library organization asked for permission to use the poster, its contents or some facsimile. By now you have guessed there's another shoe to drop.

If you do any sort of writing, you know that such things last only for a while; and sure enough, *abyssus abyssum invocat*, one bad thing follows another, and suddenly, those heady days gave way to headaches. I sensed something was not quite right about the poster and began looking around.

Boing, Boing, the ezine of the cyberpunk culture, so to say, posted a short notice of the poster in 2011. *Boing Boing* is an online group blog that began as a magazine and later morphed into its current blogosphere existence. The blogger simply said he had found the sign in a "quaint library" that had "maybe" six people, three of whom were elderly folks. It's clear what the blogger was trying to say—the poster was wishful thinking. But the comment is as silly as saying that the Internet is a vast wasteland of pornography and online ads. Another blogger posted that it came from a book (which was untrue—the book came later) and that the book was an "amusing read." What followed was a torrent of dozens of comments, some of them, when not outright hateful, were simply sharply critical.

Every critic is, of course, more brilliant than the person he or she criticizes. The unhinged, hysterical nature of some of my critics was troubling. I didn't expect anyone devoted to the Internet to accept without comment any criticisms of it. If you doubt that, look at what happened to Nicholas Carr after his article and subsequent book about the Internet making us stupid appeared. Or Mark Bauerlein and his dumbest generation book, or, before any of us even thought about these matters, Sven Birkerts and his elegies.[4] But I did expect more than mere *ad hominem* arguments.

It's one thing to be criticized by those who worship the Internet and all things digital, but quite another when your own family, in a manner of speaking, takes you to task. I didn't escape that kind of criticism either when Greg Landgraf took off on the piece by damning it with faint praise. While still valid (that is, libraries aren't obsolete), he said that the 10 reasons "had not aged well." All of this got me thinking. Are the 10 reasons no longer true? Was I right then but wrong now? I decided to take another look at the Internet and the ten reasons, and see whether my earlier musings about the web and all things digital are today completely wrong-headed. And that's how this book came about.

REVISITING THE 10 REASONS

The first part of this book will cover the ten reasons again, with an eye to ferretting out whether what I said is still true. Without spoiling the ending, let me say that the reexamination is worth the effort.

The second part of the book can be thought about in one of two ways. Either it can be thought of as more reasons why the Internet is no substitute, or things that libraries either encourage or prevent. These things are critically important because as we inch deeper and deeper into the digital ocean, we need to do so with our eyes wide open. I fear we are going into the deep end of the ocean with our eyes wide shut.

The final part concerns where we are now (Chapter 13), and offers two views on the future (Chapter 14) using a template of strategic analysis to help guide us to see what may be on the librarianship's horizon, and where it might all end up. I'm no scryer, but I think some events, like so many tea leaves, are useful predictors of the future.

As much as anything, readers need to know what this book is not. It is *not* a Luddite screed. I say that every time I write about the web, and it would appear that those who take offense to the holy grail of the Internet being criticized ignore it. It's easier to call names than to dissect arguments. I am not opposed to the Internet, digital documents, online texts, ebooks or the rest. I do think, however, that one has to be aware of what one gains and loses with each new piece of technology. For example, when the printing press rolled around, many feared we'd lose the gorgeous illuminated manuscripts, which, of course, we did. Some argue that their loss was so much good riddance, while others thought losing manuscripts in favor of more books a fair tradeoff. In exchange for cars and the ability to go various places quickly, we got smog, traffic, fatalities and so on while eliminating horses. It isn't that we chose these antipathies; rather, it's what we got when we chose one thing instead of another. Ideas have consequences, both good and bad. To criticize cars doesn't mean you favor the horse and buggy over them.

My interest in writing about the Internet is to bring to the foreground the consequences of moving in this direction, to highlight what we are going to lose in this exchange, and to make sure we think the tradeoffs worth it. If we can't have such conversations without trying to shout down those trying to have them, we're going to be the poorer for it.

But pointing out some risks is no reason to shoot the messenger or question his heredity. If we are going to get this right, we need to know there is a chance it can go really wrong, that it can end very badly. There are times when our exuberance for things digital puts us at risk, and minimizing the inherent risks of the web puts us at greater risk still. For example, the efflo-rescence of hate groups of every stripe has one thing in common other than hate: their once esoteric nature threatened their existence to obsolescence. Unfortunately, with the Internet, that's no longer the case, as it is no longer the case for a considerable number of other awful things, as we shall see.

In a *very* small way, I'm asking in this book the same question T. S. Eliot asked in his great poem "The Rock": "Where is the wisdom we have lost in knowledge? Where is the knowledge we have lost in information?" This isn't merely a trick of the poet playing on words. Some of what we lose on the web is in fact this wisdom, this knowledge, all in favor of nebulous "information." For some, there will be gleeful shouts of joy that we are no longer at that place. Now we can have *everybody's* thoughts and opinions. Perhaps that is so, but do we know that what we're getting is unquestionably better, and that the consequences of the changes outweigh the downsides?

THE WEB IS GREAT, BUT ARE WE ON THE RIGHT TRACK?

While we have certainly gained more with the World Wide Web than perhaps we have lost, has it made our knowing impossible? Weinberger makes a similar point when he argues, "Rather than knowing-by-reducing to what fits in a library or a scientific journal, we are now knowing-by-including every draft of an idea in vast, loosely collected webs."[5] My argument throughout this book is *not* that we need to go back to pre-web days, but that if we are including every "draft of an idea," then we certainly don't need to discard libraries the way many web aficionados advocate.

Alvin Toffler warned about our current state. Years ago, he worried that we will acquire too much information and it will impede our ability to think.

Toffler said that when we are "plunged into a fast and irregularly changing situation, or a novelty-loaded context ... [our] predictive accuracy plummets." We will no longer be able to "reasonably correct assessments on which rational behavior is dependent."[6]

The point Toffler and Weinberger make is that we can become too distracted by information overload. We seem to have forgotten this along the information superhighway, thinking that it does not matter what the threshold is; we can always take in more. As Nicholas Carr argues, however, quite the opposite often occurs. Our minds begin to bail information like so much water from a leaky boat. We not only are unable to hold on to new things, we cannot even follow those things we once took in easily.

While the web is wonderful and provides us with much to which we did not have access before it came along, it also saddles us with much that we may not want but get anyway. We may well be losing the wisdom we have lost in knowledge, as Eliot argued, and the knowledge we have lost in information. The question remains, do we care, and if we do, what are we going to do about it?

We are gored on the horns of a proverbial dilemma. On the one horn, we have the vast information on the Internet. The ability to buy most anything, check a diagnosis, find a support group for something we may be struggling with, pick up new friends we would likely not have met in several lifetimes, and access everything from the genome sequencing, to a map, literally, of the galaxy. On the other horn, an equally pointed one, we have "the unedited mash of rumor, gossip, and lies."[7] We have the web's monstrous mental baubles: Kardashians 24/7 the stupid animal tricks, cats everywhere, and some idiot setting fire to his flatus. Sadly, the web even has the power to distract us completely as with the horrific story of a young couple in 2010 who let their real baby starve while they played a marathon video game of nurturing a virtual baby.[8]

Even those who have great hope for the web, like Clive Thompson, have little hope for the public web, like Facebook, Twitter, and really any source that attracts millions to it because they are too large to make a dint in our social intelligence. But Thompson thinks that, rather than making us stupid, the Internet *could* make us smarter. "At their best, today's digital tools help us see more, retain more, communicate more. At their worst, they leave us prey to the manipulation of the toolmakers."[9] Ah, there's the rub.

The web has become our new "repository" of experts. It is the "go to" source for everyone seeking information. We "Google" our physicians, our ministers, our children, our spouses-to-be. We get medical information, news, hate mail, and pornography. Universities are giving way to the "university of Google" while "librarians are enmeshed in a struggle for a workable vision of a future for their institutions, not only debating the merits of new techniques for navigating collections, but wondering how to weigh the expertise of the crowd against that of those with credentials."[10]

ARE LIBRARIES OBSOLETE AFTER ALL?

This book asks if this is the right way to a secure our library future. Should we jettison libraries in favor of forging ahead with the scant resources we have in the manner that the web provides them, or is there a middle way that extracts the best from both? Everyone has a "megaphone as large and as powerful as the *New York Times* and that includes both geniuses and seriously troubled individuals."[11] Meanwhile, as it connects us with everything and everyone, it is also threatening to shut down newspapers, close libraries, end print publishing, and redirect our most trusted sources of gaining information. Should it ever be controlled by any one person or a group of people, we'd be in serious trouble, indeed. When knowledge access is fragmented, it is hard to control. When it's all in one place, it's easy—or at least easier—to shut off, shut down, or otherwise influence with or without permission, as we are already seeing in totalitarian states. Recall that in Huxley's "brave" world, things are discarded merely because they are, for no other reason, old. In the new world, we're attracted to things because they are elegant, beautiful and, well, new. We don't want people to be attracted to old things.[12]

Knowledge is adiaphorous with respect to the web; it is morally neutral about where it should be housed. But how it is preserved, and where, becomes the debate. Many web aficionados believe that digital is the *only* way to go. That may well be the case eventually, but it is the argument of this book that we aren't there yet. We don't know enough about how this is going to work decades later, and we certainly have many symptoms that suggest it isn't working nearly as well as we thought it would by now. Print may well be on its last legs, a charge we have heard before, but it isn't dead yet. As digital increases with each passing year, the question becomes whether we are preserving it well enough for future generations. Can those future generations get access to it years, decades and centuries from now? Until we know for certain, we need to continue to preserve materials in the near and long terms.[13]

We have very little understanding of the impermanence of the web in our brave new digital world, or we no longer care. The view that the Internet is the be-all and end-all of every information equation is in keeping with the American notion of "one best way" or a silver bullet to solve all problems. The Internet solves one of the many complexities in the information calculus. But to argue that it is the solution to all of them is as silly as saying there is only one solution to any complex issue. Closing libraries or curtailing them because of the Internet is to throw the proverbial baby out with the bathwater. While the Internet may help solve some of the problems in libraries, it may be just a case of exchanging one set of problems for another.[14]

Even space problems in libraries cannot be relieved by the Internet *unless* it remains stable and materials are accessible not only today, but also ten years from now. This potential space-relieving feature of the Internet is likely one reason it has such an appeal to libraries, and why, if it is ultimately unstable, it can become the Achilles heel of librarianship. More than a half a century ago, we knew that the then current growth of libraries was unsustainable. It was predicted then, for example, that the Yale Library would, by 2044, have more than 200,000,000 volumes and occupy more than 6,000 miles of shelf space. If the card catalog had not been replaced, it would contain close to three quarters of a million drawers.[15] Libraries must change, of course, but in what direction and to what extent?

OVERRELIANCE ON CROWDS?

Do we turn everything over to unknown crowds, trusting them to create a better library of knowledge than so-called experts?[16] I don't know the answer to that question, but I do wonder why it must be an either-or question in the first place. Why can't we collaborate? Both groups alone will make mistakes. The Internet, for example, may make us more connected than ever, but while we're talking to more people than ever before, we're also not necessarily communicating.[17] We Americans tend to love the flourishing anecdote and gravitate to that. The web is filled with them, stories of individuals finding their way, finding solutions to problems, getting proper treatment, finding love when it had eluded them for decades. No more celebrated anecdote exists than the one told about Mark Zuckerberg and his art course at Harvard.[18] Zuckerberg had not gone to class, he had not studied. The final was coming up and he was going to flunk the course. So he went to the Internet, downloaded all the images he thought would be on the test and then sent them out to his network of Harvard undergraduates (recall that this was long before

"Facebook" began). They filled in the blank spaces and Zuckerberg "aced" the exam.

Great story. Is this the best use of the web, not cheating exactly, but also not exactly doing your own work? It's one thing to look up the number of miles the moon is from the earth. It's another to use the Internet to pass an exam, answer questions during a phone interview, or cut and paste a paper without attributions. But let's put his act aside for now and ask another question. What, exactly, did the famous Mr. Zuckerberg learn about art history? Granted, he is a very brilliant young man, much smarter than most people even at Harvard. But can we count on his art history background, should we ever have to rely on it? Will his act influence how he thinks about art and its importance in culture, should he ever come to control an important collection of art or even art images? Will it influence how he thinks about storing art in specific or preserving images in general?

I think the same argument can be made about much that we "learn" from the Internet. It *can* be very helpful and provide a solid beginning. It can also be flippant, cursory, error-prone, at least as much as any human endeavor can be, and it does mix together without distinction solid information, misinformation and outright error. Or, as Plato once put it, "everything that deceives may be said to enchant."[19]

AS INFORMATION DOUBLES, KNOWLEDGE HALVES AND WISDOM QUARTERS[20]

The point is that knowledge is not a static body of unchanging facts. Knowledge is more a living organism, growing more or less endogenously, changing shape and size, sometimes modestly, sometimes completely. Sounds like a pitch for something like the Internet, doesn't it? But we will still need those who can help us interpret what we find, and show us where to find it all, and that sounds like a pitch for both libraries and experts. For all the brilliance of Google's algorithms—and it cannot be doubted that the algorithms are brilliant—they still cannot replace human interaction, something Google forbade opting for in favor of a fully automated approach.[21] I would argue that we need both. The Internet can help us get to the jungle faster, but we still need those guides who can help us ferret our way through the underbrush. As Robert Darnton put it, "Information has never been stable. ... It should serve as a corrective to the belief that the speed-up in technological change has catapulted us to a new age...."[22]

I think there is room for both libraries—differently configured with adaptable space for the changes underway and those we anticipate—and the Internet. Both are required and both serve a much needed function that could not otherwise be accomplished without the other. Some will see this as a truism, and perhaps it is. But as Chesterton once said, the trouble with truisms is that they are often really true.[23] We can use both to our best advantage.

Some will doubtless think it hypocritical to criticize the web as I do here in places and yet use it for research. But you don't have to be against healthcare to be against Obamacare. My *cahier de doléances* isn't so much a book of complaints as it is a plea for looking for a marriage instead of one best way. I think we can marry the two approaches to information gathering and preservation—libraries and the web—without having to criticize the one while exalting the other, without having to poke fun at one while praising the other.

Libraries, when compared to the fast sleek and spiffy Internet with all its flashy trappings, appear stolid, somber, lethargic things, filled, at times, with wizened faces and white hair. That shouldn't be a reason to dispense with them or to think they are no longer useful. America worships youth, but given that the vast numbers of baby boomers are hitting retirement, most of America is going to look like a nursing home instead of a playground. Perhaps grey is the new black.

What I fear most, however, is not that libraries are obsolete after all. What I fear is that we are going to make them so, regardless. Marshall McLuhan famously said (he didn't really but it is attributed to him) that we shape our tools, and they shape us ever after. It's hard to think of another case in which his words resonate as prophetically than in this new digital age. We shaped our digital tools, and now they are reshaping us; or perhaps I should say more precisely, they are reshaping our nation's libraries. I do not think this is merely some academic argy-bargy between hysterical librarians on the one hand and Internet lickspittles on the other. These technological tools reshaped our nation's libraries only at the edges at first, but now they are doing so at their very cores. Today, these digital tools are reshaping our libraries by methodically removing them altogether. Whether an unintended consequence or not, the loss of all our nation's libraries may not be merely possible so much as it appears inevitable, despite our once irrepressible print. The question we must ask ourselves before they are gone is, is this what we want? Is this the future for information access we desire?

I would hasten to add that these technological tools are doing the same in virtually (okay, pun intended) every area of our lives that they touch. For example, Massive Open Online Courses (MOOCs in shortspeak) are rapidly changing higher education, for better or for worse. Opinion makers like Thomas Friedman strongly endorse their success.[24] The well-respected American Council on Education (ACE) has endorsed for credit at least five of these courses offered by Coursera, one of the major companies developing such courses, lending more than passing credibility to such classes.[25] It didn't hurt that the initiative had Gates money behind it. So, my question is more than a capricious one academics are wont to make. We're poised not only to change dramatically the way we preserve information, but we're also on the cusp of changing entirely the way we deliver education.

THE INTERNET: PANACEA OR TOOL?

The web isn't wrong-headed. It does, however, create unintended negative consequences that we need to think through. The questions I raise in this book are those about the Internet as a sufficient source for our future nation's repositories of information and/or knowledge. Shouldn't we all rejoice over all these changes? Information is cheaper and literally everywhere. But does this distract us from developing wisdom, as Theobald (the "...Wisdom Quarters" fellow) had it?

In the midst of all this, we're still trying to determine the effectiveness of online reading (more about that in Part Two). Early studies imply it isn't the same, or as robust. We wonder if Google is making us all geniuses or stultified stooges, but we know it compromises our ability to remember (why bother when "everything" is at your fingertips)? Sherry Turkle, meanwhile, argues that while 750 million of us are on Facebook and other social networks, we were all together there, alone, echoing what a decade before Putnam had said about our bowling alone.[26] Perhaps we can agree that the web is an overall good, but does that good exceed all the bad it has wrought?

What troubles me is that none of these things seem to matter much to anyone anymore. We brand individuals who bring up these questions as Luddites and exile them as far from us as possible so their musings won't disturb our cyber-utopia. Digital is our future, no matter what, so shut up, log on, and click your troubles away.

For more than a millennium now, libraries, as most of us over 40 have known them, have served us quite well and quite efficiently. The fear isn't replacing them as most things eventually pass with time: *habent sua fata libelli*. Books have their fates, sure, but must it be an inferior one? My fear is that we are replacing libraries with something writ on water, or rather in cyberspace, which is, by the way, nowhere. Are we replacing libraries with a future that is really better, or only with one that is the easiest to reach? We have to get that part right because we aren't likely to have a chance, or the fortune, to make that decision again.

The biggest roadblock to the future of libraries is that the generation that built these grand things has bequeathed them to a generation that uses them less and less, doesn't particularly like them, and despises the cost involved in keeping them up. While I remain certain that the Internet is no substitute for a library, my view is increasingly a luxury, if not a conflict of interest. Libraries are, to coin Prospero's words, "... such stuff as dreams are made on, and [their] little [lives are] rounded [now] with a sleep." My abiding fear is that we won't really know what we have lost until they are all gone. We're staking everything on this digital age.

I, for one, hope we get this right because we cannot afford to get it wrong.

CHAPTER 2

Everything Is Still Not on the Internet

The first claim I made nearly a decade and half ago is that *not everything is on the Internet*.[1] That assertion was an easy one to make then, and the least criticized of any of the reasons. The Internet was still very young back then, and Google an infant.[2] Of course, everyone still made grand claims for the World Wide Web. Amid all those prognostications lay but a small amount of supporting evidence, as if wishing made it so.

VANNEVAR BUSH AND HIS MEMEX DREAM

The idea of what the web could become, however, was not something everyone had just dreamed up fifteen years ago. Vannevar Bush's dream of Memex as long ago as 1945 may well have started it all.[3] Bush, who was then director of the Office of Scientific Research and Development, envisioned something a little less than a World Wide Web, but one that would function in the same manner. Believe it or not, people in 1945 complained of all that we had to know. Bush wrote:

> There is a growing mountain of research. But there is increased evidence that we are being bogged down today as specialization extends. The investigator is staggered by the findings and conclusions of thousands of other workers—conclusions which he cannot find time to grasp, much less to remember, as they appear. Yet specialization becomes increasingly necessary for progress, and the effort to bridge between disciplines is correspondingly superficial.[4]

What intrigues about Bush's lament is that we are "bogged" down by specialization. It isn't that we will quit thinking for ourselves, or allow others to do it for us, but that we will find a machine that will aid our reflection and

19

education. Moreover, Bush focuses only on *knowledge* that we need to know. Nothing here about stupid human tricks:

> Consider a future device for individual use, which is a sort of mechanized private file *and library*. It needs a name, and, to coin one at random, "memex" will do. A memex is a device in which an individual stores all his books, records, and communications, and which is mechanized so that it may be consulted with exceeding speed and flexibility. It is an enlarged intimate supplement to his memory.[5]

This "memex" device Bush foresaw as something to resort to when we cannot recall something, an *aide-mémoire* if you will, an aid to our reflection, not as a substitute for it. Bush did not necessarily think it would contain everything, but let's allow that he did. He still did not see it as the be-all and end-all. Google on the other hand does see it that way. Its mission from the beginning has been to organize all the world's knowledge, or, rather, "organize *all the world's information* (my emphasis) and make it universally accessible and useful."[6]

Has Google succeeded? It certainly has made a dent in the body of information but hardly exhausted our knowledge. We are a long way from organizing *all the world's* knowledge, and the lack of a discriminating eye on the web makes it far more likely to fail than to succeed. In fact, others are finally seeing that after all. Google just isn't cataloging the world's knowledge as it is simply selling banner ads.[7]

Of course, you have to be *very* careful how you say this. Those who love Google will tell you in no uncertain terms that smart people use it, and if you're not using it, you're an idiot.[8] In point of fact, what's mainly on the web is Western information. Even Google's massive book project has not come anywhere close to what its founders hoped. While it has made headway, moving from a handful of libraries in the beginning to now more than a few dozen major research institutions, it hasn't completed the project. It did, however, deal the sockdolager to copyright when Judge Denny Chin handed it a win under the "fair use" clause.

This isn't the chapter to go into that mare's nest of problems; that will come in a later chapter. But Google, by ignoring copyright, discovered that even a couple of cool dudes in Mountain View can still run aground on a crotchety thing like copyright. The case has only recently been settled in Google's favor, pending appeal. Even with Google's multimillions of digitized books, the complete ones are those in public domain (not unlike the Project Gutenberg before it). The rest remain for now in snippets until appeal.

Collectively, those snippets and those in public domain constitute the world's knowledge... In English.

KNOWLEDGE VERSUS INFORMATION

Further, the question of both "knowledge" on the one hand and "information" on the other is still a debate. This is by no means a new debate, either. Although he meant something a bit more pedestrian than do we, William Cornish wrote about the distinction in his 15th century "A Treatise between Information and Truth."[9] It may have been more pedestrian, but it was no less important and ended in a battle for life and death, literally. Cornish had been beaten up but not officially charged for spreading what were thought to be rumors about Henry VII. Writes Cornish, "For by fals enformacion many tymes among Right shal be reweled and the rightiwuse shall do wrong."[10] That is, false information will even make the righteous do the wrong thing. He goes on to point out that truth has a very difficult time getting things right in a context in which false information is allowed free play. His "cumbrous songe/ [is] priked with force and lettered with wronge."

While our arguments may be about different things—his political, mine informational—they are not so different. When the information calculus is as likely to go wrong as right, right needs all the help it can get. Cluttering the information calculus with a great deal that is either wrong, slightly off base, or simply imbecilic doesn't really help anyone get to knowledge, much less to truth. And yes, I know there are some Pilates out there saying aloud, "What is truth?" Let me say to them what Johnson said to those who would dally in such sophistry: We'll count our spoons when he leaves our table.

For this argument, information appears to be more casual in nature and covers so much ground that it can be anything from the number of square feet in a football field, to videos of cats playing with their tails, or to humans doing, well, unmentionable things. I mention this only because the rise of information to its current glut levels has caused many to call for an Internet 2 that would be free of advertisements, silliness and cute cats.[11] While that characterization is more than a little hyperbolic, the idea was to make of the World Wide Web a more sophisticated educational tool. Think of it this way: Internet 2 is to the Internet what PBS is to television. Internet 2 isn't meant to replace the Internet but to distinguish it from a more popular, and therefore less scholarly, World Wide Web.

But if you combine all of Google and all of Internet 2, and so on, don't you have all of the world's knowledge, or at least enough of it to make the claim that everything really is on the Internet? The answer is still no. Because of the way most people search the web, not everything can be retrieved from it. Although most search engine companies argue that their spiders or robots scour the web daily, weekly or monthly, the fact of the matter is that they do not, and they really cannot, at least not now. Furthermore, no search engine company really wants to. What's missing from these searches is a lot of proprietary information, especially of scholarly work.

Now, some attentive readers are doubtless thinking, "Hasn't he heard of Google Scholar?" The answer is yes, and I am including it in this assertion. Google Scholar, while good, contains only a very, very small fraction of information available on any given topic. It is also, at least for now, more sciences-heavy. To rely only on Google Scholar is to limit oneself to, say, a ready reference shelf in a small science library. The reason I find this a drawback is that too many young people rely only on Google. A few of the smarter ones may move to Google Scholar but stop there. The problem doesn't end with just a matter of falling short, which we could possibly remedy with better training throughout the educational process. Many young people have fallen victim to the hype that everything is on the web.

What's Missing: Proprietary Databases, Invisible Web and More

I work in an academic library. We pay about one million dollars annually for proprietary databases. While *some* of this information is in fact on the web, it's only a tiny percent of the total, and nowhere near all of it. That's because those companies charging for it own it and aren't ready to let it go for free. By virtue of my job, I have access to much of this information; an unaffiliated general user would not. Moreover, it is becoming increasingly common that even those general users, if they gain access inside an academic library, might still not have access to every proprietary database. Some of these databases are so carefully controlled that if a user is not *matriculated* at an institution, he or she cannot gain access to that information.

But let's suppose that one can gain access. Can we then say that Google, or the World Wide Web, has all of the world's information, or at least access to it? Again, no. Almost no surface search engine can seine what is called the "deep" or "invisible web" (the deep or invisible web isn't the same as the dark Internet, which contains sites that can no longer be reached at all). Search engines miss the invisible web because of its structure of a mix of file types—media, graphic intensive, sometimes referred to as "dynamically generated sites"—altogether.[12] Most surface search engines, like Google, cannot search in the manner required by the deep web. While this has changed somewhat since 2001, it hasn't changed dramatically enough to drop the claim completely.

Perhaps a larger question is whether users should care. That is, is there enough information in the deep web to matter? When examined last in 2001, Mike Bergman, founder of BrightPlanet, (a deep web company) and coiner of the phrase "deep web," estimated it to be 400 to 500 times larger than the surface web.[13] Today, it's virtually impossible to say how large it is (some estimate that there are fewer than half a million websites), but let's grant that it is smaller than in 2001. Still, the material on the deep web covers everything from agriculture to education, and lifestyles to literature, and so on.[14] Devine and Egger-Sider, two researchers who wrote first about the invisible web, have looked at it again and contend that it is so rich, and so detailed that it should be a staple subject in information literacy courses.[15] Considerable value indeed.

Much information about companies, too, is just not available. Some companies prefer not to publish their information, at least not on the web. While the number of companies not disclosing is much smaller than a decade and half ago, the point remains true. Too often, companies publish only PR, feel-good reports on the web. This material, if not blatantly propagandistic in nature then certainly not the whole story, leaves users to fend for themselves to find the truth.

A more serious problem for the web is its crowd-pleasing ways. Even when material appears on it, there is no guarantee that it will be there in a month, two months, a year, much less fifteen years later. Moreover, there is no guarantee that it will appear again in a search performed the same way a week, a month, or a year later. Individuals post materials, but they do not always continue to tend these posts later. We all begin energetically enough, then we fall away with other more pressing concerns. Even companies owning proprietary databases will add certain items only to remove them later for more current or popular ones. Digitization projects, which add immeasurably to the web, may begin one way and end another, leaving the material hanging in cyberspace. Microsoft, it will be recalled, began a large-scale book scanning project only to drop out after several years.

Those with tastes outside the mainstream will also find the web not much to their liking. This may sound strange since it is the web after all that brings together so many individuals—including some that should *not* be brought together. Still, esoteric tastes may well find a home on the web, but they will likely have to build it first.

Earlier in this chapter I quoted from William Cornish's 15th century text on information and truth. The citation is to a website. Let me say that the richness of the web is a marvel to anyone paying attention. The web is a rich variety of the scholarly, popular and terribly inane. I would be the last to dismiss the web as ineffective or otiose in any degree (save as a substitute for a library).

Moreover, if you continue to search Cornish, you'll even find a link to the British Library and one of its 15th century texts of the actual poem or song. One can even page though that text. Granted, I could have found this citation through various traditional text searches and may even have found the poem itself.[16] That certainly would have taken much longer than the few minutes it did on the Internet. Isn't this enough to discount my contention that not everything is on the web? "Okay, okay," some of you are saying, "maybe not *everything* but close to it."

Yes and no. The web is great in its enthusiasms, but those enthusiasms have a way of waning. Maybe not today, but next week or next month, or next year, it may well no longer be there. How long materials have been on the web often determines whether it remains. Despite what politicians might think, one cannot digitize materials without immediate and ongoing costs. Once online, without continued care and visitation, the site will go dark. I'm not arguing that this problem is one that threatens the existence of the Internet. On the contrary, it's hardly noticed until you look for something you found last month but cannot find today.

It is a problem, and one that commercialization of sites is not helping. Commercialized sites crowd out those without any support at all, and once again only the most popular survive (survival of the most liked, as it were). I'll save the disappearance of digitized sites for a later discussion, as well as the subject of re-mastering what's already been digitized.

Some may argue that the very presence of the deep web militates against my argument that not everything is on the Internet. I can understand this argument. It is certainly better that the deep web is present at all than missing altogether, but given the way surface engines work, it may as well not be on the web for the vast majority of Internet users. Many researchers are missing detailed helpful knowledge from the rich detail of the deep web, either because they are unaware of it, or think surface engines are capturing all they need to know. I'm not discounting that even the deep web will appear on surface engines but until then, not everything is on the web.

Even the presence of Google Scholar, mentioned earlier, and other academic attempts to add to the web fall short, and they do not begin to provide both the access and the breadth and depth of a strong library. If we are able to realize fully Robert Darnton's "Digital Public Library of America" (http://dp.la/), it will not be dollars alone that shortchange us but a combination of funding, legal issues and user preferences.[17] Meanwhile, I submit that there is a difference between looking at a computer screen and thinking that's all there is, and looking at multiple floors of a library building and knowing you've only touched the surface.

So Let's Just Scuttle the Web? Of Course Not

Now, none of these things taken separately—misinformation, for lack of a better word, disinformation, the deep web, and impermanence—add up to much, but added together they do create a sizable gap in the loss or lack of oversight of information. To pretend that the web has all one needs is to define research needs narrowly.

The web is abundant with information. It is also abundant with so much schlock and nonsense that it often boggles the mind. We have apparently made the decision that we prefer convenience over everything else and so will take the one and tolerate the other, but the point I made years ago is still largely true. Take away all the nation's libraries and all you'll have is a surface web. Make no mistake about it: That surface web is very generously filled with a great deal of information (and misinformation as well as disinformation) that will suffice for most elementary searches and some slightly more in-depth ones. *Wikipedia* has its place and makes for a wonderful *starting point* for any beginning research. To rely on it or the web as if that's all there is, is to be satisfied with the first aisle in the vast storehouse of knowledge. As Weinberger argues, "Our system of knowledge is a clever adaptation to the fact that our environment is too big to be known by any one person."[18] It is also too big to be known by any one version of the web, either.

This brings us to another point that Weinberger focuses on, what he calls "the new institution of knowledge."[19] What libraries house and what the web now provides are really two different ways of looking at knowledge. Or rather, one looks at knowledge, the other at information. One can argue that they are the same, but I prefer to think of them as the difference between raw data—the web—and analyzed information, knowledge if you will—what libraries have traditionally housed. I say this because for all of my career, now covering the last thirty-five years, no academic library I worked in gathered vanity knowledge. Self-published materials were the bane of our existence. Public libraries, to be sure, defined the base more broadly while special libraries narrowed the definition further still. Libraries collected the best and brightest, though some less charitable individuals will call that elitist. Think of it this way: the Internet collects so much noise, while libraries have always tried to collect the signals.[20]

The web makes everyone equal to Einstein, or Einstein equal to everyone else. Such an approach appeals to the American sense of equity and fairness. We're all the same, really. But honestly, we're not. We have those in the top 2 percent of intelligence, income, and so on. I cannot do what Bill Gates does or the late Steve Jobs did, and neither can I make money like Donald Trump (or Gates or Jobs). These are distinctions with rather large differences. And to argue that any child can become Bill Gates or Steve Jobs or Steven Pinker or any number of other highly talented individuals is simply to ignore a host of factors that make us all different.

Knowledge is the same way. Some of it is worth knowing while other parts of it are just so much intellectual clutter. To contend that what *The Onion* provides is equal to what *The New York Times* provides is just to be argumentative. The "boundary free" (Weinberger's phrase) web creates a new kind of information source for us that can both hinder and help. The fact that everyone, regardless of his or her abilities, can add something, however slight, is a new way of thinking about how we build on what we know. It also makes, as Weinberger's other famous book had it, everything miscellaneous.[21]

Further, this approach, which favors any of us over the expert, or to put it another way, makes anyone equal to an expert, also provides a new way of looking at knowledge. It means that we will accept something that we may later have to reject. It isn't that we haven't had to do this before. Immensely intelligent and expert individuals have had really bad ideas.[22] But it does mean that we will have to kick-start our information base more often than not because not everyone brings to a subject the same background and education.

This will lead us to yet another way of thinking about how we build our information base: relying on the non-experts (Weinberger calls them "other-credentialed"). Many web commentators not only think this is great news for us but also that this is the only way to go. Clay Shirky, Jeff Jarvis, Peter

Morville, Clive Thompson, and Bill Tancer see this democratization as a better approach to our ongoing knowledge-building. But others, Cass Sustein, Shirley Turkle, Mark Bauerlein and Nicholas Carr, aren't so sure. I can't speak for anyone but myself, but I find the approach of using the less informed or the ill-informed to be less precise and more error-prone. Not exactly a recipe for getting at the world's *knowledge*, but more at the world's *chatter*.

THE UNSETTLED NATURE OF KNOWING

Lastly, this approach leaves all of knowledge very unsettled. Some might laughingly say that it was never anything but unsettled, and that may be true to a certain extent. But I would argue that before the web, we developed the knowledge base, perhaps not always linearly but certainly fully, and we always knew we weren't *there* yet. I'm not so sure any more that we understand this when we look at the web. The fact that some say we no longer need libraries is a good clue that some think we are already there. If everything really is miscellaneous, then perhaps there isn't a base of knowledge, just a morass of data, of information, made up of the good, the bad and the ugly. Weinberger and others would say I am simply feeling the effects of a new regime. I would agree, but I feel it more along the lines of what the Romans must have felt when the Visigoths arrived. Well, okay, not quite that bad.

Those who are under thirty will laugh at this and say this is only a function of my age. Yet to jettison the very structure which got us to this place— libraries—in the pursuit of knowledge for a structureless, loosely coupled approach isn't so much wrong as it may be careless. Libraries appear as plodding, crustaceous barnacles on the sleek, fast-moving Google ship. We need the ramped up web that can undo a mistake in a matter of nanoseconds. While that is very true, no one seems to mind that it can also create a spate of errors in the same amount of time. The web, when humming well, is fast and convenient. When off-kilter, it remains very fast but also very inconvenient. In another time, plodding won the race. Today, only speed matters.

But if everything is not on the Internet, can one really argue that libraries are that much better? Even if our "model library" is the Library of Congress—and not just anyone can use it easily—would we be so ill-informed to argue that it contains all there is?

Of course not. Libraries don't have everything either, and this would be especially true of those that are in every hamlet in the country. So, isn't the web, right there at your fingertips, much better?

Quite possibly, but that assumes everyone has access to the web, which of course is untrue. In fact, *libraries* account for almost 35 percent of all Internet access outside the home. Take libraries away and replace them with the Internet and the gulf between those who have and those who do not, just doubled in size. Then there is that 15 percent who have not been on the web and never intend to go on it. Do we just count them out because they refuse to drive the Information Superhighway?

Libraries have never held everything, and librarians have never argued they did. No one argued that what's housed under library roofs is all there is. On the contrary, they remained symbols of what is possible, of our progress toward knowledge, of what is the beginning but also the best one could find for just about any research project. Although the web has certainly made research easier (i.e., more convenient, especially when it comes to quick facts), I would argue that book for book, an academic library, even a small one, is better for ongoing research than the sprawling web alone. Our university students prove that to us every day when, after hours of searching on Google, they come to the reference desk, typically frantic, asking and even begging for help. They do not always get it in nanoseconds, but they do get the guidance they need quickly enough. Unfortunately, this is but a small fraction of our students. Many of them are content to use whatever they find on the web, take all of it as fact, and hope for the best.[23] Of course, we can train students to work better and smarter. But no amount of hectoring from librarians will change what students regularly do when pressed for time, and what their culture encourages daily. When everyone around them is pointing and clicking, they feel they have to do the same. And it isn't just students, but everyone seeking information. Part of the problem is the fault of librarians and how they have sold themselves to users (more on this later). Even granting this, our poor sales job isn't the whole story.

This says nothing about *how convenient libraries are,* but it does say that if you're doing research, serious research, and not quick facts or factoid hunting, a library with librarians overrules the unfettered Internet. Perhaps you can't do all your research in your pajamas in a library (students at our institution disprove that claim every year at exam time), but is that so bad? My main point then and now remains unchanged: Too many people think everything is on the web, and that assertion hurts everyone, especially those who are led to believe they can rely exclusively on it. This isn't a question of either-or. We need both libraries and the web.

Isn't All This Just Stuff and Nonsense?

Are arguments of this kind so much stuff and nonsense? Do people really think the web has everything? Sadly, it is true, and said by people who should know better. Even professors make the case, although they are about evenly divided between those who think the web is the devil in disguise, and those who see it as the new messiah. *My argument is that it is neither.* It is, rather, another tool in a large toolbox that helps us find our way through the arabesque of knowing. My complaint against the web is that its promoters seek to offer it up as a substitute for libraries, a replacement for them. My argument is quite the opposite. It is surely a grand and wonderful *addition* to our efforts to democratize our pursuit of knowledge. One would be silly to avoid it, and stupid to overlook it. But to take it, even in all its glorious, chaotic, capricious topsy-turveydom, as a very good substitute for a library is simply nonsense. It is a fabulous tool, but it should not be the only tool, and we certainly should not grab it alone and throw away the toolbox. It helps enormously on some things, on others, much less so. In that way it is much like everything else in the world, *including* libraries. Libraries are wonderful repositories, but as we shall see in the third part of this book, they have their own inherent problems. Can't we all just get along, as the late Rodney Strong once famously said?

Apparently not.

Sociologist Aleks Krotoski's book on untangling the web makes the case that web has its faults but is on balance an altogether good thing.[24] I would add that the web has brought us as much bad as it has good. While it has made access to information, data, easier, it has also made more complex our lives in dealing with that data, trying to find out what it means, and keeping ourselves private to any extent at all. Amid all the benefits are gallons of bilge water unfit for human consumption. In any case, it isn't a substitute for a library.

I believe that the Internet has certainly made a good claim for providing access to much more than many libraries could ever hope to. At the same time, I hope I am making a case here that even in the 21st century having this access alone is hardly the panacea for our knowledge deficit. In fact, it may even worsen it.

CHAPTER 3

Searching the Web

Next in my *cahier de doléances* is the contention that the web is a mile wide and an inch deep, and searching it isn't easy. When I asserted this in 2001, the bone of contention could not have been more solid. The Internet is larger now, of course, but is it any better? Certainly is has improved (its depth, to be treated later), but it is not, as asserted in the previous chapter, the sum total of all knowledge, *Wikipedia* notwithstanding. While the previous chapter dealt with the width of the Internet, this chapter focuses on searching results. Regardless of which one is under discussion, despite the robust algorithms in many search engines, how one searches the web, and how those results show up, make all the difference.

KNOWING WHERE BUT ALSO KNOWING HOW

One of the complaints I and others have had about the web is the impression it gives that we can simply plug in what we want and get it instantly. In some ways, this is true and it would be silly to argue otherwise. Looking for a fact or factoid, it's likely many users will turn to the web first. It's quick and convenient, and often accurate. And while it is not altogether as reliable as a scholarly study, depending on the topic, the web proves reliable enough for most searches, especially if the search is one the user has some knowledge about.

The trouble comes when users step outside their intellectual comfort zone. This is less likely the case in printed sources but not altogether absent. There have been, in recent years, a number of bone-headed mistakes made in print. Let's face it: fact-checking at publishing houses is not what it used to be. Some would argue that this loss of solid fact-checking is a product of an omnipresent web. Since anyone can do it, why should publishers pay to have someone else worry over it? The web, after all, is at *everyone's* fingertips, and since *everything* is on the web anyway (or so the argument goes), publishers, looking hard for ways to cut costs, have cut them in the area of fact-checking. It's a plausible argument, as far as it goes. Fact-checking, however, began to wane long before the web was up and running, so the web isn't to blame completely for this loss. In any event, because the Internet makes searching easy and because we like to think it is without error, searching outside one's intellectual comfort zone can create problems.

The free text language of the web makes it a wonderful tool for searching various kinds of information. In some ways, online searching spoils us for using other search interfaces. For example, proprietary aggregate databases of scholarly articles most certainly *do not* permit a search in this manner. Almost every one of them requires some learning curve—some databases are easy to search, some difficult—in order to master them with any degree of efficiency. So, web-searching makes it very difficult to search other interfaces. Users get into the habit of searching one way and fail to remember what is required in another, thereby losing out on valuable information, although it's available. But this is less a problem with the web and perhaps more the problem of those other interfaces. Perhaps they should adopt a more open and accessible "ambient findability" that the web has.[1]

So, what's the matter with searching on the web and the results it returns? First, the how of its searching. In Google's case (and just about all other search engines), it's a combination of things: it's Googlebot, algorithms, page rank, web-crawling and more.[2] Google doesn't crawl the entire web, nor does any other search engine. But Google, and many others like Bing, cover billions of individual web pages. We can carp about how many—there may be as many as a trillion pages on the web now—but suffice it to say that with the exception of the "invisible web" (a point made in the last chapter), pages generated on the fly from large databases, pages from large newspaper pages on forums or blogs (although you can search blogs separately on Google), the searching interface is robust, searching a sizable portion of the web. Most search engines take some months to crawl the web, too, but most of them accomplish this task in a few weeks, perhaps a month or so at most, and any updates are a few days to a few weeks, to a month old.[3] This is both good and bad news. While it certainly may be more *current* than information one might find in a print encyclopedia, it may not be as reliable.

GOOGLE: THE LIBRARIAN'S FRIEND OR COMPETITOR?

With the addition of Knowledge Graph, Google provides yet another layer of searching.[4] The results appear just to the right of searches in a box or frame-like display. This provides much more to the novice searcher, trying to predict what the user wants and providing her with possible solutions to the query. It's a very bold and strikingly successful approach to interpreting the results. Google has for a long time matched the query with web results that were close. But the results are best guesses. Knowledge Graph now goes one step further, acting as an interpreter, but isn't without its own interpretation problems.[5] In a way, Knowledge Graph, which appeared with little fanfare outside of Google (as Google's video rollout made grand claims), elbows its way into the arena of reference librarian. As one critic observes, "Just as it is critical to understand decisions Google makes on our behalf when we use it to search the web, we must be critically aware of the claim to a newly authoritative, editorial role Google is quietly staking with Knowledge Graph—whether it means to be claiming that role or not."[6] It's a very important step that infringes—if that's the right word—on the role of the librarian. While the results are robust and quite good, the question remains whether the unwary user has the knowledge depth or understanding to know which of the results to peruse, and which not. Or, even whether to question the results at all. It is this kind of interpreting without human intervention that may have led to Amazon's infamous t-shirt debacle of "Keep calm and rape a lot."[7] Even with Google's new and more robust so-called "Hummingbird" algorithm, the changes made to fit the mobile environment may not yield the best results for more than mere casual searchers.[8]

Some results on search engines refer to *Wikipedia*. *Wikipedia* has undergone significant changes since 2001, and it is much more reliable now than it was then. Back in 2001, the entries had a higher than average yield of errors, misinformation and disinformation. This is less and less true, and that's a good thing since Wikipedia is now one of the most used encyclopedias in the world. In 2011, studies of *Wikipedia* and *Britannica* using mainly scientific articles yielded similar results. The longer *Britannica* articles were more thorough and more accurate on balance, but not by very much. In fact, it may be a distinction without a difference. *Wikipedia* has also improved its reliability. It still suffers, however, from what I'll call the Seigenthaler Effect.[9]

SEIGENTHALER EFFECT AND HOW IT ENTANGLES THE WEB

In May of 2005, an article about John Seigenthaler, the famous newspaper editor, appeared in *Wikipedia*. One of the biographical facts about him linked him with the assassinations of both Robert and John Kennedy, a particularly virulent and defamatory bit of rumor especially since Seigenthaler was devoted to the Kennedys and served on Kennedy's presidential campaign. Although this egregious error was later corrected, some similar, though less inflammatory errors have appeared about various individuals over the years, causing significant hurt, some damage and considerable misinformation. While the articles are generally corrected sooner rather than later on various online encyclopedias, the damage is often done and takes considerably more time to undo the error than to create it.

Wikipedia has gone to great lengths to correct problems of this kind and has successfully minimized—though not eliminated—the possibility of errors. Unfortunately, the open web, because it is both uncontrolled and very large, is much less likely to correct errors. Moreover, information about political candidates, especially during elections, is not as reliable as good printed sources. The argument in this case is that one is less likely to be slandered in print because of the inherent controls that prohibit that possibility. No one impedes the disgruntled voter from posting whatever she wants to. The web prides itself on being unfettered and uncontrolled. It further prides itself on the lack of any quality controls. This has become its blessing and its curse.

The problem for the unwary user is this: Which sites can we trust and which not? In a world of literally *millions* of sites, which ones can we rely on when our own knowledge base is weak in a certain areas? In a library, we're told. On the Internet, we are also told, but our informant may as easily be the Unabomber as easily as some budding Einstein.

The simple answer is that there is no simple answer, and searching on the web, while not a crapshoot by any stretch of the imagination, is risky. We cannot hope for a 100 percent error-free source anywhere. Infallibility is for theologians, but we like to think every effort has been made to prevent errors from creeping in. In the case of the web, the argument is less about errors and more about voices and convenience. As Weinberger points out, it's a choice about how we look at information. If democratization (though not necessarily discrimination) of information sources and many, many views are what we want, then the web is infinitely better than any printed source. If an error-free, authoritative source is more to our liking, then print sources are the avenue of choice. The problem today is that the choice is less between those two and more along the lines of a kind of ultimatum: we have the web, we don't need anything else, so learn to live with it. Well, we're trying.

In the absence of permanent uniform resource locators (PURL), searching the web isn't easy for most search engines, or at least for those that 95 percent of us use. While this is not an inordinately large problem, it is a problem; and until the web moves to permanent URLs (it's getting there), some information will be missed. Worse, it might show up one time and then, a week later, won't be in the search results at all, making you feel for a moment as if you've lost your mind.

Page ranking plays a role in web searching, too. While many search engines create an index not unlike the one at the end of this book, returning those results alphabetically would not be very helpful. Nor would other ways you could think of: size of the site, number of times the words are searched for, when searched, and so on. Search engines like Google rank the pages, and Google's page ranking has become legendary. It's so legendary that the full details of how that ranking works are a proprietary secret. It's the main reason that Google is one of the most effective search engines around.[10]

Suffice it to say, the rankings in Google (PageRank Algorithm) are a popularity contest, and they deliver surprisingly good results. But there's a problem. Intelligent web users can make their pages artificially more popular. Early on, one element in the rank of page had to do with referrals. If the referrals were all from noted scholars, it would be hard to find a better source. The referrals are not all made up of subject experts, of course, but, well, of anyone.

Underlying all this, however, is an overlooked fact. What comes up first, or even in the first dozen hits, aren't necessarily the best ones available. And Google's "I'm feeling lucky" approach, while funny and so very hip, may not be the best way to go, unless what we want is commonly known information anyway. Herein lies the problem from a researcher's point of view. The fact of the matter is that very few of us go beyond more than three screens. In fact, *one* screen of returns is pretty much the limit for most people searching the web. What happens if the best links to what you want to know are on the second screen, or fourth or fifth one? Well, you just got unlucky. When it's a needle we're looking for and the haystack isn't even in the field we're looking in—or even one nearby—then we're not going to find it. In fact, we may never find it, but we won't know that unless we're willing to plod through multiple screens of "hits" and look closely at each of them to be sure.

Wanting a Fish You Get the Ocean

This could well be a case of *embarras de richesses* but it's really more of dropping a net for fish and getting the entire ocean. Although the "I'm feeling lucky" approach can work, it's a toss-up when what we want is a bit more recondite than the mere factoid. Many search engines like Google dismiss word order and capitalization, but these can be important in more specialized searches that look for specific information. A quick look at any search engine's "about searching" should clear up things, like when and when not to use quotes and how to use Boolean operators. Misuses of these terms can short-circuit a search. But really, how many people read these pages before searching?

Nothing, however, beats a good search strategy. This is, of course, something librarians live and breathe, and nothing can make a search faster and more efficient than having a good librarian at your elbow. Like some lesser search engines, not all librarians are equal, but most of them are quite well-versed in searching databases and can be immensely helpful in directing a search.

Some useful tips that librarians know only too well include things like spending a few minutes thinking about what is being looked for. What are some key words and/or terms that best describe it? What other words or terms could be used to describe it? Often looking up what is known about a topic in a thesaurus will help suggest other terms. Google, for example, allows up to 32 words in a search.[11] Better yet, take a quick look at an encyclopedia article to get an overview of the subject. Well, yes, *Wikipedia* is acceptable, but it might not be as quick as looking it up in a print encyclopedia only because the print version will not have four dozen links to other subjects that may or may not be relevant. Rather, the print article will have an in-depth overview with related subjects at the end. What can be gleaned from that article coupled with the related articles provides ample background to search a subject with which one is only remotely familiar. Moreover, such a strategy helps the user to eliminate sites that are not authoritative.

Next, put this together in a query. A quick look at the first few screens should provide enough information to know whether a restart is needed, whether the search is headed down the right track, or what fine-tuning is required. It's a good idea to save search strategies in case they are needed later. Most search engines allow saved search approaches that run periodically and notify the user.

What I have just described is not what most people do when online. In most cases, the search or "information gathering" relies on prior knowledge.[12] Since most web browsers may in fact impede this process, users are left with whatever they find by hit or miss, literally. Many either find the whole experience frustrating, or they will "settle" for whatever comes up, even though it may not be what they wanted. The fact of the matter is, however, that what we search for online is rarely this complicated. When it isn't cute cats or vampires, a celebrity or a celebrity scandal, porn, a purchase of some kind, the number of research queries is small in comparison. For most web users, this is fine, but when the subject matter happens to be something more than marginally important, the need for precision becomes more than casually important. Once that occurs, it then becomes a matter of both reliability and verifiability. It's one thing to find fifty links to a certain topic; it's another to know which of the fifty links on, say, evolution are by scientists, which are by creationists, and which are by eighth graders.

One might argue that this is an easy step to discern, but it isn't. North Korea and China have been duped by something as plain to Westerners as satire. What is not as plain are the kinds of mistakes that can be made by quite intelligent people. Pierre Salinger, for example, once famously based his public comments on what happened to a site constructed by, for lack of a better word, nutcases. I made passing reference earlier to the Seigenthaler Effect, but the web's "problem" with reliability and verifiability goes deeper than this because its glory is its insistence on giving everyone a voice, whether that voice knows what it's talking about. Think again of Peter Steiner's famous *New Yorker* talking dogs cartoon: on the Internet, nobody knows you're a dog.

Google "knols" provided a better avenue for reliable information. These were pages written by experts on a wide variety of subjects. While a very rich and helpful source, one first had to know they existed, secondly to know where they were located.[13] Google knol was Google's answer to *Wikipedia* in some ways since each page gave users a chance to see who wrote the page and to review his or her qualifications. At least that was the original idea. Some now argue that it began as a Wikipedia killer and became little more than a Craigslist.[14] At least it tried to be helpful. One annoying feature was the rating scale (1–5) that appeared on the page, allowing users to rate the contribution. "Annoying" because it could not be known who these users were and what *their* qualifications were for making the ratings. Joe Six-Pack may weigh in on cold fusion, but I'd like to know more about his background before I trust his lead. Unfortunately, Google knols are now defunct.

The Web's Strength Is Also a Weakness

The open web on the other hand isn't like this at all, in the sense that there is no attempt to make it less anonymous. If anything, we want it completely anonymous. Anyone can post anything, and users are ill-equipped to know whether what they find is from a reliable, qualified individual. Again, if looking for common knowledge, a factoid, or checking on the latest tidbit about *American Idol*, this kind of crowdsourcing isn't much of a problem. But for more important and critical knowledge, it does become increasingly important. Of course, given our current state of K–12 education, even the so-called common factoid might become a *pons asinorum* for some. In at least one case, there may be evidence of bias on the part of Google News results. Robert Epstein, whose work examines how search engines can influence elections, argues his articles do not appear in the results of Google News, the largest of news aggregators, although articles referring to it do.[15] Google declined comment on the story when it appeared. If true, this would add yet another layer of online searching imbroglios.

Contrast all of this with what one might find in a good academic library. Not only will there be ample sources not yet on the web to consult (at least for the near term), but there will also be knowledgeable librarians on hand to assist in that process. Further, most libraries will have something akin to federated searching in which one can use a single search strategy to cut across multiple databases to return the best one to use. This not only saves times, but it also provides at a glance where the best haystacks are that are also likely to hold the needles sought.[16]

Search engines like Google understood this, and when Calacanis compared Google's early attempts at searching to a steam roller without any humanity in it, Google took exception.[17] But it did not change the fact that the searching is based on 1s and 0s and not on any human element. The reference interview, of course, does just this. Reference interviews are *démodé*, out of date, in our brave new world. Users have jettisoned them in favor of the speed and convenience of search engines and instant gratification, even if that gratification later turns out to be wrong.[18] We cannot blame the web for this but we can bewail the loss of the human touch, the human interaction, and the human collaboration that brings about well-refined results.

What libraries cannot do, however, in the search context but may well have to in order to keep up, is analyze what users are searching and why. Librarians have long looked at failed searches in online catalogs to ascertain why they failed, but only large search engines on the web gather data and mine it in ways that may or may not be useful.[19] Data mining is becoming—make that has become—a new cottage industry that is no longer in a cottage but rapidly becoming its own palace. Looking at what people do online tells us something about ourselves and our culture, including some things we do not necessarily wish to know, or rather wish we didn't. While the data isn't yet tied to particular users (but it is on Amazon and other sites, a trend that will be reexamined in Part II), it is interesting enough even in the aggregate to look at. Exactly what it tells us is another story.

HUMAN INTERVENTION ISN'T A BAD THING

Libraries, as mentioned above, have been looking at what users search for in order to make the search calculus more successful, yet knowing what you have in those results isn't the whole story. For example, we look at failed searches routinely but cannot really tell why they failed. Were students just meandering about, looking for something specific that we didn't have, or just shooting in the dark? How does one tease out from these results those who really want this information, and those who are merely curious about it? Data-mining by search engines and others may yield data they can sell, but what it tells the buyer may be useless. In any event, is this what we want from our knowledge provider: our searches used against us?

Add to this what Jakob Nielsen calls "participation inequality."[20] While he uses this term in reference to blogs, it spills over into what people search for. Those who search for celebrity information may, for example, have more time on their hands and hence can surf more often than those looking for information on alternative energy, or Dante's *terza rima*. I know in my own case that I am more likely to write a critical review of a bad restaurant or retail experience than I am a very good one. I don't think I am necessarily any more carping than the next person. It's just our nature to be unhappy about an occasion when the *expectation* is to be satisfied. But this tendency slants the negative over the positive in most cases. For this reason, we should be wary of choosing books or movies based on reviews of both found online in either "Amazon" or "Rotten Tomatoes." It's not that either one is always wrong but because those willing to write such things may not be the best qualified to do so. They may have an axe to grind, or may not have read what they are commenting on in the first place.[21] It's possible to get the right information, but we must (a) know that the more easily found places may not be the best and (b) be willing to look for them carefully, not just accept what appears first.

In any event, it is my contention that an information delivery systems made up of mainly this kind of information will be hard-pressed in the long run to replace a library. I will leave off, for now anyway, any of the philosophical discussions of whether we should want this to be the main source to help us produce a "well-informed" citizenry. Web users are at the mercy of an ocean of links and most, when they know what they're doing, find the experience overwhelming. We must do what most of us are unwilling to do: cull through many hits until we find the best ones.[22]

WANTING MORE, BEING SATISFIED WITH LESS

I can hear some critics carping already that even if this is the case, so what? Many people are satisfied with this approach and find what they need well enough. But this is not my experience in working with young people on an academic campus. For example, many students come to the desk frantic after searching Google for literally hours and finding nothing. After ten or fifteen minutes with one of our reference librarians, they have exactly what they want. The reason for this is that what they want is very specific and very detailed information, something the web can generate eventually, but a skilled researcher can help find in minutes.

While both approaches are needed, the more detailed and precise approach takes time, effort and human intervention. As the web matures, so will its content and discovery tools. Until then, what we have on the web will work for some and not for others. Still, it isn't ready to replace our nation's library network or its librarians. At the same time, I am fully aware that "the owners of information no longer own [or control] the organization of that information. Control has already changed hands. The new rules of the information jungle are in effect, transforming the landscape in which we work, buy, learn, vote, and play."[23] The overriding question of this book is this: Is this what we want, or is this rather what we are settling for?

In addition to ranking issues, there is also the problem of commercialization, an issue in web searching that is escalating. Google, Amazon, Bing and more all use search inquiries—yours, mine, others—to generate *their* income. In one sense, we're all working for them since we're helping pay their way. And protestations to the contrary, while it may not be a big deal to some, gathering data on my searches for a search engine's profit is not exactly what

I bargained for. Perhaps a case could be made that placing ads strategically on pages based on data analysis is helpful to some. What isn't helpful are the banners, ads and whatnot that clutter search pages so maniacally ADD as to make the experience more than a little unpleasant. Yes, some search engines have made concerted attempts to reduce pop-up ads. But replacing these ads with results that have been otherwise manipulated to get their first isn't much better. *Some* better alternative must be sought to monetize the web, but we're left with this one because users have allowed it and not demanded better.

The astonishing amount of money made by these companies, too, creates another problem inherent in the search calculus. It reduces to two or three the really effective search engines. Further, what they buy or are willing to buy out, reduces our options. I am, for example, delighted that Bill Gates decided to buy and preserve the 20 million or so photographs and negatives of the Bettmann Archive. What I'm not so happy about is what he may do with it and how he will control—and he must really, to get a return on his investment—access to it. This is our life now in the digital world. Information in all its glorious, anfractuous abundance is now controlled on the web in ways we users have little say in. Some may argue it has always been this way, but it really hasn't. Information made its way to us through a series of checks and balances, for better or for worse. Because those checks and balances have been abolished by our digital lives, the only way to control them now is to control the controllers. But, *quis custodiet ipsos custodes*?

The short answer is, of course, no one. We exult that the web is free from any control—or that's what we tell ourselves—and we are free to put any sort of information up, from the good, to the bad, to the ugly, and it can get *really* ugly. *Caveat emptor*! Let those who search the web beware. But the fact of the matter is that the web *is* controlled, and rather well. It's controlled by those who make its tools and by those who construct its indexes and use it for returns on investment. This isn't necessarily bad, but it can be; and in some cases, it impedes what can be found, by whom and when. Again, this makes it ineffective as a single tool to replace our nation's libraries, not just entirely, but even a little bit.

GOOGLE ÜBER ALLES?

On the one hand, the web has given us more power over information "to foment a revolution in business."[24] It is empowering us and now we, the consumers, are armed with more *information, more data,* than ever. We can look at anything, any product, and find what we need and, moreover, find what others are saying about it. But this very gift also exacts a greater price. "We are forced to play a more active role in evaluating our sources of information. Whom do we trust? Amazon? The manufacturer? Some random customer?"[25] My argument in this chapter is that few users of the web understand this, and so they are guided by a great deal more misinformation than information. We search blindly, hoping to find the right sources, not those by cranks or crackpots. Expert knowledge is no longer a guiding light on the information highway but at best, a small signpost. It is crowded out by all the other voices trying to carve out their own niche, either merely to be heard, or to make a living.

We need more navigation help, and one of the best places this can be found is with a knowledgeable librarian.[26] While it would be logistically impossible to train everyone who uses the web as precisely as I would like, it is possible to train them at various grade levels, something we do not now do with any consistency. I realize that the future may bring us such features, making our searches more accurate and valuable. Further, it is to every search engine owner's benefit to make those searches better and more effective to improve the process, improve the search algorithms, and improve search results. We are not there yet, however. In any event, it underscores the importance of libraries and librarians at each juncture of web usage.

It's safe to say that a decade or so ago, this charge against the web had more than passing merit. Web searching then proved, at best, clunky and successful only in fits and starts. Today, web searching is much more refined and far better at returning useful results. I hope I have shown, too, that it's far from perfect, far from great, and has enough pitfalls in which even the web savviest among us can slip and fall. To some this charge will seem much ado about nothing, but to those of us who attempt to help young people use the web effectively, we see it every day, every week, all year round. To argue that the web is now the electronic panacea for libraries in this regard is at best premature.

We turn now to a more serious problem, that of quality control. The lack of any quality control on the web has always been seen as one of its charms, one of its more striking benefits. The question is whether this is merely a philosophical point of pride, or one than undermines the information calculus to such a degree that it short-circuits the entire process. To that problem we turn in the next chapter.

CHAPTER 4

Quality Control,
or Lack Thereof

This chapter deals with the lack of web quality, not its quantity. Some may wish to cavil, but the contention here is not that the Internet is empty of good information. The point of this chapter is that the real good of the web is often overshadowed by its startling bad. Further, because it's a mixed bag of information, misinformation and disinformation, it cannot possibly be a good substitute for the current network of libraries, the collective contents of which have withstood the test of time. Some of my detractors mistook my original article and the subsequent book for a Luddite sentiment. As I indicated in the introduction to this book, nothing was further from my mind.

Critics thought I was just being hysterical, but the only reason I wrote the article in the first place was a growing—and now full-blown—sentiment that libraries are obsolete. I wrote mainly against a vocal sentiment in our legislature that we "could zap a book from one place to another across the web." In some ways, the comment reminded me of Senator Ted Stevens's description of the web as so many tubes that got filled in various ways.[1] The trouble isn't just a handful of legislators saying libraries are obsolete. It's much more.

INFLUENTIAL VOICES CLAIM LIBRARIES ARE OBSOLETE

Today, many other influential voices are also touting this notion of the web. For example, Adrian Stannier, a very intelligent man and chief technology officer at Arizona State University, said at a 2008 conference in Boston:

> Burn down the library. C'mon, all the books in the world are already digitized. Burn the thing down. Change it into a gathering place, a digital commons. Stop

air conditioning the books. Enough already. None of us has the Alexandria Library. Michigan, Stanford, Oxford, Indiana. Those guys have digitized their collections. What have you got that they haven't got? Why are you buying a new book? Buy digital. Enough.[2]

Now I think I understand what Stannier is trying to say. He is, perhaps, encouraging libraries to recreate themselves, to think outside the proverbial box. By couching his comments in provocative language, he hopes to be heard. Underlying his comment is, however, the simple fact that he thinks the web *already* has made libraries obsolete. In any event, he wants to make all books digital. The implication seems to be that if libraries cannot be this new thing, then we need to get rid of them. Some might think that these are the musings of so many technocrats, but it isn't just technocrats; it is also some librarians. Cory Doctorow, of *Boing, Boing,* had this to say about the Stannier types:

> Every discussion of libraries in the age of austerity always includes at least one blowhard who opines, "What do we need libraries for? We've got the Internet now!"
> Facepalm.
> The problem is that Mr. Blowhard has confused a library with a book depository. Now, those are useful, too, but a library isn't just (or even necessarily) a place where you go to get books for free. Public libraries have always been places where skilled information professionals assisted the general public with the eternal quest to understand the world. Historically, librarians have sat at the coalface between the entire universe of published material and patrons, choosing books with at least a colorable claim to credibility, carefully cataloging and shelving them, and then assisting patrons in understanding how to synthesize the material contained therein.
> Libraries have also served as community hubs, places where the curious, the scholarly, and the intellectually excitable could gather in the company of one another, surrounded by untold information-wealth, presided over by skilled information professionals who could lend technical assistance where needed.[3]

Libraries can coexist happily with web. We just need to get the parties involved to give the other its space. The trouble often comes, as they say, in the details, and too many who like the sound of their voices, blurt out too often that the web is a silver bullet, a panacea, for all our information needs.

WEB QUALITY ISN'T A CESSPOOL, BUT IT ISN'T DRINKING WATER EITHER

So, now a decade later, is quality still an issue on the web? Sadly, it is. Clifford Stoll pointed this out early on:

It's an unreal universe, soluble tissue of nothingness. While the Internet beckons brightly, seductively flashing an icon of knowledge-as-power, this nonplace lures us to surrender our time on earth. A poor substitute it is, this virtual reality where frustration is legion and where—in the hold names of Education and Progress—important aspects of human interactions are relentlessly devalued.[4]

The web has always prided itself on being controlled by no one, which may contribute as much as anything to its knowledge-as-trivia effect on our minds. Efforts to control it through COPA (Child Online Protection Act) and other Internet bills have been met with the fiercest resistance, not the least of which by the American Library Association. But this love of the unfettered, uncontrolled web is its blessing and its curse. Blessing because it is now populated with millions of pages of information. Curse because it is also populated with millions and millions of pages of highly questionable, debatable and downright awful websites.

Some think the web has made libraries obsolete because it allows for instant collaboration, and that collaboration is much easier than face-to-face collaboration; hence, the quality of the web's answers is better than that of experts. This celebration of crowdsourcing has given rise to a spate of books like Surowiecki's *The Wisdom of Crowds* (Anchor, 2005), Jeff Howe's *Crowdsourcing: Why the Power of the Crowd Is Driving the Future of Business* (Crown, 2008) and Winograd and Hais's *Millennial Momentum: How a New Generation Is Remaking America* (Rutgers University Press, 2011). All of these books make very good cases for crowds and crowdsourcing, but they do not tell the whole story.

For example, groups do better (large or small) than individuals only when certain conditions are met.[5] This is not always kept in mind. It would be far better to survey cardiac surgeons on a cardiac matter than merely surveying the population of Americans in Iowa. Asking everybody with a computer what to do about a health matter (which happens sometimes in medical chatrooms) may be the worst thing we can do. While the web is an excellent tool for finding those with similar ailments and talking with them about their experience with treatments, it is not necessarily a good place to diagnose and assign treatments, unless those individuals can bring expert medical opinion to bear. Tens of millions of Americans search Google for medical answers (and additional millions for advice about their pets' illnesses), only to fall into a quagmire of tens of millions of answers in 3.2 nanoseconds.[6] If patients are looking at only the first few screens, then they are possibly not even getting information, but disinformation or worse, misinformation.[7]

ARE GROUPS ALWAYS BETTER?

Groups *can* be better under certain conditions, even when the group in question may not likely be consistently right. If the group is large enough, it can come up with the right answer, but the higher number of possible answers, the higher the failure rate. The good news is that in groups where the right answer is more likely to be chosen than not, and errors are randomly distributed, the average answer will be right. The problem is that we cannot always know this ahead of time. In fact, as Sunstein points out:

> [C]onsider a situation in which the answers of 51 percent of the group are likely to be *worse* than random. In that situation, the likelihood that the majority of the group will err increases toward 100 percent as the size of the group increases. The same problem can beset pluralities, if the plurality is more likely than not to err and if the judgments of those outside the plurality are random. Under those unhappy circumstances, the likelihood of a mistake will move toward 100 percent as the size of the group expands.[8]

Sunstein goes on to say that the blunders groups can make can be disastrously bad when there is a "systemic bias," giving rise then to two cases in which group judgment is to be avoided. This holds true even when the groups happen to be especially intelligent. Sunstein asked a number of his Chicago Law School faculty members what the weight, in pounds, was of the fuel that runs the space shuttles (4 million pounds). The median response was 200,000 pounds; the average was 55,790,555 pounds, owing to *one* wildly wrong guess. So, even in a very intelligent group of individuals—far more than a random number of individuals walking a randomly chosen street—the average and the median responses proved not only wrong, but also worse than a random selection might have been.

The other rather startling (and disturbing) area regarding homogeneous groups is that they are "more likely than individuals to escalate their commitment to a course of action that is failing—all the more so if members identify strongly with the groups of which they are a part."[9] The reason this *could* be a problem on the web is that many homogeneous groups have like-minded members. Second, many web users are looking for just this sort of homogeneous tie-in to a group of like-minded individuals. Before, when our choices were more limited but also more diverse, the chance of a conservative coming into contact with a liberal view, and vice versa, may actually have been higher than it is now, when individuals are self-selecting their like-minded groups. This infection, if one can call it so, is largely owing to the very thing that gives strong impetus to the web: social influences and information homogeneity. So, in point of fact, it is the social dynamic of groups that aggravate group error rather than attenuate it.[10]

So, crowdsourcing for its own sake is one small way in which the web can provide both good and bad answers. On the web, we tend to think that the more minds we consult, the better we will be. Crowdsourcing can yield solid results, but the make-up of the crowd is everything; it simply cannot be numbers. Crowdsourcing is only one minor flaw with the web's quality. Many other factors contribute to that lack of quality, as well.

THE GLUT OF WEB PORNOGRAPHY

A discussion about web quality requires a brief mention of pornography.[11] The web is awash in pornography of all kinds. Now, some will argue that this sort of information was available in print long before it was online, and that's true, but in order to see it, an individual had to order it, knowing full well what would arrive on his doorstep. This is not always true with the web. Moreover, pornography, at least on the U.S. version of the web, is rampant *and* ubiquitous. According to a recent study, the U.S. hosts 60 percent of the world's porn, or just over 400 million pages.[12]

Mentioning sex is always dangerous. Once you bring it up in anything but a "let it all hang out" attitude, you're branded as a Puritan, a fool, or both. Be that as it may, the issue of the "glut" of Internet pornography has been downplayed (certainly the American Library Association is quick to shelter it under its "intellectual freedom" wings), because many see it as so much hype. According to media organization XBIZ, however, pornography sales exceed $50 billion worldwide, which hardly seems like hype.[13] What makes this number so staggering is that we all know how much "free" pornography there is on the web. While Google has, to its credit, tightened its search parameters so pornography does not come up early and often with as many searches, Bing and other search engines are less refined and will reveal, well, everything, even with the most innocent of searches.

The scale of the widespread attraction to pornography is even more staggering. That $50 billion represents more revenue than CNN, ABC, CBS, NBC and FoxNews, *combined.* Its revenues are also larger than Amazon, Google, Microsoft, eBay and Apple, again *combined,* with over $3,000 being spent every second, and more than 28,000 Internet viewers looking at pornography ... *every second.* China leads the world in pornography users, at least according to dollars, but the U.S. isn't very far behind. In fact, as a nation we are, per capita, leading the way. Sadly, it isn't just a few highly populated cities, either. (For a state-by-state overview of the nation's voyeuristic fetishes, click the link to the map in the endnote.[14])

Regardless of the figures, I think most will agree that pornography was a social nuisance before the web. Now it is a monstrous imbroglio. Individuals who would never have bought a girly magazine are now taking a peek online at home, at work, in planes, trains and automobiles, and wherever their iPhones, iPads and iPods allow them.[15] Child pornography, even though illegal, remains a staggering problem, and the dark corners of the web (that come to light all too easily) reveal human sexual deviancy in heart-stopping, hair-raising detail. Now, we have a new form of pornography, called "revenge porn" wherein jilted or disgruntled former partners can get back at each other online.[16] Indeed, most states do not even have laws against revenge porn, much to the great chagrin of its victims.

The web prides itself, as said before, on being under no one's control. Regardless of all the legislation (both the marginally successful and the failed) to prevent online pornography, especially child pornography (Child Online Protection Act, Children's Internet Protection Act, Child Pornography Prevention Act), pornographers continue to get their nocent wares in front of all noses, whether we want it or not.[17] Apparently we want the Internet unfettered more than we want to protect our children. And while I am under no delusion about these bills and their effectiveness, their presence at least makes it more difficult for pornographers. The more barriers we put in place, the better off we will be. Oh yes, libraries have what many might call pornography, such as *Lady Chatterley's Lover*, Joyce's *Ulysses*, or de Sade's *Justine*. Whether these books are a kind of literature or thinly disguised pornography isn't the point. No one would argue that these books, or any like them, would ever be preferred, by those who view pornography, to scantily clad women or "Girls Gone Wild."[18] But even if readers cannot agree with me about pornography—and many I know do not—then at least we can agree that with "quality" of this sort on the web, it cannot, it should not be our sole source of information.[19]

NEWSPAPERS TAKING A BEATING, TOO

News has taken a beating at the hands of the web. Internet news has replaced, or is, replacing all print-based news, but its quality is suspect. One of the largest sources of Internet news is Arianna Huffington's *Huffington Post*, often referred to as HuffPo for short.[20] HuffPo is read by more than 20 million people a month, is growing at a phenomenal rate, yet has fewer than 200 paid staff but over 3,000 contributors.[21] Readers also have a share in the content (but not in the pay), making two million contributions a month. The fact is that "the vast majority of stories that it features originate elsewhere, whether in print, on television, or on someone's video camera or cell phone."[22]

Is this a fair assessment? Is it a vast empire built on the backs of bloggers? Nate Silver argues against this assessment.[23] Silver contends that much of the traffic is made from the paid contributors. In fact, he says pointedly, much of the unpaid blogging traffic is not worth much. He goes on to point out, rightly I think, that most misunderstand the HuffPo business model. It is not a news organization; it's a technology company. That raises the issue of whether we want our news replaced by technology companies. Many argue, and some even convincingly, that this is the wave of the future, and newspapers (and the rest of us) must ride it if we are to get our news. Only time will tell if this is the right choice. Some might think that sacrificing news to the mercy of the popular isn't exactly the way to a well-informed citizenry. As far as the HuffPo argument goes, the lack of pay turns out to be moot. Much to the delight of Arianna Huffington, a judge upheld her inalienable right not to pay bloggers.[24]

While much of the HuffPo content sounds wonderful, HuffPo isn't for everyone, even for those who share its left-of-center politics. It can be crude, offensive, and push the envelope. In any event, when it becomes the main source of news for most, I think it has to be of more than mild concern for all of us.

JOURNALISM ALSO TAKING A NOSEDIVE

What should be of more concern is the survivability of solid journalism. Not only have newspapers staffs shrunk, but so have their pages. Critics will complain that this is just a stodgy medium unwilling to move with the times. Certainly there is something to that. Advertising revenues funded many newspapers for years but as more and more of them went virtual, print ads dwindled, shrank and have all but disappeared. Newspapers could see the handwriting on the wall, if only faintly at first, then boldly later. Many newspaper publishers were in denial, others in wishful wait-and-see attitude. Now the future has caught up with them and they are the victims of their own hidebound, myopic ways, or so some might say. Granting all this does not remove the fact that the quality of journalism is also failing.[25] We are rapidly approaching a time in which there will be no journalists in the sense of the term understood for the last fifty years. We are fast approaching a time when spectators who write brief stories outnumber those who investigate them. Too harsh? Perhaps. But,

> As journalism declines, there will still be plenty of "news" but it will be increasingly unfiltered PR. The hallmark of great PR is that it is not recognized by the public as PR; it is entirely surreptitious. We're supposed to think it's genuine news. In 1960 there was one PR agent for every working journalist. By 1980, the ratio was 1.2 to 1. In 2010, the ratio stands at *four* PR people for every working journalist. At the current rate of attrition, the ratio will be 7 or 8 to 1 within a few years. There are far fewer reporters to interrogate the spin and the press releases, so the likelihood that they get presented as legitimate "news" has become much greater."[26]

Aren't we moving backwards? Even with tens of thousands of bloggers on hand, once print newspapers are gone, bloggers will have nothing to write about since only an infinitesimally small number of them do any sort of investigative reporting now. With fewer print or online choices of investigative reporting, users will be forced to outlets that are more suited to their own biases.[27]

The potential loss of the kind of quality that investigative reporting gives us, combined with the increasing shallowness of most online news, and the steady drift of many readers to their own biased sites for reportage of any kind, does not spell a bright future for an informed citizenry. Is this really the fault of the web? While we cannot lay all the blame on the rise of the Internet, we must admit that until the web put "everything" at our fingertips, no other competitor existed. Now, however, all that has changed. We want everything free and convenient. Well, you do get what you pay for.

STUPID HUMAN TRICKS—FOR ALL THE WORLD TO SEE

Less serious but nevertheless problematic issues of quality also plague the web. *YouTube* videos of young men acting the fool, or worse, young girls imitating what they think might be appealing at some level to someone, crowd the Internet with one-hit wonders. Michael Buckley, for example, began his career using *YouTube* and an initial investment of about $2,500.[28] This investment turned into a $100,000 a year job that led to other opportunities. His rants on *YouTube* became famous, not for their factual nature but for their notorious nonsense.

What about the Internet's ability to bring us together to help with various disasters, famines, tsunamis, oppressive governments, and so on? The Internet does this. Yet with every disaster relief there are nearly as many fraudulent websites rushing to bilk the unwary of their money. As quickly as we can learn of them, there are the quacksalvers with their nostrums competing for legitimate funds and, often, in the end making us leery of any web charity. In May 2013, F5 tornadoes hit Moore, Oklahoma. Within 48 hours, there were postings on the web warning those who wanted to help to be especially careful of web-based solicitations. As Eric Schmidt and Jared Cohen say in their new book, "[The Internet] is a source for tremendous good and potentially dreadful evil, and we're only just beginning to witness its impact on the world stage."[29] Suffice it to say, for all the good the web can do quickly, it can also do just as much harm and as quickly. Again, that does not make the Internet evil or worthless, but only offers another argument against its becoming a serious replacement for the libraries we have had in place for the last two millennia.

Even with something as powerful as web collaboration, a benefit which we had before but never to the extent the web allows, the web does not come away unscathed. Just as quickly as great minds can come together to plan for a better world or solve some problem inflicting humanity, so also are predators, villains, curmudgeons and the nefarious-minded able to band together quickly to do quite the opposite. True, we've always had the sordid working their evilfare before the web. Now, however, it is the speed with which both the good and the bad can rush to aid the common good, as well as to unravel it. Both occur now with lightning speed and deadly accuracy. Sadly, many of those on the web and up to no good target the young, the unwary or both. This makes web access in schools K–12, when not prohibited, then highly circumscribed.

HATE GROUPS PROLIFERATE

One area of web quality that cannot be celebrated is the proliferation of hate groups.[30] Hate groups once functioned almost solely by word-of-mouth. Small numbers of individuals willing to be associated with various and sundry sordid groups would tell others, but growth was slow; and prior to the Internet, many groups fell by the wayside because of a lack of communication among members. The U.S. Postal Service became too dicey to use as many members simply were not willing to run the risk of getting caught with hate materials.

With the advent of the Internet, however, all of these groups and many more have either been born or reborn. Using encrypted emails, spam and various other cloaking devices, these groups can now recruit many new members, and reports indicate that they have done just that. Anyone with access to the web is fair game. While these groups have proliferated, thanks to the web, so have their fortunes. Some of these new recruits are also sending in donations in record numbers.

These hate groups run along the lines of what most would expect: white supremacists, homophobic groups, and basically any anti- (fill in the blank) imaginable. Even when the unwary search for legitimate information, they can easily encounter these sites, which often mask what they are doing, using the very tools that the web makes available to place them in easy sight of potential recruits. For example, students looking for information during Black History Month are directed to white supremacist sites. Ditto that for web users looking for sex education information only to be sent to pornography sites.

This is not true for teenagers alone but all of us. It's what William Dutton, the director of Oxford University's Internet Institute, refers to as the "knowledge gap hypothesis."[31] Those who are better educated or otherwise better informed will benefit more from what's on the Internet and will be better able to take advantage of it while avoiding what is erroneous or misleading. This may be why there is so much data-mining going on, and why Google, Amazon, Facebook, Bing and other sites are working to refine that data into dollars.

For example, Amazon uses it to refer users to other books, but how well it does this is debatable. And what it omits may be more important than what it selects. How many reviewers of books on Amazon have critically read the books they recommend, or have they merely read reviews of them? The sheer number of books some reviewers claim to have read raises doubt. This is true for sites like Yelp where critics recommend restaurants that they may or may not have been to.[32] Obviously this would extend to all such sites—music, movies, clothes—that offer advice or reviews about what *you* should do. Some may argue that something is better than nothing, but I disagree. Bad or poor advice is not better than no advice at all.

THE WEB MAY NOT MAKE US STUPID BUT IT MAY MAKE US AFRAID TO THINK FOR OURSELVES

The Internet also opens up to us new avenues of abuse by placing them "at our fingertips." Take for instance, Internet gambling. In 2005 alone, according to the Annenberg Policy Center, more than $60 million was spent on online poker *alone*.[33] It's estimated that more than two million college students and more than one and a half million young people under the age of 22 are gambling online. If, on the Internet, no one knows you're a dog, then they also can't know you're underage, or are much too impressionable to be there. *Science Commons* founder John Wilbanks argues that searching online doesn't work as well "for finding science as it does for finding pizza."[34]

THE EXPERTS VERSUS EVERYMAN

Larry Sanger of *Citizendium* believed that real names needed to be associated with real people, that experts needed to weigh in on topics they had researched, and that the general populace needed guidance by these experts, not just the opinions of tens of thousands, some of whom may know what they are talking about. "Our community is built on the principles of trust and respect; contributors, or 'citizens,' work under their own real names, and all are expected to behave professionally and responsibly. Additionally, experts are invited to play a gentle role in overseeing the structuring of knowledge."[35] Readers will be quick to point out that *Citizendium* failed.[36] Today the site still exists (http://en.citizendium.org/wiki/Welcome_to_Citizendium), and it appears that traffic is ongoing though, perhaps not at previous levels. Some will argue (they already have) that this is the triumph of the democratization of information over the elitism of experts. But is that fair? Certainly *Citizendium* struggles for cash (as does *Wikipedia*), and the number of contributors has fallen below 100 with fewer than a dozen or so edits being made in a day's time. Compare that with *Wikipedia*'s millions, and some will argue (again, they already have) that *Wikipedia*'s numbers have triumphed. Perhaps it is more that narcissism has triumphed over expert knowledge? It's America! We have a right to be wrong.

While *Wikipedia* may be riding high today, its future is anything but certain. A business model like *Wikipedia*'s "grow[s] only if enough people care about [it]."[37] While *Wikipedia* has never been at a loss for content contributors, it still struggles for funding. Now it appears that even *Wikipedia*'s funding has been ill-used, according to one outgoing CEO.[38] What happens if it all disappears? Are we certain that web content will survive as long, when no one cares for it, no one updates it, and no one mends its links? In the end, the main thing *Wikipedia* may have taught us, as Weinberger claims, is that "a miscellaneous collection of anonymous and pseudonymous authors can precipitate knowledge."[39] Setting convenience aside, is it really an improvement on or over traditional libraries with expert encyclopedias?

Why not just "trust the people," as Jeff Jarvis implores us to?[40] Why not just let them decide? We saw earlier that crowdsourcing does not work in every case and can founder rather dramatically in others. Moreover, any search of the web and any surfing of television's 200+ channels can at least make a case against trusting the people in every case.[41] Reality shows continue to dominate ratings, celebrity blogs dominate the web, and all sorts of nonsense and silliness reign supreme about the Internet. Should we try to save ourselves from ourselves, or simply hope it all comes out in the wash? That is a philosophical question for others. As the late Daniel Patrick Moynihan, brilliant intellectual and quondam politician, once famously said, "Everyone is entitled to his own opinion but not to his own facts."[42] Moynihan spoke from the older tradition when facts weren't considered a form of elitism.

Some readers will argue that I am criticizing entertainment, and I will be the first to agree. That, however, is part of the point about Internet quality. We cannot allow a mostly entertaining venue to replace serious information in the pursuit of knowledge. At the risk of being a stick-in-the-mud, I say we are raising a generation of young people whose sole source of information is a blend of fact and fiction, but mostly fiction, if the data from search mining are any clue. According to Google's top ten searches in 2012, Whitney Houston, the Korean rapper Psy and his gangam style dance, Hurricane Sandy that ravaged the East, Kate Middleton, a young Canadian boy who allegedly committed suicide after being bullied, actor Michael Clark Duncan's death, and BBB12, a Brazilian show featuring scantily clad men and women living together "Big Brother" style, topped the list.

Now before anyone else says it, let me be the first to say that no one expects the top ten searches, or even the top 1,000 to include "inscapismic episodes in Hopkins poetry" or "categorical imperatives and Rawlsian morality." It is my contention, however, that an informational source so heavily weighted in favor of entertainment and the frivolous cannot also be expected to mature into a serious resource for knowledge, not to mention scholarship.

As for countries undergoing political unrest, it is enough to say that for every country that has seen unrest, the web has helped its oppressors as much, and in many case more, than it has helped the oppressed. We hope that those in oppressed nations will rise up to become "digital renegades," but instead they have fallen "digital captives."[43] We often forget that the sheer power of the web to do good is only equal to, and sometimes exceeded by, its power to do harm. While the web can do some of these things, it cannot do all of them equally well, and not nearly as well as the libraries that dot our nation's— and really the world's—hamlets throughout our planet.

The web's quality is also mired by its exaltation of everythingism. The web's banalities are endless. Internet cats have become proverbial. An ailurophile myself, I love a cat story, photo or video as much as the next person, but I hardly think that adds to my day so much as its diverts me from getting things done. I have not mentioned, either, the enormous number of games on the web, a separate issue from gambling. It's one thing to lose half your paycheck in an hour; it's another to lose your entire day to "Angry Birds" or whatever else happens to be on your screen at any given time. Some will complain that this is separate part of the Internet and should not be included in a discussion about quality. I would counter that anything that comes up in any search is fair game for discussing the web's quality, so this includes any number of social networking sites, everything from Facebook to LinkedIn. While the latter tries to be useful in every way, one can still waste enormous amounts of time updating a profile, adding talents, and communicating with others. Is this the information vehicle we want to replace our nation's libraries?

ARE WE BECOMING THE TOOLS OF OUR TOOLS?

So, is the web making us stupid, are we creating a "dumbest" generation, as both Carr and Bauerlein argue? Perhaps not as profoundly as they contend, but something is. (Who would have guessed that the city of London found it necessary to embark on a program to pad its lampposts in order to protect the heads of its many text-messagers.[44]) Nietzsche argued that our writing equipment takes part in forming our thoughts. Thoreau argued that we have become the "tools of our tools."[45] Thoreau goes on in *Walden* to argue that "Our inventions won't be pretty toys which distract our attention from serious things. They will be an improved means to an unimproved end which it was already too easy to arrive at...." Author John Culkin, writing about McLuhan, famously said that we shape our tools and afterwards they shape us. We cannot deny that our "tools" in this case, our technology, is shaping us. What is in question is how much and to what extent. But it is safe to say that we are all undergoing some measure of change from these tools, and that, for better or for worse, these changes are creating some level of havoc in our acquisition of knowledge. Perhaps it is as Weinberger points out, that it is merely a change from the old tadpoles to the young-footed frogs in an evolutionary scale of things.[46] Meanwhile, we need to be certain we aren't leaving a generation of "young-footed frogs" behind because they happen to fall between two evolutionary chairs.

Preservation on the web is little discussed but much needed in a conversation about web quality. While it's well known that digital media are not a preservation medium, it is less and less discussed and more and more assumed that they will work as one. Digital preservation is far from "settled" and a critically important point of conversation.[47] Currently we do not know what will be saved. It appears clear that the most popular will subsist *as long as it remains popular*. It is equally clear that those things that are little used (but remain nevertheless important to scholars) may not remain. Librarians know this only too well as proprietary aggregate databases field numerous titles, only to drop the less used, and certain titles are removed by their publishers. In neither case are librarians alerted quickly or even routinely. Whether the matter is one of a very little used title, or if the publisher has found a better deal elsewhere (either making it available through that publishers' own vehicle or another), the instability can wreak havoc on scholarly communication.

This is one reason that libraries seek to save what is important, what is needful from a research point of view. It's why there are various kinds of libraries so no one library is saddled with the task alone. And although the Digital Public Library of America (DPLA, http://dp.la/) is trying to remedy some of the problems I have raised here, we're not there yet, and I do not think we will ever be to the place where we can dispense with our network of physical libraries.

We have a choice, however. We do not have to be defined by the convenience of the trivial and capricious. If we want the web to be our sole source of information, then let's make it what it has to be to occupy this role. We can either let the digital future find us and live with the consequences, or create the future that we need and that scholarly communication deserves. It's very old-fashioned to point out that we who are living now are dwarfs sitting on the shoulders of giants. We have the benefit of history behind us. Why ignore it so that we destine ourselves to relive much of it? Why not take the best of what we know and fashion it into something that is the best for all us, not a mishmash of mostly silly entertainment. What I fear the most is best captured by Clifford Stoll:

> No, I don't worry about the bookless library, an efficient, money-saving edifice, housing only shiny banks of modems, disk drives, and books that talk to each other. A place without visitors, children's story hours, or librarians....
>
> Instead, I suspect computers will deviously chew away at libraries from the inside. They eat up book budgets and require librarians that are more comfortable with computers than with children and scholars. Libraries will become adept at supplying the public with fast, low-quality information.
>
> The result won't be a library without books—it'll be a library without value.[48]

We can invent that future for ourselves. But we have to love our past enough to create a better future.

CHAPTER 5

Rotting from Within?

NOW YOU SEE IT, NOW YOU DON'T

Number four on my list of reasons why the Internet is no substitute for a library I phrased thusly: "What you don't know does hurt you." What I meant by that, in the earlier book and now, is that the web, owing to its instability as a medium for enduring knowledge, allows for various eccentricities to occur. These eccentricities run the gamut from electronically displayed articles that either appear in less than their print form, or appear in full, only to disappear—vanish altogether—in what is sometimes referred to as "link rot." Anyone who has used the web for more than ten minutes knows this to be true, and the problem still plagues the web. Sites that show up a few weeks ago vanish altogether later. Articles bookmarked a year ago now turn up as "404 File Not Found." It isn't what I would characterize as "widespread," but it occurs often enough to make the search experience frustrating.

In the chapter on web searching, the focus was on various peculiarities about the web's structure that cause some things to be overlooked. The chapter also treated algorithms and how they can not only be gamed but can also overwhelm users with a glut of useful and useless hits or anticipate what is only distracting. The endgame is that users become mindless spectators, being told what to like and dislike, what to look for and what not to look for.[1] Knowledge Graph, whether Google intends it or not, is an intrusion into what librarians do, if not supplanting them altogether. Further, there are ways of searching that effectively eliminate critical hits or display them beyond the first or second screens so as to make them effectively eliminated. Finally, some search engine results end up being a mix of misinformation or disinformation that makes the search exercise pointless.

THE WEB'S CONTENT IS WRIT ON WATER

The complaint of this chapter is one step beyond this: it is the impermanence of the web owing to link rot and the nature of web's desire to be incessantly current. The web is, as Stoll called it, "an unreal universe, a tissue of nothingness."[2] Well, okay, let me quickly say that *it can act like this*. It can appear as capricious as the weather, as whimsical as the flight of a butterfly. As two MIT researchers discovered recently, the Internet is disappearing, 11 percent a year and 27 percent in two years.[3] The good news is that researchers have discovered a way "that works reasonably well" to get back deleted materials. Not what you want your skydiving instructor to say about your parachute but perhaps this is acceptable for research?

I don't want to give the impression that every search query or search calculus encountered ends in link rot, or in disappearing links, or nowhere, but it does happen, and with increasing frequency. Only careful examination of the results tells a user how valuable his results are. Unfortunately the snatch and grab mentality of the web robs us of our "careful" gene. From a scholar's point of view, because web searching *can* be a snipe hunt, it makes the *Quellenforschung* experience something to be despised.

Before readers email me that the same thing can happen in a library, too, let me hasten to add that a missing or lost book is an equal annoyance. While in a well run library, this does not happen very often, when it does, if the patron knows more than the color of the book, it can be found elsewhere with relative ease. But I should also point out that because libraries are relying more often on the web, and are finding ways to eliminate print materials, this will continue to be a growing problem in physical libraries, too.

Before focusing on link rot, a word about proprietary aggregate databases in libraries is in order. Excuse this necessary divigation that some will surely see as too much inside baseball. It really isn't, especially for scholars looking for specific materials. If you're a casual web user, or if your needs on a given day are along the order of trivia, then this problem, while it can still occur, will likely not be of much import. But if you're doing serious research on the web, this problem will occur with annoying frequency. It is important because it is an additional sticky wicket of online scholarly communication.

PROPRIETARY AGGREGATE DATABASES: PROBLEMS

Almost every library of any size offers proprietary aggregate databases. These are databases the library purchases for patrons to use, and they contain hundreds, sometimes thousands, of electronically delivered journals. These are not web materials per se, but web-*delivered* materials. So, everything that can go wrong on the web can also go wrong here even though the materials are in a self-contained database not accessible to surface search engines.

Over time, we have learned that these databases also behave whimsically, which makes the job of delivering materials harder than might be imagined. No, no one really wants to go back to the "olden days" when all journals were in print, if for no other reason than the problem of space and the loss of trees. But the ease of access of electronically delivered materials is not exactly all that easy. It just looks that way.

First, these aggregate databases drop journal titles routinely. Sometimes this occurs because the publisher of said journal wants to make that journal available through that publisher's own portal. While this is understandable, it wreaks havoc on delivery. Sometimes, libraries are notified about the problem. Often, they are not until a red-faced and furious scholar accosts a librarian to tell her a thing or two about her ancestry for cancelling a title when she did no such thing. Rather, it is the publisher who pulled the journal, but libraries are left holding the empty bag.

The title can also be dropped because it lacks activity, and the aggregate database, like the web itself, is all about what gets the most hits. Although a journal of esoterica, wherein there are only a few journals to begin with, might well be the only avenue for a certain scholar's intellectual work, the titles, or title, might be dropped, leaving that scholar to find her own way. Sometimes copyright conflicts obtrude but not as often as they once did. Since there isn't any choice about buying these very expensive aggregate databases—either the library provides access, or not, libraries comply and hope for the best.

The problems do not end there. The other annoyance with proprietary aggregate databases that libraries encounter is that the electronic version may differ from the print one, if in fact there is a print one. This is particularly true when the journal is graphic-laden either with pictures or formulae. These are dropped altogether, or present as online yet missing when printed. Instead, the print copy the patrons look at, typically after they are back home, reads "graphic removed," or some such verbiage that indicates something was there but isn't in the print version. This presents something of a conundrum for the library: does it buy the database and let patrons fend for themselves, does it avoid the database and buy the print copies, assuming they are available, or does it buy both, doubling or even tripling its cost (frankly, given the static or declining budgets of libraries, this is rarely the choice)?

But the fun doesn't end there in our brave new electronic world. Perhaps some allowances are made for math journals or art journals but surely databases that focus on general readership aren't at issue, right? Yes and no. Yes, because in a scholarly context (an academic library as opposed to a public one), those ads and other graphics might well be the very thing the user wants. For example, a research project might involve comparing ads today with those ten, twenty or even fifty years ago. And no, because providing this kind of twofold access (print and online) may not be an option the library can financially afford. Further, even in scholarly journals, footnotes may or may not be present *in toto*. None of this is, of course, so tragic and problematic as to make the problem insoluble, but they are enough of an annoyance to make the decision to purchase a proprietary aggregate database not as easy as it might first appear.

PROPRIETARY DATABASES: HIDDEN COSTS

I wish I could say that was all with respect to libraries and their databases, but I cannot. At least two other issues remain: cost and link resolvers. The cost of these aggregate databases is considerable and range from a low of a few hundred dollars to a high of tens of thousands. Because the databases contain multiple journal titles, purchasing one means having to make a careful decision. First, of what's there—what the exact journals are and where the duplication, if any, is. Again, because budgets are static or declining (mainly because administrative bean counters think everything is on the web anyway, so no need to buy expensive databases), libraries have to make careful decisions. Second, the databases are vetted for what's not there. Perhaps it's a humanities database that's purchased, so now a science one must be purchased, as must a social science one. These databases have to be purchased and dollars add up in the tens of thousands because, contrary to popular belief, not everything is on the Internet. Furthermore, libraries are the only entities buying them. If they are gone, there is no access to any of these materials.

The final curtain on this drama cannot be dropped just yet. Assuming vendors have delivered everything perfectly, no provider has gone out of business, and savings have been realized through a consortium purchase, we're done, right? Not quite yet, as one of my granddaughters likes to say when you ask her if she's ready for bed. All of these hundreds, perhaps thousands of journals have links to them, and these have to be checked to be sure they are "live." If libraries purchased only one database, these could be checked manually. In our case, a medium-sized library, we offer just over *100* databases, many of them containing hundreds and thousands of journals. Not enough hours in the week or enough people assigned to the task could check them all, so an additional cost—a link resolver—must be purchased.

All of these things make providing electronic access via the web not so easy after all, and not without some hiccups along the way. These complaints really come under the heading of niggling details, but they are the kind of details that make the difference between success and failure on the part of the scholar. These issues cannot be dismissed with the wave of a hand, or sneered at by those who think the web has all you need. In fact, these databases are purchased *because* the Internet doesn't have all that scholars need. Remove them from academic libraries and you will hear the wailing from where you live. While these are only some of the issues fraught with difficulties, we leave them now to turn to more web-based issues that offer a different set of problems.

LINK ROT: KILLING THE BLOOM OF THE WEB?

The main difficulty with open web-based materials is that they are subject to link rot, as indicated earlier. Link rot is defined variously but for our purposes we'll define it as referring to individual links or to whole websites in which the URL, the uniform resource locator, points to something that is no longer available. Link rot, sometimes written as one word, is also referred to as link death or link breaking, but they all mean the same thing. While it isn't exactly the same thing as a broken link, a broken link can look the same and cause the same sorts of problems. The difference is that a broken link *might* begin working again. Link rot generally refers to links that are no longer working—dead ends, as it were.

Usually what happens is that the link that has been clicked on is now pointing to a site that either no longer exists or is no longer available. This happens for any number of reasons. It could be that the domain has been changed or that what was once held by one individual is no longer, and the link points to different content. It could be that some of the material is now archived elsewhere, or that it has simply been allowed to fail. The real problem is that no one really knows why this happens. Further, we don't really know just how big the problem is. Because this is a relatively (more on that qualifier later) small problem, web proponents dismiss it as a non-issue. All that can be said with certainty is that it is a problem, it occurs often enough, and there isn't much anyone can do about it.

Web proponents argue it isn't really a big deal since sites like the Internet Archive (archive.org) can, through its "wayback machine" search feature, get users back to just about any page one wants to get to—so long as that user remembers the URL. Other sites also offer archived webpages, but these are not generally well known, and it isn't likely that someone will know to search there. Then there's the problem of when you do know to search, will the archived pages have the content you're looking for?

LINK ROT: IS IT REALLY A BIG DEAL?

Is this a big deal? Two law librarians recently wrote a paper on the "rotten" state of citations. Trouble is, when they went back to get the citation, it was gone. The link had migrated to another URL, and they could not find it without a great deal of searching. Yes, this is a nuisance, but as McLemee rightly points out, it remains "a serious problem for the disciplinary production of knowledge, which relies, in part, on the existence of stable and documentable sources of information. Citation allows others to examine those sources—whether to verify them or assess how accurately an author has used them, or as a basis for further research."[4]

Anecdotal, right? Not exactly. Link rot can be a very big deal for some information, especially legal information when the history of the law is important, or healthcare information when the physician can't find the treatment information needed. In a recent article in the *New York Times*, researchers Kendra Albert and Larry Lessig reveal that *half of the links* to Supreme Court cases no longer work, or point to something else. A link used by Justice Alito on violence in video games led to a site that read, "Aren't you glad you didn't cite to [sic] this Web page? If you had, like Justice Alito did, the original content would have long since disappeared and someone else might have purchased the domain in order to make a comment about the transience of linked information in the Internet age."[5] Of course, citations are the law's precedence, and when footnotes are missing or simply vanish, the court case suddenly sinks in the vastness of cyberspace.

Our white-hot lust for what Morozov calls "Internet solutionism" is forcing us to rely more and more on the Internet. Because of its ubiquitous convenience and its apparent cost effectiveness, more and more of what we consult is in electronic, digital format. Consider what happens when this is the *only* place material is housed and links to it are, for whatever the reason, lost. What then?

The imbroglio reminds me a little of the morality tale that Alasdair MacIntyre told in his book *After Virtue*. He provides a think piece in which he says to imagine some grand scientific experiment goes wrong and utter devastation occurs. The backlash against scientists and science libraries is great, as both are run out of town on a rail. After a decade or so, tempers cool and, realizing our hastiness, we try to get back what we lost. But it's too late, it's all gone. So we rebuild it from faulty memories. MacIntyre uses this as his backdrop to what has happened to morality. I see it happening to information in general after we over rely on the web, only to discover links begin disappearing. Soon we will be left with reconstructing what we used to know from memories weakened from lack of use.

I'm not a doomsayer and I don't think anything like this is in our very near future. If faulty links become more numerous, however, I can envision a time when a combination of them and crowded bandwidth create a less than happy situation.

Link rot is a problem that *Wikipedia* reports on regularly.[6] I chose February 2013 to do a random check, and at that time more than 4,000 articles needed some sort of cleanup. I don't doubt that the *Wikipedia* folks were on this and will probably get it cleaned up quickly, but it does represent a bit of a problem and something of an annoyance factor. Obviously, just over 4,000 out of millions of articles is a small percentage, but how many other websites purporting to provide access to information pay this much attention to the problem? Of course, 4,000 is 4,000 more than you'll find in a print encyclopedia. It is obviously in *Wikipedia*'s best interests to keep the link rot number low, but how much interest is there in link rot on the open web?

It certainly isn't one for content that appears free for a time and is later archived behind a pay wall. For users who cannot gain access, that information is no longer available to them. This isn't, of course, link rot per se, but it may as well be. That information is now off-limits to the user. The reason for the lack of access is different, but the frustration is the same. The user knows the content he seeks is there, just not for him to see. By virtue of my work in a university, very little is off-limits to me, even sites requiring a subscription to their content, but that is the fact of my employment and hardly the access available to the average user.

So is link rot really a problem? Or is this sensationalism not unlike what the television news often does (especially local news) to entice you to tune in, only to discover that there was "nothing to see here, move on?" Not according to some scholars. Michael J. Bugeja, director of the Greenlee School of

Journalism and Communication at Iowa State University of Science and Technology, considers link rot a "major" concern. Simple web redesigns of the *Chronicle of Higher Education* caused Mr. Bugeja, a frequent contributor, not to be able to find some of his contributions. According to Mr. Bugeja, he advises, "Solid sources rather than servers," arguing that link rot is "a warning shot that if we don't figure out a way to preserve original sources, we are going to erode the scientific method and peer review."[7]

Surely this is the hysteria of an older scholar who does not "get" the brave new world we live in? I wish that were true. It is now a staple in all writing guides to indicate which month websites were accessed. It's required because we all know some web-based citations may not be there when readers refer back to them. A point of reference is needed so readers will know that at one time the information was available. Talk about a needle in a haystack! It's almost like saying, "The blue book, fifth floor, aisle ten, right hand side, third shelf, second from the right."

Footnote Flight

Link rot doesn't just erode links; it also erodes footnotes, what Bugeja calls "footnote flight." In this case, the footnotes simply begin disappearing. I mentioned this problem in *Fool's Gold,* but it continues to be a problem on the web today. With open access a growing influential source of information, a trend I wholeheartedly endorse, this could be a significant problem instead of just a niggling detail (but where devils hide). Mainly only scholars think footnotes are important, but footnotes are vanishing at a rapid rate, even in texts these scholars write for electronic publication, and the pressure to avoid them when writing is growing. Of course this isn't entirely the fault of the web; part of the problem occurs because of link shortening sites like Bitly. Whatever the reason, or whoever is to blame, the web is a contributor to this maddening problem.

Publishers are indeed working on possible solutions to both of these problems but no failsafe mechanism has emerged. One way to avoid link rot is through DOIs (digital object identifier), an alphanumeric code that is uniquely related to the content and provides a persistent URL, or PURL.[8] For every solution on the web, there is, as we have seen, an attendant problem. Not everything is published in scholarly venues that scholars want access to, such as nongovernmental reports or the so-called "grey literature." And DOIs do require publishers to sign up with CrossRef, the international, nonprofit group that began this process in the early 2000s. DOIs can be faulty, too, so it isn't as if this solves everything.

Another effort is underway by 301Works.org and devised by the Internet Archive to resolve link rot issues.[9] None of us like long URLs, the kind that are impossible to remember and even harder to copy and paste. Sites that shorten URLs have been a lifesaver, but they also raise questions about how long such links last. The 301Works.org is partnering with many of these companies to provide a persistent link and so maintain those links in perpetuity.

Link rot persists not only on the unfettered Internet where the problem is most pervasive but even in scholarly journals maintained by scholarly publishers. I mentioned legal materials but both chemical and medical literatures also suffer from this same problem.[10] While it is improving, no major electronic chemistry journal is immune. Further, about 16 percent of the medical literature in Medline abstracts is found to be corrupt. Granted, 16 percent may seem small to some but it's not if what you are looking for is in that 16 percent and is critical to your research. In *Fool's Gold*, I mentioned the story of a researcher who had used Medline, the online database, for his search only to discover much later that a print paper outside the online coverage warned against the protocol he chose, especially for certain patients with certain respiratory idiosyncrasies. Sadly, one of his trial patients met these conditions and died from the protocol. It is not a stretch at all to envision a time when a similar thing might happen, not because it isn't on the web (though that will always be a possibility), but because it was once there and has fallen off the radar owing to link rot. It goes without saying that one may be a small number, but when it relates to the death of someone, that's too many.

Other journals are also at risk. Indeed, any journal publishing in electronic format must not only be aware of link rot and footnote flight but must also be working to do something about them. No one will deny the convenience of the 24/7 nature of electronic journal access, and I have yet to encounter any scholars who want to go back to print journals. From a library standpoint, they are not only costly to purchase but also have hidden costs, such as storage, binding, personnel to acquire, manage and preserve them, and others still to aid those trying to find and use them. Even in a small library, it is not possible to place every bound periodical on a shelf because space quickly becomes an issue. Some will fall into disuse and so will need to be moved to an area to allow space for materials that are used daily or weekly. But such a decision, whether onsite or off, requires dollars and personnel, and contributes to the inconvenience of the print format. Further, the whole print enterprise isn't exactly what anyone would call green.

Link rot, footnote flight and the panoply of problems associated with electronic access is no small beer, either. Electronic access is hardly an easy economic decision for publishers or for libraries. They are more convenient and provide almost instant and ubiquitous access, yet when they are dropped from databases, fall victim to link rot, or appear in less than a complete form, their value attenuates. Tenure issues related to online journals also obtrude, but not, admittedly, as severely as only a decade ago.[11] Blogs, wikis and other online publications still create problems for those seeking tenure who offer them up as evidence of their scholarship.

When I wrote "10 Reasons" a decade and a half ago and followed it up with *Fool's Gold*, the issues of link rot and footnote flight emerged as somewhat of a surprising and complicated mess. I did not anticipate finding problems like these of such formidable import for scholars. When I reviewed the "10 Reasons," I did not expect to find this an ongoing problem at all. Of course, these issues have been greatly improved upon, and I would be the first to say that I would not be surprised to find in another ten years they will no longer be a problem, surely. Nevertheless, discovering that now, a decade and half later, these are still issues of serious concern surprises me. While I am still optimistic about the web, I must say that a decade of observing what happens to materials online, especially scholarly materials, does not inspire much confidence in its permanence in the future. The growing presence of monographs online, however, and the massive ebook collections now being made available to libraries, give me pause. Will we find the same problem with these texts? It's too early to say, but some not entirely unrelated problems have already emerged, such as useless metadata (think of it as the electronic version of the printed card catalog cards), perfectly erroneous subject headings, and some (maybe 5 to 10 percent) subject headings that describe a different book altogether. We leave to one side the matter of whether gigantic electronic ebook collections are the best collection development tool (a kind of one-size-fits-all approach).

We can only hope these are not a portent of bad, careless or shoddy things to come. Even so, none of it makes a good impression when we think that this is the backbone of all information—past, present and future. And it especially furrows the brow and raises the hackles when we hear some loudmouth unequivocally contend that libraries are obsolete because we have all we need on the, well, vanishing Internet.

CHAPTER 6

En Masse: Mass Digitization

AMERICAN ABUNDANCE

A founding principle of Americanism is abundance, or so it would seem. If one is good, one hundred is better. We apply this to almost everything: cars, boats, guns, dollars, Starbucks, wine, women, song, and, sadly, our government debt. We believe that you can never get too much of a thing, even when you can. And let's be serious. How many of us haven't secretly thought, even if we never acted upon it, that if two aspirins work quickly on a headache, four will work with the celerity of lightning? The web is our excess writ large, our noise over all the signals. One website is a good thing, so a trillion must be a trillion times better, right?

It's only upon reflection—something we Americans are not very good at—that we begin to rethink our presumptive assumptions. Suddenly all those cheeseburgers aren't sitting so well, or, rather, sitting all too heavily, on our hearts. All that wine is weighing not too lightly on our livers, and all those Starbucks coffees feeling a bit too sugary for our pancreata (not to mention the multiplicity of the buildings themselves looking more and more like too much of a redundant thing). Of course, by the time we get to the reflection part, assuming we ever do, that runaway snowball is too big even for the sun to melt it before it flattens everything in its way. Apparently we never got the moral of the Midas story all that clearly.

In thinking about this abundance, I tried to characterize the exultation of bean counters everywhere when they looked with covetous eyes at the web. Legislators in nearly every statehouse thought that the web, coupled with digitization, equaled "zapped" books from one locale to millions. Infrastructure be damned, we could do this if we wanted to. We're Americans! With the success of electronic texts (minus those niggling details in the last chapter), it appeared that legislators had finally proven Twain wrong after all.[1] Libraries that cost tens of millions to run in a given state would now cost almost nothing in every state. Three cheers for the web: hip-hip-hooray!

I don't mean to characterize legislators as footling fools. I cannot tell you how many times, while looking over budgets more strained at than a gnat swallowing a camel that I had wished it were true to a certain degree, to any degree. How easy it would be to provide services so no one would have to get out of bed to become a neurosurgeon! Why, the would-be surgeon/physician could just lie back in bed and "spectate," watch her way to wealth and happiness.

INFORMATION HIGHWAY NOT EXACTLY THE HIGHWAY TO HEAVEN

It hasn't exactly worked out that way. From a distance, the Internet Superhighway looked like the perfectly constructed road to paradise. Sure, we might lose a few jobs, but we'd create hundreds more to replace them. Like the magic tree that for every chop you made, three chips grew in its place, there would be jobs, not in exactly the same places, but some place nonetheless. Once *on* the Internet Superhighway, we discovered that the road to paradise had a helluva lot more potholes than we thought. Hope, however, springs eternal nowhere else like it does when discussing the Internet. If you're reading this and not thinking that we're going to fix all these tiny, minuscule problems with the web, then you're a fool, and a Luddite to boot, so there!

My fifth argument, not so much against the web but rather as an explanation why the smooth ride to heaven was so teeth-clatteringly bumpy, had to do with this idea of abundance. If we could digitize one poem, we could digitize one million books. And so, we just about have, but not yet, and not really. Mass digitization has occurred on a massive scale, but it has not exactly panned out as we hoped, or even as Google promised. At least not yet. We acquired some difficulties along the way to mass digitization, and these difficulties remain A few of them we'll consider here.

MANY MASS DIGITIZATION PROJECTS ARE EXCELLENT ADDITIONS TO KNOWLEDGE

Before getting too far along with this discussion, however, I want to be quick to point out that many of the vast digitization projects underway, including Google's, are a tremendous benefit to all of us. Just yesterday, as I was preparing for this chapter, the news came across my desk that the *entire* Vatican Library is to be digitized "[in] 2.8 petabytes of storage."[2] For most of us, 2.8 petabytes may as well be "a bunch of storage" the number is so incomprehensibly large. But how large is it? Experts guess it will be over 40 million pages and will take, assuming no difficulties along the way, about a decade to accomplish. The Vatican, as we all know, holds rare and wonderful treasures, including its "forbidden" collection. Something tells me that those volumes may be the last to be digitized. Regardless, this is grand news indeed.

Only a curmudgeon would find something wrong with this. Since I have established my *bona fides*, let me, without trying to protest the name-calling, insert only a small word here. Yes, I want to see that collection. I've only been to the Vatican once and stood with about 1,000 others looking with awe and reverence at the ceiling of the Sistine Chapel. I had looked forward to doing this for years, but somehow standing there with those 1,000 chattering, camera flashing, water-drinking masses, the effect was a little—just a little—less awe-inspiring. I would go back and do it again, however, and much prefer seeing it in person to the scores of times I have viewed it online. Some years ago I set foot in the Strahov Library in Prague for about three hours. I was inches from Averroes commentaries on Aristotle. It was a horribly cold, rainy day, in July believe it or not, so my wife and I (we're both incurably bookish) nearly had the place to ourselves.[3] Yes, it was a spiritual experience.

I go on like this because I want to underscore just how much I would like to see that Vatican collection and any other collection like it. Having access to such collections anytime would give me even more to look forward to in retirement. And yet, and yet...

Many who saw that story on the Vatican rejoiced, including those who do not read a great deal. Some of the online comments, while a little bathetic given the news, did give some indication of the universal embrace of all things digital. "Wow," said one, "that's a lot of work," or, "Cool." But some of the commenters may not have read the very short article all the way through. At the end of the story, there appeared two very important points not even hinted at in the headlines. A company that specializes in storage and security, EMC, has made the storage space available. It has handled religious materials before and done a very good job, but this digitization "does not guarantee preservation."[4] In an effort to overcome this, EMC will use a format that is certified by the International Standards Organization. So, it's fine, right?

Not exactly. The story continues, "even so, digital files can break down or become outdated and unreadable." And guess what? Neither EMC nor the Vatican has any plans on record about what will be done as a phase two follow-up. *Sic transit gloria mundi*, shall we say?

ARE ALL THESE GREAT PROJECTS SO MANY TICKING TIME BOMBS?

This illustrates my point about mass digitation in general and any given digitized collection in specific. If this is the case in 2013 for a company at the height of storage and security, following what are considered by everyone as the very best standards available, then what about all the other mass digitization projects everywhere else that are, each one, one or more steps removed from the one above it in security, preservation and care? And what of those thousands upon thousands of digitization projects in hamlets all across the globe that are following next to nothing with respect to standards, and have no plans at all for preservation or for re-digitization? What is to become of them after five years, a decade, two decades? The purpose of any preservation project is to make the contents available now and in ensuing decades, if not centuries. But this is exactly what is not happening, and the fear is rising that these libraries are sitting on digital time bombs.[5]

At this point, no one knows. We wing merrily along our way and hope all of this will somehow come out in the wash. Is there any reason to believe that it won't? Possibly. We drove down a road similar to this only a few years ago. When the rush of CD-ROMs hit the scene, just about everyone was using them for data collection preservation. Disks would last forever, including some that were specially designed to last for hundreds of years, or so we told each other. All of a sudden, everything came on a CD: music, databases, even books.

But the indestructability of CDs turned out to be a myth. Not only could these devices be easily scratched, but CDs made one year might not be readable on new machines made just a few years later, something libraries buying ProQuest on CDs discovered all too quickly. Reasons why this problem emerged were legion: software installed improperly, files not transferred correctly, or some not be transferred at all. In some cases, one might find the disks worked perfectly one week only to have them fail repeatedly the next. It proved a nightmare to researchers who depended on those disks, making every turn of ProQuest on disk as much a gamble as any roulette wheel. As we'll see in Part Two, the evolution of knowledge from print-based to web-based is creating new reading habits, some good, some less than good, some downright ugly, the outcome of which is anything but clear.[6]

What these transitions—CDs, databases, digitization—mean, however, is that there has been a rapid destruction of some print. When print isn't being destroyed, it is being sent to solitary confinement, i.e., storage facilities, where it resides until it has been forgotten (and why not, they are out of sight?); then it's destroyed. Nicholas Baker's *Double Fold* discusses this problem in connection with an older technology, microfilm, as well as the digitization and our nation's archive of newspapers.[7] But digitization did not begin and end there. In fact, printed books are being tossed out everywhere, and for no other reason than they are "in the way" or the space for them too costly.[8] It no longer appears to matter if they are needed; what matters is that they are in the way of progress and need to be set aside.

Hold on. Isn't this what we need now? Shouldn't we get rid of these space-consuming, tree-hating, old-fashioned technologies to make way for the new, easy and convenient digital information artifacts? Of course we should, but only if the new technologies are an improvement over the old and are as easily managed and as consistently used. Unfortunately, this has not been the case so far. As a strong proponent of ebooks in libraries, especially academic ones, I find the data so far uncompelling to make me think all we need are ebooks. I keep asking myself, am I building a barber shop in towns inhabited by bald-headed men when I hold on to print? To make sure ebooks have the best possible chance of survival and use, we not only purchased them in large quantities, we publicized their existence in every manner possible. While use data rises each year, I find that based on the data alone, we likely would not have implemented any other technology with so many underwhelming results so far. It will get better, I'm sure.

Talk like this will get you labeled a crank faster than criticizing the web, at least in library circles, so let me hasten to add further that not only have we added ebooks, but we have also weeded our collections of items that are no longer being used by anyone (for at least for two decades). Moreover, I have done so in every library that I have had the pleasure to lead. Books, especially reference tools that sit on shelves and gather dust for decades, are books that, for that library, were the same as if they had never been purchased. Clearly, collections have to pruned of dead wood; *habent sua fata libelli*, as Joyce said about his books in a letter to his publisher. But to remove books only because they are in the way, or because a new space no longer has room for them, or because a struggling new technology needs to be the only source in order for it to succeed, is to my mind an alarming trend, to say the least.

I see these things as cautionary tales. Let's try to learn from our past and not be doomed to repeat it. Web-based information is, in the short term anyway, the wave of the future. But let's not just say that and be done with it. Let's be certain.

DIGITIZATION IS NOT PRESERVATION

Sadly, we aren't certain. We're digitizing tens of thousands of materials (in Google's case, twenty million), and we're not sure what's happening to those original printed texts. In some cases, we know they're destroyed in the process.[9] In others, perhaps not so much.[10] So, while we may be able to rest contentedly knowing that Google and other mass digitization projects are keeping books safe, more or less, other projects of both unknown value and unknown worth may be destroying them in the quiet of some suburb.

Loss of printed materials isn't the only problem with mass digitization projects. Even in Google's case there are quality control issues in which pages are missing, blurred, or the resulting text unreadable.[11] While every assurance is given us that these will eventually be corrected, no one seems to know when "eventually" will, well, eventuate.

I should hasten to point out that mass digitization had invigorated many texts that were either out of print or essentially lost to readers. Further, the early fear that mass digitization would spell the doom of publishers or copyright holders turns out to be only partially true.[12] Some small publishers have felt the pinch of the web, to be sure. But others, with texts long forgotten, are realizing something of a rebirth. So, on balance, is this unequivocally good news?

Yes and no. Certainly, for those texts forgotten but being rediscovered, it is good news. Some authors *may* experience a renaissance of reading, but the matter is complicated by what exactly these texts are for. We know, for example, that few people read an entire book online unless it is with a device they can carry around with them, and even then there is no guarantee all of the text will be read or even skimmed (see Part Two, on reading). No one reads a voluminous e-text while sitting at a desktop, or even from a laptop. Neither the desktop nor the laptop makes for an easy reading experience. What they do make easy is rapid scanning ... of the first few pages. This is moreover true of tablets, or phablets or whatever the new handheld device is. Readers on these devices are not typically *reading* the texts for comprehension, another matter taken up in the chapter on reading and literacy.

Mass digitization projects take funding from other areas, too. Celebrated cases of libraries (San Francisco Public Library and the National Library of France, to name but two) diverted huge amounts of money to digitization and away from other costs as a standard operating procedure. The cost of digitization presents itself as a savings feature only to eat up all available resources. Part of the reason for this is the relative ease in which digitization can be undertaken. It is only on further reflection that unanticipated costs emerge (copyright restrictions, orphan works, optical recognition needs, etc.). By the time these do appear, however, the project is "in blood steeped in so far that ... returning were as tedious as go o'er."

Many digitization projects cherry-pick materials to digitize. This only makes sense, of course, because one wants to undertake projects that will have little use. Choosing the popular has both advantages and disadvantages. Materials compete in a kind of popularity contest. There is nothing wrong with this approach per se, except that it relegates to the dustbin materials that ought to see the light of day. Critics will argue that we must begin somewhere, and nothing could be more true. The problem isn't beginning at this place so much as this place also becomes the end. Funding, energies, enthusiasms, all flag, and the end result is less than the optimistic beginning. Again, this is not a reason to suspend all digitization projects, but it should at least be understood before embarking, and every effort made to prevent it.

COPYRIGHT STILL OBTRUDES, SORT OF

The celebrated copyright imbroglio that Google encountered has been reported on so often and in so many publications that to rehash it here would be to recount the obvious. Google recently finally won its eight year old U.S. copyright battle and will be able to scan any book it wants to for as long as it wants, and publish snippets of books still under copyright protection, as "fair use." Orphan works still bedevil that project, but more on that below. The short version of the story is that Google set out to digitize all the world's books, a goal it set as long ago as when it went by the name Backrub. Google, in one of the many places the story is retold,

> ... devised an approach that combined diplomacy to borrow books gratis from the leading research libraries in the West, ingenuity in devising its own speedy work-flow technology for collecting digital images of the printed pages and

low-wage temporary workers to perform the labor-intensive work of turning pages. The human touch was literally visible in some images—fingers can be seen holding the book in place.[13]

Google later automated the book-turning process, too, to allow for the economical digitization that some sources put as high as $900 million. It cannot be thought, nor should it be expected, that Google would simply do this out of the kindness of its heart, despise its almost Hippocratic oath to information: first do no harm. (It's the thought that counts).

Somewhere along the way, Google determined that copyright did not apply to it and decided on an opt-out strategy for authors who did not want their books digitized. Google began with agreements to digitize the collections of a half dozen large university libraries. That number soon doubled, then tripled. By 2005, however, several groups, including the Authors Guild, determined to put the brakes on Google's project. After much wrangling in court, an agreement was reached with a $125 million settlement to cover books they had scanned without permission, the plaintiffs' court costs, and the creation of a Book Rights Registry. But the decision was rejected by Circuit Court Judge Denny Chin. Further, Google also incurred legal debts and a river of bad publicity.[14]

The matter is no longer unsettled, as Google has won its case. Judge Chin recently found in favor of "fair use," citing the many benefits, and many are ecstatic over the ruling in late 2013. Google has not helped its case by acting imperious with respect to copyright, discounting privacy issues, and behaving as if the world owes it a favor for undertaking this work. Non–English speaking countries have weighed in against Google's overreliance on works in English. No one, it appears, is very happy. Well, almost no one. Many other groups have either doubled their efforts or since taken up mass digitization projects (HathiTrust, JSTOR, Open Content Alliance, California Digital Library and Gallica in France), but at least one major player, Microsoft, dropped out.[15]

What troubles me about all this isn't the projects themselves. Authors whose works have been digitized are getting more reader exposure (if not always royalties). Copyright is again coming under attack, and our copyright laws (which I have referred to as draconian) are again the subject of scrutiny. Unfortunately, the real scrutiny of copyright is the bailiwick of Congress. Its track record on copyright has been to worsen it, not to ameliorate it. What *is* troubling about this project is what will happen now. Now that Google has won, will it begin to charge everyone for access? Are we sure we want to preserve the great works of culture (one of the reasons Google co-owner

Sergey Brin argued for the project in the first place) only to read them along-side ads for Viagra? And what of privacy issues? Are we forced to embrace the fact that we must live without privacy in order to be online?[16]

Projects like the Open Content Alliance (http://www.opencontentalliance.org/), and to some extent the HathiTrust Digital Library (http://www.hathitrust.org/), are attempting to provide an alternative to Google. The HathiTrust Digital Library now has contents that rival Google, with close to 11 million volumes digitized (over 5 million titles), and it makes these available to libraries for noncommercial uses.[17] But how long it or any or the other such project here or abroad can rely on foundations, volunteers, cost schemes and funding support is anyone's guess. And what happens if they fail? No one knows because no one is thinking that far ahead. The Digital Public Library of America (http://dp.la/), with its admirable ambitions, should also be included in this group. This will be a national crowdsourcing test if it is successful, but it is by no means a sure thing, and it's already had some trouble getting off the ground.[18]

BUT WHAT ABOUT THE ORPHANS?

Then there is the matter of orphan works, alluded to earlier. Orphan works are copyrighted works that have no clear copyright owner, and, further, have no means of ascertaining who the owner or owners are so that the work could be used for other purposes.[19] No one knows for certain how many orphan works there are, but some estimates place it at about 20 percent of all copyrighted works.[20] The picture is unclear because this is a moving target. Most mass digitization projects (save for the Google type) would remove such works in deference to copyright, or until copyright ownership could be established for certain. Meanwhile, orphan works remain orphaned in digitization projects for the time being.

It is the philosophy, not the projects themselves, that I hold up for criticism. Nearly all I have examined are worthy projects and ones that many researchers will benefit from. But if they were presented as choices between better on-site library services, a larger and great variety of existing resources, longer operating hours, and the dangers of relying on digitization as an acceptable preservation tool, it isn't clear which of these projects would be funded. Certainly not all of them would be. Some would surely be discouraged, especially by smaller institutions that do not have the requisite resources to pull off a successful project, however small. Rather, so many of these projects are, in

Graham Greene's fine phrase, "like a dumb leper who has lost his bell, wandering the world, meaning no harm."[21] And yet, like that leper, they have the potential to harm whether wishing to or not. It isn't so easy a problem to solve, despite all the calls to do away with copyright and make everything free, as if we all have a right to everyone's work and can take what part of it we want without attribution or notice. Making everything free sounds good in theory. It's the practice of it that makes it so costly in the end. I hate to be a stickler for the Constitution, but nothing in it demands that we make available everyone's ideas for everyone else to use as they wish. Our rush to make everything free may well push us headlong into a free-for-all.

The idea of mass digitization and global collaboration is applauded by many as the way to utopia (to save everything click here). But,

> While the sharing of data is made possible by the technology of digital libraries and the Internet, it runs counter to the practice of many [academic] fields. Researchers often are reluctant to share data with others until they have finished mining them and publishing their results. Ownership rights in data may not be clear or intellectual property laws may vary across the multiple jurisdictions in which data are held.[22]

In addition to copyright restrictions, permissions and the rest, we have yet another difficulty: the way scholars work. Without doubt, we can make this work in a new way but what we cannot do is try to make it work in a new way before all the pieces are in place. We must encourage sharing but not before the new infrastructure is equal to the old one. It does no one any good to tout a new strategy that is more convenient, surely, but less effective in the long run. In many ways, we have declared a new way of driving on the Information Superhighway, on the left side instead of the right. But we forgot one very important feature along the way: we forgot to alert the Department of Transportation, if you will, not to arrest anyone driving on the left side of the road. All we have managed to do so far is make changes that have created a crisis in scholarly communication and then walked away, as if that detail fell to someone else to clean up. Since all these changes strike at the heart of what scholars do, it's a bit callous to demand such changes when reward alternatives are not yet in place, and, moreover, all the penalties still are.

INNOVATION AWAITS NO READER

Technologists will argue that they cannot wait because innovation waits for no one. That is very likely true, but acceptance of those innovations will

likely be ignored if technology makes itself as welcome as a bull in the proverbial china shop. If we want this future, let's change copyright. If we want
global collaboration, then let's reward scholars not for original scholarship
but for collaboration. And if we are to replace our libraries with digital ones
only, let's make certain that readers for whom they are designed can use them
at least as well as they can in traditional libraries.

The last point I wish to make is one that I fully anticipated but thought
would not eventuate this soon in our digital history: the disappearance of
digital libraries. Literally hundreds if not thousands of digital projects are
underway. Most of the larger ones, and some of the smaller, too, are a boon
to researchers, as already noted in this chapter. This trend is likely to continue.
But what happens when all our best intentions fail, when—dare I say it—
technology runs aground on its own invincible folly? Then what? Making
money on the Internet is hardly easy, and monetizing content turns out not
to be the get-rich-quick scheme everyone hoped it would be.[23]

I can almost hear the mocking from here, but let me hasten to say it's
already happening. I made brief reference earlier to Microsoft's mass digitization project that flagged early, after just under 800,000 volumes.[24] It also
ceased its funding of the Internet Archive. Some will immediately point out
that Microsoft did this because Google already had the clear advantage and
was better at it anyway. Others will also point out that whatever Microsoft
had digitized, others took up and made available. So there's nothing to worry
about? In the words of Vint Cerf, "It's absolutely true that the Internet is getting bigger and bigger and more ubiquitous, it's going to be in just about
every appliance we can think of. The question is, does that mean it's all going
to collapse. I don't think so."[25] Not exactly a ringing endorsement.

In a recent TED (Technology, Entertainment, Design) talk, scientist
Danny Hillis makes a compelling case that the Internet *is* all going to crash
after all.[26] A small group of people created the Internet (no, Al Gore wasn't
there), each of whom knew the other. By the early 1980s, most of the names
and addresses of people then on the Internet could be carried in a small,
pocket-sized address book. Today you'd need an 18-wheeler to carry it around.

According to Hillis, "The Internet was designed with the assumption
that the *communications links could not be trusted*, but that the people that
connected computers to the Internet were smart and trustworthy. Those
assumptions no longer apply."[27] What Hillis goes on to describe is a combination of several of the worst disaster movies you've seen. Security holes are
everywhere, but everything we know is tied into this faulty security: gas and

water utilities, transportation grids on ground and in the air, not to mention the backbone of what is supposed to become the greatest library the world has ever known.

I'm little worried that a web that brings us games, amateur night and thousands of other even more dubious diversions doesn't have the same interest in preservation that others of us do, those who are used to millennia being the standard benchmark. Honestly, if these diversions were all we placed on the web, then it wouldn't matter what happened to it. But in addition to these diversions, we place on the same medium everything we know, and it appears we're hoping for the best in terms of its preservation. The good news is that there are people working on fixes for the bad security. The bad news is that Hillis found out after his talk that the problems are worse than he described. None of this inspires confidence, especially since past performance is generally a good indication of future behavior.

At the risk of sounding like Ted Stevens and his "tubes" of the Internet, or an *Onion* headline ("Internet Collapses Under Sheer Weight of Baby Pictures"), let me say we get the impression that we are fast approaching (the objects in your mirror are closer than they appear) a point of no return. Over the last decade I have heard, read and written about Internet 2, a nonprofit consortium of educators and researchers in government and industry.[28] Internet 2 is the Internet without all the ads, idiotic videos, cats and girls gone wild. Whether one can say it has succeeded is not the point; the point is that it was created because universities found they could not get enough bandwidth to do what they needed to do and host all of the inglorious glories of the unfettered Internet.

INTERNET DESTINED TO FAIL?

Is the Internet going to fail? I don't have the expertise to say one way or the other, but I think it's a safe bet that it cannot go on the way it is without making some significant changes in infrastructure. I put great faith in things like LOCKSS (http://www.locks.org) for digital sustainability.[29] But so far it aims mainly at dissertations and theses, two kinds of documents some might think are the last items we should worry about saving.

Let us assume it won't crash and that the subsequent changes in infrastructure will not be so costly that only the elite can afford it. What about all those hundreds or thousands of digital libraries out there? Can we be certain they will last forever? Let's hope so because we have placed all our proverbial eggs in this basket that we hope is not a basket case. Do we have the certainty that these digital libraries will be self-supporting before too long, even though it's pretty clear that making money on the web isn't as easy as everyone thought? Will the smaller mass digitization projects be subsumed into other projects and maintained with the same enthusiasm that the original founders had for them?

I don't have answers for these questions, but I want to believe that *something* will be done to preserve them in perpetuity. We've put too much into our digital existence to have it fail. But are we preparing for, or at least working against that possibility? I would have to say that it appears we are not. Moreover, whenever anyone raises questions, he is hooted from the public square for doing so. This will only make a coming disaster harder to prepare for and even harder to accept.

We have not yet reached the stage in our technological world in which any book or a facsimile of information can simply be zapped to all who need it wherever they are. I doubt anyone would dispute this. And yet, it is very common to find such sentiments in the literature everywhere we look. Bookless libraries are no longer an innovation put forward for shock value. They are considered the standard for any newly designed library—that is, of the few new libraries that are still being built. Almost monthly, we read of "the new future coming" and how "bookless" libraries are here to stay, as if that is a matter to celebrate (by the way, did anyone check with readers?).[30]

It is not my wish to stymie the future. More than most, I understand that the current model in traditional libraries with their expensive databases and costly operations is no longer sustainable. But let's be sure we're moving in the right direction, keeping what is good about the "old model" and strengthening what is good about the "new" one. Let's make sure, before we discard the "old model" that the new one doesn't discourage reading or, in fact, prevent it. Let's work for a future that works not just for a handful of those whose desire is only in the fact that "we can do it" but also for those who desire to use the information in the resulting medium.

So, is this charge that mass digitization is not a panacea as valid today as it was a decade and a half ago? I have made the case that, while much has improved, we still have a way to go before the technology we need overwhelms the problems that exist today. Until then, is it too Luddite to want to hedge your bets?

CHAPTER 7

Copyright

COPYRIGHT, THE BUGBEAR OF THE WEB

Copyright, next in my list of arguments why the Internet is no substitute for a library, remains unchanged. Nothing much has occurred with copyright in a decade and a half that now makes me want to backpedal about it, regardless of the current tensions being placed upon intellectual property rights by the web, and the current information-wants-to-be-free sloganeering we hear so much about these days, or the recent Supreme Court decision.

Let's begin this chapter with an easy concession with which no one will disagree. The United States has the most restrictive and draconian copyright laws of any industrialized country in the world. The terms of limitation are extraordinary so as to be nearly limitless. These laws are also virtually incomprehensible without a legal cicerone, and even then, nothing is certain.[1] Is confusing too strong a word? Let's see. A work created after 1978 comes into public domain after the life of its creator, plus 70 years, so good luck tracking that. But if it is a corporate work, then the terms become 95 years, or 120 from the point of creation. Got that? Wait, don't answer yet. If created between 1923 and 1963 and with a copyright notice, then the terms are 28 years but can be renewed up to 47 total years, now extendable by another 20, so a grand total of 67, unless renewed. If after 1963 with a notice, 28 years but now automatically extended to 67. Don't put away those slide rules yet, kids. If created before 1978 but not published, then life of the creator, plus 70 years, or 2002, whichever is greater. We're almost there. If created before 1978 but published between 1978 and 2002, then the life of the creator plus 70 years, or 2047, whichever is greater.

Now that was fun, wasn't it, and we didn't even touch upon orphaned works, or works without a clearly discernible copyright holder. How is it possible to find a given copyright, or even know which works are in or out? Is it any wonder Google just ignored all this folderol and did as it pleased with Google Books? And how are laypeople supposed to be able to pick up a work, easily know whether it was created before or after 1978, had a notice or not, and then when its creator died, plus 70 years, not forgetting to account for the social worker? It's ridiculous, isn't it?

When I wrote about copyright a decade and a half ago as one of the ten reasons why the Internet is no substitute for a library, I felt certain copyright would not change very soon. I was right. So far it hasn't, but it is under a great deal more scrutiny than ever before. That scrutiny could force a change, given recent and tragic events in the lives of Aaron Swartz, Julian Assange, and Edward Snowden, but more on those later.

INCREASINGLY, COPYRIGHT IS BEING IGNORED

With the rise of MOOCs, massive open online courses, the problem of copyright and permission has magnified.[2] Duke University got into the MOOC business in a massive way, so to speak, in 2013. Duke discovered that even when a reply regarding permissions is received, it's often the wrong response, or one that clearly misunderstood what was being asked. Writes Smith from Duke, "From the perspective of one asking a rights holder for permission to use some content, the process has a lot of frustration.... Sometimes, however, it is even more frustrating to receive a reply, because those answers often confirm that we are not dealing with a well-managed or carefully-administered process.... [O]ver and over the rights holder's staff replies with inapposite questions or, amusingly, a grant of permission to do something else entirely."[3]

We do this because both Congress and lawyers have intimidated us into thinking this way. Certainly infringement of copyright is enough to scare anyone witless: innocent infringement is $750, not a lot but nothing to sneeze at. Willful criminal infringement, on the other hand, is $250,000. When Congress gets its hands on copyright, things get immeasurably worse, and this has been true every time Congress has addressed copyright. As for attorneys, for whom I have the utmost respect, we do have a lot of them, and some would say too many. Depending on the source you use, for every 250 to 300 people in the U.S., we have one attorney. We have about 50 percent of all the attorneys on the planet, but we also have a smaller population, further skewing the ratio. No matter how it's calculated, we have a lot of attorneys. Is it any wonder the U.S. is also the most litigious society on earth?[4] Again, this is skewed since we allow anyone to file a lawsuit. But the sad fact of the matter is that Americans tend to solve their differences in court, possibly the worst place in the world to settle disputes.

IGNORED, BECAUSE IT'S COMPLICATED

Copyright is, after all, *our* law, and it's pretty straightforward in the abstract—well, as straightforward as one could hope when constructed by attorneys and approved by Congress. The U.S. Code Annotated, Title 17, section 102 reads as follows:

> Copyright protection subsists, in accordance with this title, in original works of authorship fixed in any tangible medium of expression, now known or later developed, from which they can be perceived, reproduced, or otherwise communicated, either directly or with the aid of a machine or device. Works of authorship include the following categories: literary works, musical works, including any accompanying words, dramatic works, including any accompanying music, pantomimes and choreographic works, pictorial, graphic, and sculptural works, motion pictures and other audiovisual works, sound recordings and architectural works.[5]

If all of this were not help enough, we are reminded in the same place that, "In no case does copyright protection for an original work of authorship extend to any idea, procedure, process, system, method of operation, concept, principle, or discovery, regardless of the form described, explained, illustrated, or embodied in such a work." In other words, creations are protected but not so much facts or ideas, as for example recipes that list ingredients. The law is an attempt to match incentive with innovation.

If we want to change copyright laws, then we should work to get that done (remembering that the other three or four times we asked Congress to address it, the end was worse than the beginning). And are we sure we want to weaken or relax our laws governing intellectual property rights? No one has said we need to be more like China (I mean no one other than Thomas Friedman) with respect to copyright in which, if there are Chinese copyright laws, they do not apply to non–Chinese materials so far as anyone can tell.

Having said that, we have to recognize that nothing else is pushing the issue of copyright or intellectual property rights aside into a free and unfettered free-for-all faster than the World Wide Web. I don't think it's too harsh to say, as one academic has, "The Internet makes it shamefully easy to copy other people's [works]. It all seems to be just sitting there, right on the screen, begging to be borrowed, re-appropriated, pirated—and it is, big time. But copyright law has lagged behind the speeding traffic of the information highway."[6] I agree wholeheartedly that copyright has lagged behind our digital-based world. In fact, many make a big deal concerning how "Technology, the marketplace and social norms often get ahead of law, especially in times of rapid change."[7] This is like saying that because cars go faster than ever before, there shouldn't be speed limits, or that we should be able to drive wherever we want, when we want, because vehicles are now unrestricted in what they can do. Until Congress changes copyright, however, we're stuck with it. We cannot get around copyright by arguing that we thought new devices were an exception, especially if we pay close attention to the words "either directly or with the aid of a machine or device," words composed long before there was anything like the Internet, much less Twitter, Facebook, texting, smartphones, iPads, iPods, or whatever else we can think of in use today. But U.S. copyright is very hard to bypass, even when Goggle's prevarication, or sleight of hand, was made clear by one insider:

> In truth, Google was not dealing with publishers in an upfront manner. During those first meetings, the Googlers did not even hint at their plans to digitize and index the vast holdings of huge libraries, regardless of copyright status. "We knew that was going to be an issue," says [Google team member Cathy] Gordon. But Google does not disclose these kinds of things early. Ever."[8]

Copyright, Google notwithstanding, still obtains as attorneys say, and because of that, what we are able to do on the web, beyond the silly cats and stupid human tricks, will have to bow to copyright until that law is changed. While intentions may mitigate the outcome, if we violate copyright, we unleash its consequences.

EVEN GOOGLE COULDN'T TRUMP COPYRIGHT— OR COULD IT?

Google discovered this the hard way when it was taken to task by its opt-out policy for authors. When others began attacking Google, Googlers were aghast. Their view was that they were doing this literally for the common good and bewildered when others didn't see it that way.[9] But who is kidding whom? Unless Google thinks making money on its various projects is evil, then its intentions were never altruistic only. Altruism may have been a factor, but it was a small factor. Judge Denny Chin of the Second Circuit's Southern

District in New York felt the same way, if momentarily. We can rail all we want at copyright and call it all sorts of names, but as long as it stays in place, those who wish to use material not in the public domain will have a hard row to hoe. As one observer writes about the Google Book Case,

> Google had created as astonishing tool that took advantage of the interconnected nature of the burgeoning World Wide Web, a tool that empowered people to locate even obscure information within seconds. The search engine transformed the way people worked, entertained themselves, and learned. Google made historic profits from that product by creating a new form of advertising—nonintrusive and even helpful.... It even warned shareholders that the company would sometimes pursue business practices that serve humanity even at the expense of lower profits.... But that didn't matter to the objectors in Judge Chin's courtroom.[10]

Google isn't the only one striving for weaker copyright laws. Grokster, a peer-to-peer file sharing site, tested the copyright laws, as have *YouTube* and the Electronic Frontier Foundation.[11] Regardless of how the argument is made—whether for the common good, for the children, for free speech, or even for God and country—if the project infringes on a copyright holder's right, then it is a violation. Regardless of who you are, *you* cannot remake the laws on your own caprice. Violators with unlimited resources, like Google, struggle but plod on, and plodding has won the case for it. The little guys, however, carry the heaviest of penalties without recourse.

WHY INTELLECTUAL PROPERTY MUST BE PROTECTED

Consider the case of two independent filmmakers, Ellen Seidler and Megan Siler.[12] The two made a niche movie, *And Then Came Lola*. The movie is about a romance between two lesbians, limiting its appeal to a certain audience. After cobbling together enough money from every source imaginable, including their personal credit cards, to make the film, they released it via DVDs, Blu-Ray discs, and digital downloads. Only days after its release, Seidler found pirated copies all over the web, and not just via Nigerian scam sites, but Netflix, RadioShack and Deutsche Bank. Once it became available for free, no one wanted to pay for it. Even when Seidler sent Digital Millennium Copyright Act takedown notices, things didn't go her way. One company told her she needed a new business model for the digital age! Eventually, she had to file in court—more costs—to get her film taken off sites that had pirated the movie.

THREE TRAGIC FIGURES

Earlier I mentioned three tragic figures who have pushed copyright by pushing the idea of information-wants-to-be-free, either by default or by design: Julian Assange, Aaron Swartz and Edward Snowden. Assange became famous over his Wikileaks website, not to mention his dangerous liaisons, so to speak. Wikileaks, an online nonprofit group, seeks to publish information that would otherwise be secret or classified. Wikileaks also survives on leaking news about events, people, places and things that might otherwise not have been reported. Wikileaks is political, to be sure, but it also buys into the notion that everything ought to free and freely known, without regard to context.

In some ways, Assange is like Edward Snowden, a former National Security Agency employee, who spilled the beans about PRISM, the mass surveillance projects that the United States and Great Britain engaged in. The real surprise in this case should have been that too many people were shocked that surveillance is ongoing, even in an administration that touts its openness and transparency, both of which have been in short supply. Snowden also thought that all information should be both free and freely available. What those who embrace these men and their illegal behaviors forget is that if a society is to remain free, not everything can be known by everyone or the enemies of that society will have the advantage. It's hard to win a poker game if you show everyone else your cards, no matter how high-minded you may be. Nor can we demand all information be free to everyone, regardless of who creates it. Nothing in our Constitution demands that the rights it guarantees are absolute (i.e., without exception), including and especially, the Bill of Rights. If this were the case, you could shout "Fire!" in a crowded theatre, never restrict guns at all, and always be able to search and seize without due process, to name but a few rights. (The issue of privacy is taken up in Part Two.)

Of the three men mentioned, Aaron Swartz and his tragic story are much closer to the information-wants-to-be-free mantra. Swartz, among his other activities, began making JSTOR articles freely available. Actually, that doesn't begin to cover his escapades on behalf of the information-wants-to-be-free crowd. He began downloading over 400,000 licensed articles off JSTOR from a computer he hid in a basement and covered with a box.[13] Swartz obviously was a very troubled individual, and it's doubtful his prosecution had anything to do with his death, the media and proponents of his actions notwithstanding. None of these men make the perfect case against copyright and for information-wants-to-be-free. If anything, all three give us good reasons to reexamine it.

Copyright Versus Information Wants to Be Free

All of the three men and their activities, however, serve to underscore the tension that exists between information and knowledge, and why one is not copyrighted and the other is. Information is data; it's what's there for anyone to look at, not unlike the clay that can sit on a clay wheel. But knowledge is the fashioning of that data, that information, into something useful that no one else saw, or that no one saw until you put it together. It looks like it ought to be free because it was derived from a free product—but it can't because until it was fashioned into knowledge, it would have forever remained as a data-set, just sitting and waiting to be sculpted into knowledge. Or, put another way,

> On the one hand, information wants to be expensive, because it's so valuable. The right information in the right place just changes your life. On the other hand, information wants to be free, because the cost of getting it is getting lower and lower and lower all the time [except, of course, to the individual that works to make it knowledge]. So you have these two fighting against each other.[14]

Didn't the Digital Millennium Copyright Act (DMCA) clear up all this controversy with respect to digital creations?[15] If wishing could make it so. The DMCA of 1998, signed into law by President Clinton, did make an effort to clear up our online copyright mess; it just didn't end up that way. Some argue that it only made it worse. The act implements intellectual property right treaties from the World Intellectual Property Organization (WIPO), the copyright treaty and the performances and phonograms treaties. It creates certain limitations of liability to online service providers, allows for the creation of copies of software for maintenance, and miscellaneous provisions for libraries, distance education, webcasting provisions and collective bargaining agreement obligations in the case of motion picture transfers. Oh, and it creates a new form of protection for the design of vessel hulls. Yes, it is the making of sausage, so cover your eyes.[16]

The DMCA, enacted in 2000, is reviled by many but not by all. Some see it as the salvation of the Internet because it protects the evolution of the web into web 2.0 and all its interactivity, so social networks, forums, blogs and more could flourish.[17] It also is the cause of numerous takedown notices. The anti-circumvention provisions that have allowed the web to flourish have also created much controversy because they generally prohibit anyone from circumventing the DMR, digital rights management devices.

An example of the problems with DMCA surfaced when the Library of Congress issued a new rule making it illegal to unlock a cellphone in order to switch to a new carrier.[18] Lo and behold, Congress enacted reform legislation that narrowed the circumvention rule to refer to what infringed directly, or made it easier to infringe directly on copyright provisions. (Perhaps, now, I should retract my do-nothing Congress claims?) The episode serves to underscore two things. First, having this oversight of the Library of Congress is not a good idea. Second, Congress must act to create long-lasting and permanent reforms of both DMCA and copyright.

The DMCA wins enemies for many reasons, not the least of which is that many believe it failed in its intent to help determine copyright in the digital age. Further, some believe it left infringement liabilities too high, made security provisions too tight, and finally failed as law because it left exemption provisions to the Librarian of Congress. In order to change it, it has to go back to Congress, the culprit that gave us the problem in the first place.

Is there any condition under which information-wants-to-be-free can be? Of course there are exceptions. Data sets, especially in the sciences, are well-known ones. Francis Collins and his colleagues determined early on to make their data sets on the Genome Project available, and many see this example as the poster child but ignore the subsequent problems, chiefly privacy. Not only has the sharing been difficult (they are referred to as "wars"), but the privacy issues have led to legal concerns.[19]

LIBRARIES AND FAIR USE

All of which serves to undergird the contention here that libraries are still needed, especially with respect to fair use. The fair use provision in the copyright law is clear enough but bears quoting in full here:

Limitations on exclusive rights: Fair Use
Notwithstanding the provisions of sections 106 and 106A, the fair use of a copyrighted work, including such use by reproduction in copies or phonorecords or by any other means specified by that section, for purposes such as criticism, comment, news reporting, teaching (including multiple copies for classroom use), scholarship, or research, is not an infringement of

copyright. In determining whether the use made of a work in any particular
case is a fair use the factors to be considered shall include—
    (1) the purpose and character of the use, including whether such use is of a
commercial nature or is for nonprofit educational purposes;
    (2) the nature of the copyrighted work;
    (3) the amount and substantiality of the portion used in relation to the
copyrighted work as a whole; and
    (4) the effect of the use upon the potential market for or value of the copy-
righted work.
    The fact that a work is unpublished shall not itself bar a finding of fair use if
such finding is made upon consideration of all the above factors.[20]

Section 107 makes clear that for educational purposes, copyrighted
materials are subject to fair use. Section 108, a longer section that follows
clearly spells this out in favor of libraries and archives. Readers may wonder
if this fair use exemption extends to the digital age. The answer is that recent
court cases have underscored the power of fair use in the hands of libraries.
The court case brought on by three scholarly publishers and Georgia State
University (*Cambridge University Press, Oxford University Press, Inc., Sage
Publications, Inc. v. Mark P. Becker*) with respect to its e-reserves came down
almost exclusively in favor of the library.[21] Further, in *Authors Guild v.
HathiTrust*, digitization in connection with libraries wins again, owing in
large part to the work of librarians on its behalf.[22] On the face of it, HathiTrust
appears no different from Google Books, but the judge saw HathiTrust's digitization project without commercial impingement, even given its association
with Google.[23] It's an important distinction, to be sure.

All of this is important because libraries are the safe haven of copyright
fair use. It isn't that copyright is unambiguous even in connection with
libraries. For too long, educators (mainly professors in academic institutions)
have thought that fair use meant that whatever they wanted to do as professors
was not an infringement, but nothing could be further from the truth. Professors using Blackboard and other similar features have made copyright
infringement on college and university campuses all the more difficult to
manage because they often use it as their own private digital library, something not covered by fair use, and something that takedown notices and subsequent lawsuits are making quite clear. What the current copyright law does
do, however, is make an exception for libraries and archives and provides a
way of managing print and digital. "The difficulty of protecting copyright
and intellectual property rights" writes one observer, "generally should not
be an excuse for forsaking [their] legal and ethical right[s]."[24]

COPYRIGHT COMPLIANCE OPTIONS

Since it isn't likely that Congress will take upon itself changes in copyright law, what are users to do? Creative Commons (CC) provides one way that users can steer clear of the copyright infringement. Founded in 2001, Creative Commons released its first set of licenses in 2002. By 2009, over 350 million had been issued. While some readers might think that only "has beens" and "never wases" use Creative Commons Licensing, history proves them wrong. Familiar entities using CCL are Flickr, Google, the Public Library of Science, Whitehouse.gov, and most recently, Wikipedia. According to CC creator, Lawrence Lessig,

> With the Internet, universal access is possible, but its potential is hindered by archaic copyright laws and incompatible technologies. We at Creative Commons work to minimize these barriers, by providing licenses and tools that anyone can use to share their educational materials with the world. Our licenses make textbooks and lesson plans easy to find, easy to share, and easy to customize and combine—helping to realize the full benefits of digitally enabled education.[25]

We need more sites like CC. It is not against copyright, nor is it anti-copyright at all.[26] Further, sites like CC underscore the possibility that copyright and online materials can coexist. While the "easy solution would be to "blow up" copyright and make everything free, it's far better to let the creators of that information license it themselves, rather than have a commercial enterprise determine that they should opt out if they don't want to be included. Creative Commons is a happy medium between two extremes on copyright.

Another good option for a remediation of copyright laws without actually overturning them, or worse, sending them back to Congress for an update, is open access (or OA). Open access came about, of course, as one alternative to the exorbitant cost of scholarly materials, and not necessarily as a way around copyright. The way it has worked out, it has, in effect, stymied copyright by taking the cost of permissions out of the equation. Since authors hold their copyrights in the open access calculus, open access provides a nearly seamless way of providing first-rate materials to users while also allowing creators to retain their rights. Like CC, the creators have limited copyrights. Even open access, however, isn't beyond copyright criticism. The American Historical Association recently complained, "The movement toward open access publishing is taking off without consideration of the impact on humanities scholarship ... in effect bypassing journal paywalls" which depend on that income for survival.[27]

As anyone who has ever worked in a library for long knows, the cost of periodical literature has increased enormously over the years at a rate that outstrips the inflationary cost of just about everything, including healthcare (for which, may I remind, we had a nationwide handwringing and now have "affordable" healthcare coming). Sadly, there appears to be no relief from rising periodical costs, even as libraries struggle to find a way, not so much to maintain subscriptions, but to sustain their existence! Costs routinely increase 7 to 9 percent annually, with individual databases costing as much as compact cars, literally. Most journal publishers know libraries have little alternative to paying these high prices and so charge them two, three and even four times what individual subscriptions to the same journals might cost. Copyright figures into this because publishers hold them and want to wring from them whatever return on investment they might be able to secure.

Can Open Access Save Us?

It's quite true that open access isn't new. The idea has been around for at least a decade, and it has been tried in various ways. It's also true that many of those ways attempted so far haven't been spectacularly successful. By definition, open access archives or journals do not always (though more and more do) provide scholarly vetting (peer review) but do allow free access via the open Internet to whatever materials are placed there. Peter Suber dispels many other myths surrounding open access, such as the quality is bad, it infringes upon academic freedom and that scholars to get peer-review status must publish in open access journals.[28] I mention the tidbit about peer review because that's one reason OA is having a difficult time getting traction in academic circles. If tenure track professors cannot get tenure credit for what they do in terms of research, they will avoid it. If open access cannot rise to the level of peer review status, then the likelihood it can succeed will be minimal. The good news, however, is that it does.

Open access usually allows for free downloading, printing, copying and distribution, only requiring that users attribute any materials correctly in much the same way that CC does. Open access bypasses the costly nature of access to scholarly publishing and scholarly communication conventionally conceived by making this access available on the open web. Open access archives or repositories can be journal-driven, discipline-driven, or a chrestomathy, if you will, an *omnium gatherum* of scholarly content. Suber also provides the best overview to open access, as well as a detailed discussion of the history and ongoing activity subsequent to its evolution.[29]

Out of desperation, open access began to appear, slowly at first. Today, OA offerings are more routine but hardly commonplace. With a recent so-called sting operation involving some OA publishers, OA has become messier still.[30] While one cannot dismiss the problem the sting found—fraudulent research accepted by more than a few OA publishers—the problem may not be OA alone. A recent study reported on in *The Economist* found that more than 50 percent of recent scholarly articles on cancer and other important topics could not be substantiated.[31] Be that as it may, the very existence of OA might well work against libraries, too, a matter to be taken up in the final chapter.

Other organizations and groups abound, but the point of all of them is the same. Through Creative Commons licensing, open access, and other similar options, we have a way to share information, maintain publishing tenure and promotion standards, and to provide low-cost scholarly communication, all the while contributing to the body of important academic research. Additionally, Copyright Clearance Center is helping by providing publishers a way to manage open access through its RightLink® platform.[32]

So, we have a history of open access, an already invented wheel through which we can share and possibly sustain scholarly communication. We have a means to properly attribute scholarly work via Creative Commons licensing. We also have a history of the process working more or less well enough to perpetuate itself, if barely, for about a decade. But one piece is missing if open access is really to provide any salvation from the high cost of scholarly communication. Right now only the largest of educational institutions (or only institutions with robust funding) are able to make open access work. All that is missing is a funding mechanism that makes it easier for small to medium-sized higher education institutions to get in on the act.

Money. Funding. Scratch. Call it what you wish, but it is the bugbear in all of this discussion, whether it's about copyright or mass digitization projects, the continued longevity of libraries, or even our government. This is not a laughing matter, and dollars will eventually determine whether organizations like Creative Commons and others will be able to offer an alternative to the unsustainable model we now have for information sharing. While some think the execution (as in, at dawn with guns) of copyright is required, it isn't really a solution, as Google Books has learned—they won, but in a costly fashion. It's too early to say how much blowback will result from Google's winning its case, but as one writer put it,

When each story of expansion is examined closely, the smooth façade of Google the monolith gives way, and a more complicated picture of on-the-fly decision making emerges. The official corporate culture, which places a premium on the initiative of individuals and small teams, can be seen in these stories. But there is also an unexamined confidence that the interest of Google and those if its customers are in complete alignment, and every new service is seen by Google as an advancement for humankind. Some day, when the experiments have run full course, they may be seen as the masterful fulfillment of Google's mission to organize the world's information, as farsighted vision. Or alternatively, the same stories may one day be read as accounts of misspent resources, evidence of hubris.[33]

Commercial enterprises aren't a solution either. Assuming any commercial enterprise can get around copyright—a mighty assumption—there is still the matter of how long such materials will be available and at what cost and under what conditions. Is this a risk we are willing to take with the bedrock of our intellectual capital?

BOOKS HAVE THEIR FATES

A book has its fate, as said earlier, and perhaps going the way of all flesh is one fate.[34] "Solutions" that undertake to "kill the book in order to save it" may not really have either the best interests of readers or books at heart, but are impelled by technology and the simple fact that it can be done.[35] Technology has become our "sheep" of the 21st century, to borrow a familiar line from More's *Utopia*. "Your sheep," answered More to the Cardinal, "which are usually so tame and so cheaply fed, begin now, according to report, to be so greedy and wild that they devour human beings themselves and devastate and depopulate fields, houses, and towns."[36] Modernized for our own time, might this apply to the web and everything it touches? It can't be wrong for authors to be denied royalties because of copyright, while pirates and other copyright violators make literally billions on the work of others, can it?

Think just a moment about how the web has, in a kind of self-serving way, disparaged copyright to its own benefit. Aggregators like *Huffington Post* make millions from content created by others for which HuffPo pays very little. *YouTube*, sold to Google for just over a billion, makes its income mainly off the shenanigans of amateurs while waiting for the takedown notices from places like NBC, CBS and other major media conglomerates. Meanwhile newspapers shrink or vanish altogether, journals with valuable but less-than-popular content fail, and a million little digitization projects bloom for the benefit of their creators, based on the content from others. Proponents of the information-wants-to-be-free argument complain that this is the new age and those old fogey media just need to "get with it." But how many of these web-based enterprises would even exist without the intellectual content of others? Meanwhile, somewhere a teenager is downloading 3,000 of her favorite tunes, for free. We have moved from respect for the intellectual property of others to "yours is mine."[37] But why? Does anyone really think that technology in all its granular specificity cannot devise a way to identify those items held in copyright and block them? Author Tim Kreider may have had the best summation on information-wants-to-be-free recently. Opining on those who ask him to write for free, he responded,

> Just as the atom bomb was the weapon that was supposed to render war obsolete, the Internet seems like capitalism's ultimate feat of self-destructive genius, an economic doomsday device rendering it impossible for anyone to ever make a profit off anything again.... I've been trying to understand the mentality that leads people who wouldn't ask a stranger to give them a keychain or a Twizzler to ask me to write them a thousand words for nothing.[38]

Google, Apple, *Huffington Post*, and a host of Internet companies of course *will* make money from it, again and again.

We ought to be able to figure out a *modus vivendi*, a middle way between the extremes, but no one seems to want to be the first to propose it. It doesn't have to be a choice between nothing is available to anyone without permission, or everything is anyone's whenever they want it, regardless of the reason, without respect to the creator's product. But don't we have that now, with libraries acting as that middle ground?

Web proponents—not all of them, mind you, but a vocal minority—appear to miss the fact that the nation's network of libraries offers just this middle ground. An individual can go into a library (or go online) and find much that he or she is looking for and use it, so long as it isn't for commercial benefit. Covered by copyright law, libraries can offer much of what is copyright-bound to those who use its services. An easy alliance, rather than the current seeming misalliance forged between libraries and the web where only patrons win and there are no losers, not copyright holders, not the intellectual property rights of creators, and not even patrons. It strikes me as win-win.

I am reminded of a recent ad for a data company, a data plan provider. It's only a commercial and so one cannot place too much emphasis on it, but it did strike me as emblematic of the culture's ethos about what technology can do and why they are entitled to it. A young twenty-something is looking at his choices and demands that he does not want to have to choose. He wants everything, and he can have it all: unlimited text, unlimited downloads, unlimited everything. He's going to demand it, and by golly, he's going to get it. Again, it's only a commercial, but isn't this sort of thinking that is an underlying driver of the web-based experience and its assessment of whatever we find on it? As one researcher puts it, we are a "culture fascinated with technological innovation and devoted to the religion of progress...."[39] Amen, so to say. If it's any indication, its aficionados are no less hidebound than the grey-haired lady toting a purse the size of a railcar on her way to the Primitive Baptist Church Bible study. Wrote *Wired* on its famous *The Wired Sh*tlist*,

> We think technology is rapidly opening up possibilities and revolutionizing the old order in a way that gives a chance to smaller players. We are unabashed optimists about our collective opportunities as we round the corner into the next century. We are skeptical of anyone's claims (including our own) to know what the future brings, but we look at the glass and see that it is no longer half-full but brimming over.[40]

I'm all for optimism, but with a pinch of reality, a dose of reason. It's possible that technology will cure all our ills before too much longer, but a dose of reality might help just a little. *Wired Magazine* is a kind of digital *vade mecum* for the Technorati, catering to cyberwizards and Internet geeks everywhere. It's all good to be optimistic about the future, yet it isn't optimistic but blindly foolish to think that every new technological trinket is going to solve everyone's problems, or at least all that fall within the ken of that gizmo's arena of operation. Surely history has taught us better than this with its march of time though technology's successes and catastrophic failures. We should have learned by now that for every solution to a problem one or two other problems take its place.

THE INTERNET CANNOT SOLVE EVERYTHING

We will eventually figure out a way to accommodate intellectual property online similar to the way we have accommodated intellectual property with other technologies (radio, television, copy machines, VCRs).[41] We will do that without infringing upon the rights of creators; it doesn't have to be either-or. Either we have it online and free of any entanglements, or we don't have it at all. It won't be easy, nor will it be trouble free. For some reason we tend to think the Internet requires that we change everything and every way we think and act just to accommodate it. Yet it really isn't that much different from other technologies. Perhaps the counterculture thinking and antigovernment philosophies that created the web influences our thinking now.[42] This philosophy has spilled over into public thinking as the web matured.

All of which leads me to believe that copyright will still pose a problem for the web now and in the not too distant future until we get serious reform enacted by Congress. I'll be as happy as anyone when that occurs, but until then we are stuck with it. Libraries will remain, and not only for those who cannot afford Internet connections at home but for all of us who do not have the financial wherewithal to "test" copyright infringement, or who think intellectual property should be respected. A decade and half ago, copyright loomed large in my argument that the Internet is no substitute for a library. Today, I think it still looms though there is a small fissure, if you will, in the monolithic supports for it. Even so, it isn't likely that copyright will simply go away, or that DMCA takedown notices will trend downward unless and until Congress acts, as oxymoronic as that may sound. If anything, takedown notices will proliferate, including false notices.[43] Some observers think that the more false ones there are—since it is illegal to send false DMCA notices—the better, as it might help put an end to them. This is unlikely since too much is at stake for copyright holders to let their creations go without a fight.

In any event, the library will remain infringement free, and ready to serve anyone, regardless of race, color or creed. And it will even serve even those who wish it would go away quietly, or just die already.

CHAPTER 8

Ebooks Über Alles?

Humans aren't the only species with the ability to communicate complex information; whales sometimes do this more efficiently with other whales than humans do with one another, and so do dolphins. Whales, however, do not write memoirs, nor do they pen elaborate "fish philosophies." So far as I have been able to ascertain, they haven't documented the travails of their gods and goddesses, either. Even though the writer of Ecclesiastes opined that of the making of books there was no end, this act—book writing—more than any other activity, separates human beings from all other creatures with which we precariously share this planet. Chesterton, as usual, had the best quip about this, though his had to do with art. Humans, he said, paint. A monkey can slap a stroke of paint on a canvas but we do not call it art. Well, when Chesterton uttered his quip, we didn't *then* call it art. Doubtless some university professor somewhere now claims than apes paint better than do we.

PRINTED WORD REVERED THE WORLD OVER

We humans revere the printed word, and have given great place to text, even a holy place. No wonder. To create even one Codex Amiatinus of the Bible in the 1500s cost the lives of 500 sheep.[1] And think of the painstaking effort of all those monks double-bent, copying endlessly those marvelous *Books of Hours*, psalters and the like. It's no wonder that one of them, it is recorded, appended to the end of his work, *nunc scripsi totum, pro Christo da mihi potum*, "I have now written everything—for the sake of Christ, give me a drink!"

Ancient people took text seriously, and loved, honored, even worshipped it. We often wrongly refer to the medieval period as part of the Dark Ages but only because we do not know the period well. It's true that the medieval period did not have many books. The cost was enormous and the honor rare (see sheep, above). Of the few books around (and the Bible, of course, was one), they not only knew, they knew by heart. It is often said, for example, that if the Bible had been completely destroyed and no original left, 95 percent of it could be reproduced from quoted material during the medieval period. The point is, we luxuriate in texts but know almost nothing by heart anymore.

Even down to our modern times, book reverence is hard to dislodge. Author Anne Lamott writes,

> I read both paper and ebooks, but please don't tell my publisher this. Ebooks are great for instant gratification; you see a review somewhere of a book that interests you, and you can start reading it five minutes later. At least I still know it is *wrong*. But when all is said and done, holding a printed book in my hands can be a sacred experience—the weight of the paper, the windy sound of pages turning, like a breeze. To me, a printed book is like a cathedral or a library or a beach—holy space.[2]

All of this is prelude to our next reason why the Internet is no substitute for a library: books have, or had, been in first place since forever.

PRINTED TEXT NOW PASSÉ?

In a few short years this has changed.

Ebooks not only have changed all that, they are dislodging printed books and may have usurped the special status accorded to print, and possibly forever. When I penned the "10 Reasons" article and the subsequent poster, ebooks had only just begun, to ape the once-familiar Carpenters' song. By the time I got around to writing the book, ebooks had some traction, but not a great deal, and certainly nothing like they have today. Today, almost everywhere we look, ebooks appear to have taken over, as have the devices on which to read them. From the Kindle, to the Kindle Fire, to iPads, to the Nook, to a half dozen other nondescript e-reader devices, ebooks and their accoutrements have all but replaced the once staple printed monograph. My contention then was that ebooks certainly were revolutionizing the way we read, but they had not yet eased out the printed word entirely. Is my claim still true?

While some contend that Proust cannot be read on an LED-lit screen, it is becoming more and more apparent that any declarations about ebooks may run the same fate as Darryl Zanuck's 1946 comment about television: he argued television would not endure because people would tire of staring at plywood every night.[3] In other words, it isn't likely that ebooks are going away any time soon. What isn't clear, however, is just how much traction they have, especially in scholarly research.

The contention that you cannot read Proust on a screen is less outrageous than arguing ebooks will never catch on. While ebooks haven't overtaken the entire reading market (for years they could double each year and still make up only a small percentage of all readers and all sales since so few were available early on), they appear to be quickly overrunning the market and capturing all readers, even the youngest of them.

Or have they?

Ebooks Up, Down, but Certainly Not Out

Until 2012, ebooks showed remarkable growth and e-readers, especially the Kindle, seemed to toll the death knell for printed books. At one point, industry experts said print books would not just be dead, but gone, by 2015.[4] Moreover, Amazon claimed in 2012 that their ebook sales had overtaken print.[5] A survey in 2012 revealed, however, that only 16 percent of all Americans had actually purchased an ebook. And, while 30 percent reported reading an ebook, a whopping 89 percent reported having read at least one print book. The growth rate for ebooks also fell to just over 33 percent, nothing to sneeze at, but hardly a rate to begin buying coffins for print books.[6] In any event, what we know is that 2012 began a decline in ebook purchases, e-readers, and an increase in the purchase of print books.

The number of readers of ebooks is waning, too. The Pew Internet Survey of American Life released in July 2013 its "Younger Americans' Library Habits and Expectations."[7] Younger Americans are certainly connected, but what is surprising is that many of them not only still go to the library, check out books, and are still reading print books, but also about a third of them strongly oppose moving every library service to the web, including all books, services and even librarians. So, which is it? Are ebooks growing, declining or both?

Part of the problem of perceived growth has to do with Amazon's Kindle and just how many of those devices are being purchased versus subsidized. No one knows the exact number (except CEO Bezos, and he's not telling).

We do know there are sharp increases in sales. Although early reports in 2012 showed ebooks replacing print, early 2013 reports showed flat ebook sales. Even with the number of school libraries using Questia, an ebook vendor, to replace their school library books all together, and with the first all-electronic public library poised for Bexar County, Texas, one would think the only thing left for printed books is the cortege.[8] Are we rushing to judgment? Should everyone take a deep breath?

The answer to both those questions is yes. Ebooks are a hit for those who only read for pleasure, much less popular among those who must read them for scholarly purposes. So it isn't one or the other, but both. Further, content specific e-readers are on the wane with tablets and phablets replacing them.

FOR ALL THEIR HOOPLA, EBOOKS SLOW TO CATCH ON

Ebooks have been around forever, comparatively speaking. Most of us think of them as only a decade old but that is not the case. Ebooks are now going on thirty-something years old, beginning as e-texts read on locus-locked terminals. Project Gutenberg, for example, is in its fourth decade.[9] Public domain materials are eligible for e-text formatting and widespread distribution, and Project Gutenberg struck first to make that option available. Reading early on meant reading on a desktop, and our reading became scanning. It proved just too complicated, too onerous to read at a terminal for very long. Early terminals "blinked" almost imperceptibly, interfering with the reading process. With the advent of many other kinds of ebook vendors— Questia, Ebrary, netLibrary and so on—e-books became more numerous, and the demand to read them on something other than a terminal grew.

By now, ebooks should be dominating our reading landscape and surpassing printed materials easily, but they are not. While the hype never lessens, the actual use does not match the hype. They offer the same enticements as web-based journals: ease of access, ubiquity, requiring no shelf space, saving trees, and holding thousands of books on one reader at a time, and so on. Ebooks also bring with them their own copyright demands. As the ebook market grows, so does the number of vendors. Rather than developing a strategy for distribution, publishers either create their own e-readers or offer their inventory to some e-reader vendors but not to others. What you want to read is predicated by what e-reader you purchase. The device is linked to the reader, in other words, not to the content.[10] Buy a Kindle Fire and you have X content;

buy an iPad and you have Y content, and never the twain meet, at least so far. This is frustrating to readers, to say the least. Ebooks make numerous promises to us, but they keep relatively few.[11]

Ebooks, for better or for worse, although unbounded by page limitations, still ape the form of the printed books. This may be one reason they have not fully replaced their printed counterparts. When ebooks take on their own "hyperlinked frenzy," however, they become almost impossible to read.[12] By the time the reader chases down every link in paragraph one, she has no idea what paragraph one was all about. Trying to reach a happy medium between too much and not enough has been far more difficult than we thought.

So far anyway, ebooks are facsimiles of printed books, down to the turning of the page (and at one point, even the smell).[13] This begs the question that if you want the experience of a "real" book, why not read one? The marketing trend is to "entice" readers to ebooks by making them seem more like printed ones. Whether this has slowed down the growth of ebooks is anyone's guess. That may be changing, however, as more and more ebooks become the only source for information access with no printed counterpart at all.[14]

Because the electronic text is often chock full of various other links, readers are forced to scan the text, and that's what many of us do.[15] Our concentration is more limited, our ability to remember compromised, and our comprehension weakened (see Chapter 10 on reading in Part Two). We race from line to line and link to link, as if we must get somewhere more quickly than ... well whom? We're not sure. In fact, some argue that e-reading isn't really reading at all.[16] Yes, ebooks broaden the reader base. E-readers may be the very tool needed to make reading universal the world over.[17] Ebooks connect many readers with authors, reduce the mystique of "The Author," and provide ways to correct mistakes, hyperboles and even plagiarism almost immediately. Finding what we want in an ebook is as simple as finding something online: we merely search for it. This beats looking through a printed book page by page, often the only way to find a fact, or a quote, as the index, if included, is often limited.

The Downsides of Ebooks

But there are also downsides to ebooks.

The increase in audience may not be from actual readers so much as from those who have scanned a few pages. While this is also true in print, the effect is not the same. Thousands comment on an online book immediately, while an author may go decades before hearing anything from a print-only reader. That author could be sure, however, that readers had read the book and wanted to connect with him in some way since they took the time to write a letter. Today, many who comment online just want to hear their own voices. This makes it much harder to know who really knows what she is talking about and who is just blowing smoke. Further, the multiplicity of voices makes it much harder to hear a profound one. Moreover, a printed book is a kind of third-party verification; a self-published ebook mimics a vanity press for printed books, but it is held in more esteem, further complicating matters for serious readers.[18]

Ebooks present a particularly difficult problem for scholarly materials.[19] Scholarly monographs—save for those that are in the public domain—are often the last to end up in an e-reader format, perhaps owing to copyright, or their difficulty, or both. E-readers still do not have an easy note taking mechanism, are not particularly easy to highlight in and do not provide a simple way of getting back to the notes. This is changing, of course, with tools like Dropbox, Calibre, Evernote and Zotero.[20] Each of these tools helps e-readers capture, record or remember what it is they are reading in an electronic format. Many are mobile accessible, too. The indie app Readmill may also help change for the better note taking and the interactive nature of readers and writers but it's too early to say.[21]

This is not to say that scholarly materials are not being abundantly supplied to libraries in the last two years. Ebrary, for example, makes libraries an offer that would be fiscally irresponsible to ignore. For example, to add 100,000 print volumes to the library where I work (about thirty times what we add in a good year) would cost us over $2 million dollars just to get them in the building, and that is only the beginning. We'd have to have shelf space for all of them, people on hand to open the boxes, to compare invoices with the materials received, to send back what is incorrect or otherwise faulty. Only then could we begin to catalog them (a fairly long process for this many books) before finally sending them out for shelving. Before we complete such a process, more than ten people would have touched these materials. Compare that with the same materials that cost 95 percent less (at least initially) and require only one person to get them ready for "check out." No storage, no cataloging, no boxes to open or invoices to cross check, and no one needs to shelve them.

But—and you knew there had to be one coming—as with everything digital, this, too, has its downsides.

Some professional librarians bristle at the prospect of buying a massive hodgepodge of titles. The same could be said about aggregate databases as well, but few librarians raise hackles over them.[22] What concerns all of us more is the ability to read them easily and well. Built-in readers are not always very user-friendly, and formatting on them can be, well, kinky. At the risk of getting too technical, some ebooks—though not many—contain MARC record errors. Most librarians find these errors small beer, and certainly no reason to forego buying them.

What remains a real difficulty is the ability to read these texts in a manner similar to which we read printed ones. Interruptions during the reading process are too numerous and too cumbersome to allow for sustained, comprehensive reading. Must electronic texts be read in the same manner as printed texts? That is unclear, but Part Two addresses this issue. Besides, how else are we to read them when that's the way we humans have read for millennia? If it is to change, it will take us considerable time to adapt. For now, all we know is that ebooks are changing the way we read and what we comprehend. We know that the change is both different and difficult. What we don't yet know is if it is deleterious to our reading habits.

EBOOKS DO NOT SHARE WELL

The next bugbear with ebooks is the ability to share or borrow them from libraries. This has been alluded to above with respect to which e-reader one buys, but it's more than that, too. Vendors have been all over the place, and sharing ebooks, especially through libraries, has not been as seamless as one would hope, partly because the process focuses on individuals with personal e-readers, and partly because publishers fear libraries will throw a wrench in their ebook sales altogether.[23] It appears, too, that because none of the companies are working together but decidedly independent of each other, borrowing ebooks from libraries will continue to remain devilishly difficult in the near term.[24]

Google's book project has made ebooks more accessible, though it has garnered for the search giant the dubious distinction of being a book stealer, at least according to one documentary.[25] Indeed, even after an eight year court battle, Google Books appears to have won its case, though there will certainly be some outcry.[26] Sharing content, including borrowing, as mentioned above, remains difficult and next to impossible when multiple readers are involved. This is mainly because digital right management issues (DRM) obtrude, but it's also because of the way access to ebooks on e-readers is configured. Until recently, the only way to "share" ebooks with others was to "jail-break" the DRM, not exactly the good-citizen way to go. Publishers are pressured to let go of their stranglehold on ebooks, but some experts believe that holding onto DRM strictly keeps users coming back to Amazon, iTunes and other purveyors of digital content. But there are ways for readers to share.

Ownshelf (http://ownshelf.com/), a cloud-based platform sharing ebooks with friends, began in 2012, and while it touts itself as the "Dropbox" for ebooks, some wonder if it will become the "Napster" of digital content.[27] Lendink (http://www.lendink.com/) has also now emerged, but it's too early to tell whether it will go over with ebook readers (or even survive).[28] Both Amazon and Barnes & Noble are offering some sharing of the DRM content, but it is limited, and the availability in libraries more limited still. Barnes & Noble is just struggling to stay afloat for now, something that may prove impossible since its Nook reader has failed, more or less. It is difficult to believe that this will remain the same into the next decade but for now, sharing ebooks is not an easy task unless the owner hands over his e-reader to friends. As one observer put it, "Today's major ebook proponents will not give up easily, because they see long-term value in technology and it fits well with their businesses. Quiet progress will lead to eventual success.... One day, paper-based books will be in the minority, but the full transition could take 25 years."[29] While I don't agree that print is destined to vanish, the fact of the matter is that it has *already* taken ebooks 25 years to get this far. The question now is, will it take another 25 years? My guess is yes, especially if early 2013 trends showing a decline in ebook sales prove true.

The other downside of ebooks is the variety of e-readers and how quickly their shelf-lives end. Part of this is by design. If vendors did not follow built-in obsolescence carefully, they'd be out of work. With great rapidity, the Kindle, Kindle DX, Kindle II and Kindle Fire, and now the Nook, raced through the market, some falling out of date before the "date due" on most printed books. Moreover, many vendors produced such a bad product or a product with bad traction (e.g. Sony, iRex, Kno), they simply did not make it through the year, leaving those who purchased them with useless technology. Consumers proved the guinea pigs, purchasing the new technology only to find out later it wasn't stable.

Even the so-called stable vendors, such as Amazon, iPad, OverDrive, Barnes & Noble and others, are not so stable as once thought. For example, Barnes & Noble, as mentioned above, is in financial trouble.[30] After spinning off its Nook, the company's most recent figures show a nearly 10 percent decline over the year previous.[31] While Amazon's sales are up 22 percent over last year, the cost of the Kindle subsidies via ads still troubles some observers.[32] E-ink, the technology that makes Kindle and other e-readers work, is also experiencing a strong downturn in sales. Quarterly sales fell 46 percent this year, and sales for the coming year are expected to be flat.[33] This may, however, be linked to the rise in sales of phablets and tablets. Lastly, a small point too, but ads that appeared online before, after and during the reading experience still annoy. Generations of readers who grow up reading in this environment will eventually ignore them, but those of us living in this transition period must come to grips with this troublesome feature of online life.

We are still awaiting the FTC outcome of the alleged ebook price-fixing of Amazon and Apple. It's clear that Apple wanted to set the price at some magical point. Amazon fared better, but how much better than Apple remains to be seen.[34] Furthermore, the outcome isn't going to be good for consumers. So far publishers have shelled out just over $166 million to settle ebook claims.[35] Apple price-fixing isn't the only problem. The other one has to do with ebooks leasing to libraries. Some publishers do not lease at all to libraries, and those that do gouge them with prices that often aren't affordable.[36] In any event, both libraries and ebook readers are the losers in this scheme that only recently began moving to the forefront of reading concerns. Some have gone so far as to say that this "collusion" on price fixing is driving a wedge between the literary haves and the literary have-nots.[37]

Many of these objections must seem minor to readers ready for the digital era and more than ready for the demise of the printed book. These are valid objections to those who must struggle to use these devices and to get used to a new reading milieu. Readers must grapple with a new reading environment, and for many of them the change is not only difficult but for some, almost impossible. We might want to think it is only a matter of age, but I believe it is more than just that. Even when we show our 18–24 year old students how to access our ebooks, many of them still demand a printed text for something they must study carefully.

EBOOKS AND EDUCATION, SLOW TO PARTNER

Universities piloting programs with Kindles and iPads show mixed results.[38] Although a number of universities are either giving them away or requiring them for use, some professors remain resistant to the digital revolution.

Researchers argue that the older laptop technology may make a better fit than iPads and Kindles with web access. The e-environment proffers many amenities to readers: reading comes to life as a song or a poem is heard. E-texts provide readers with an alternative to print textbooks; they store more than a book bag can hold or a human can carry. And they provide thousands of apps that are useful: grammar, mathematical, historical, artistic and so on. Further, because students are used to the smart phone environment, iPads are clearly a perfect extension of that technology. So what is the problem?

Part of it is the versatility itself. Too many distractions mean students will do much else *instead of* their work. The reading itself provides too many distractions, and the smart applications lead to too many shortcuts, helping students bypass an important learning experience. Many proponents laugh at these objections because students are no longer required, they argue, to memorize anything. It's always at their fingertips. That is just the point, opponents argue. The slower typing required on the keyboard impedes written work. Applications that an individual university may require are not always easy to run on these web-accessible devices. Some students discover that iPads are not helpful for taking notes, and some even jettison them for their more familiar laptops. Some students do not even know the very basic and elementary skills to make the simplest of deductions without the iPads or smart phones and their apps. They are, in a word, lost without them.[39] Some of these drawbacks are likely to vanish over time with improved technology (third party external keyboards for iPads are now available—and one from Apple itself may be coming—increasing the already exorbitant cost of owning one), and none are reasons to scupper web-accessible devices. What is likely not to improve is the over reliance of students on these devices for what was once considered common knowledge of every college bound student.

With libraries, the problems are similar. Kindles are widely used in libraries, but again with limited success. In order to abide by the legal restrictions, libraries have to create a number of different checkpoints for Kindles as they come in and go out of the building. Further, libraries have to devise ways to restore these devices easily after patrons have tinkered with them. This may include something as simple as erasing sophomoric pranks or as serious as deleting credit card activity.

OTHER EBOOK PROBLEMS

Cataloging materials on these devices is something of a nightmare. Do you catalog each book or just the device? Are the records to be as simple as possible, or as complex as all other library records? When devices retire, is a new record entered or simply transferred to the new device, even though the new device is surely to look a bit different and have different features? And how does the library distinguish which devices hold which content, and for how long? Finally, the formats these texts come in also present a small problem for libraries. Most of them, fortunately, are HTML and easily read on any web-enabled device. Some texts, however, require a plug-in, or have to be accessed through Adobe Acrobat, further complicating the reading experience.[40] The same difficulties with respect to using these devices for making annotations or other notations obtain here as well.[41]

While these are the most obvious problems with ebooks, getting them into the building is not easy either. Library budgets have been static or declining for the last decade and a half, yet libraries must now stretch scarce dollars even further. The various models out there provide a nice variety for readers, but the selection makes it harder for libraries to determine which ones should be made available to students, as they cannot buy all of them. The advent of demand-driven acquisitions, DDA, also provides a potentially inexpensive approach. Most DDA models allow for x number of views before a full purchase is triggered. These can range from one view to half a dozen or be associated with an amount of time in which the material is viewed or be a combination of the two. So for example, a purchase is not triggered until after the material is viewed three times or more than 30 minutes. The cost of these views is nominal. If the threshold isn't reached, the full dollar amount isn't charged.

The attraction for libraries is obvious. Until this model emerged, libraries purchased all materials at 100 percent of the cost and hoped the material would be used, eventually. Regardless of efforts made in collection development, the sad fact of the matter proved the 80/20 or Pareto Principle—80 percent of demand is satisfied by 20 percent of the collection, give or take 10 percent. So, ten books purchased for $40 each cost $400, regardless of use. The chances are very high that if those materials are not checked out by the end of the first year, they never will be.

But even given the DDA potential savings, the difficulties with e-texts are not over. What happens to titles viewed but never purchased? And how long do they "clutter" the catalog? For example, in a given year there might be 10,000 titles available to trigger a purchase. But after a year, 9,000 may never have been viewed. Are those titles left in the catalog indefinitely, or removed? Does this process confuse readers who may have seen a title once but now cannot find it? These are not easy questions to answer, but libraries are attempting to answer them in the least disruptive manner possible for users.

Some libraries share materials via consortia and this process creates its own joys and sorrows. Pricing is better via a consortium—one of the main reasons for using one—but typically someone else is making all the decisions for every library. These decisions may or may not agree with already established policies in a given library. The digital rights management (DRM) issues are still a difficulty to be addressed and solved. The technical support behind ebook consortia sharing is critical to making such endeavors successful. Because there are so few up and running, it's too early to tell just how successful they will be.

EBOOKS: PRINTING, PLAGIARISM, PRESERVATION

Printing still continues to be a problem with all ebooks, and will likely continue to be so for some time to come. Print an ebook?! Sounds oxymoronic, doesn't it? But the need remains, at least for now. Most ebooks in libraries allow some printing, but that printing is limited by the vendor. Typically, as with many things technological, the printing isn't uniform across vendors, some vendors allowing for a certain number of consecutive pages, others allowing up to a certain percentage of the book. An easing of copyright restrictions would allow for more, most likely, but that becomes a "waiting for Godot" proposition.

Another "p" for ebooks is plagiarism. Electronic texts make it especially easy for students to copy, not just portions of a text, but multiple pages, easily. I don't think that rising generations are more dishonest than prior ones, or that today's students are dismissive of academic integrity. But plagiarism, while never absent from the academy, is certainly more epidemic among today's high school and college-aged students than it was decades or more ago.

Not only do search engines allow for easy access to materials but even online books are searched quickly, too. Within a matter of minutes, our less than prepared student cobbles together a somewhat cogent paper that satisfies the assignment criteria, with a first reading anyway (unless our said student sounds like Einstein with this paper, when he has sounded like Homer Simpson on all the others). The process is so easy and so quick, it begs even the most intemerate among us to cheat, or at least think seriously about it. Some will complain this is not a fair criticism of the web. Perhaps. But even our legal system does not allow for entrapment, and the web's siren song of plagiarism is certainly canorous enough to attract many otherwise law-abiding writers. In point of fact, it has, and not just students, but the highly competent from all walks of life.

The most difficult matter to deal with, with respect to ebooks, is their preservation.[42] For now, libraries are counting on vendors to take care of this, but that is a far from certain approach, though it will mature, just as electronic journals have in the hands of vendors. No vendor will continue to offer ebooks if their value in libraries wanes considerably, any more than publishers carry titles that do not sell. Preservation is important but so is perpetual access, something that is not guaranteed even from one year to the next. No guidelines exist for ebook preservation. The preservation of print materials became the library's concern as soon as the purchase was made. Publishers had little say in preservation unless one counts the acid-free paper discussion a few decades ago. That is far from the case with electronic texts. The library is ultimately dependent upon the publisher for providing the perpetual access and the preservation, as well as for adapting the format for new devices. Hugh McGuire said in a Ted Talk in 2012 that what is collected on the web is ego noise, what is collected in books is research, edited and carefully crafted. If the web controls ebooks in the future, ebooks as we know them today will be gone.[43]

The good news is that ebooks cannot be lost (at least not in the same way as print books can be), nor can they be tossed out the window of a moving vehicle, eaten by an animal, or have coffee spilled all over them (though of course the devices they are read on are still subject to all of these misadventures). They do require bandwidth and a network over which to deliver them. These are not matters to be dismissed but they are ones that are certainly not new to the digital age.

Some preservation options for e-texts do exist: LOCKSS (Lots of Copies Keep Stuff Safe) has been around for over a decade.[44] Begun in 2000 and located at Stanford University Libraries, LOCKSS is an open-source program that provides an inexpensive way to preserve content. It is a perpetual light archive with an emphasis on locally owned content that is shared across the membership. It is a fee-based member service, but the fees are very reasonable. Portico, created by JSTOR, is another, newer fee-based program that "work[s] with libraries, publishers, and funders [to] preserve e-journals, ebooks, and other electronic scholarly content to ensure researchers and students will have access to it in the future."[45] Finally, there is CLOCKSS, "a not-for-profit joint venture between the world's leading academic publishers and research libraries whose mission is to build a sustainable, geographically distributed dark archive with which to ensure the long-term survival of Web-based scholarly publications for the benefit of the greater global research community."[46] The CLOCKSS venture is a Controlled LOCKSS and will make certain that future generations have access to digital scholarly content.[47]

Of all the "10 reasons" I outlined a decade and a half ago, my comments on ebooks proved the least reliable. Not only have they flourished more quickly than I expected (sort of), they are gaining greater breadth and depth than I imagined, even if they are "reading" readers more than ever before. Ebooks provide a number of extremely important conveniences for users. More and more ubiquitous, ebooks allow for easy searching, and they have the potential, at least, of costing a great deal less than print books (especially with respect to storage and processing for libraries). Rising generations appear ready to embrace them (but not exclusively, however), and the market appears to welcome them with open arms.

Upon this reexamination, however, it is safe to say that there are still some related issues that are at least worth a furrowing of the brow one last time. Ebooks remain a bit difficult to use when it comes to scholarly material. While many more options are open to scholars with e-texts (for example, no longer are we "stuck" with just public domain materials), some difficulties remain. We still do not have a unified format that allows any electronic book to be read on any e-reader. Publishers are still dulling Occam's razor by increasing entities without necessity. Copyright has not gone away, and because it hasn't, the cost of ebooks and their e-readers is still out of reach for most individuals. Although many of us have smartphones, no one is making the case that most people prefer to read books on them.

Literacy issues remain with e-texts. Not only are scholarly materials hard to read on these devices, but something about the devices themselves distracts readers and their ability to comprehend texts. While some proponents argue that individuals are likely to read more on e-reader devices, no one is making the case that readers actually comprehend more. I believe this issue of comprehension and literacy may well be a problem that time will erase, yet I worry about the generation of readers who are in the middle of this change. Will they lose out?

E-reader devices continue to multiply; and as they do, previous generations of devices become outdated (and by the way, where—to what trash heap—are they all going?). Content on those older devices may or may not be available on newer models. The actual cost of ebook delivery is still a mystery, and while iPads are thriving, they aren't selling as they once did. Furthermore, in 2012 and 2013 ebook purchases declined noticeably. Print books still have a strong pull for many, many readers and aren't likely to disappear soon. In fact, a recent Rasmussen poll (2011) indicates that, *nationwide*, readers would rather read a book in traditional print format than in an ebook format.[48] And it isn't just a few of them, but 75 percent of them. Furthermore, American adults do not want to see more and more library services automated to the point that librarians are left out of the mix entirely. So, maybe there is hope for libraries even in the age of ebooks.

Efforts to preserve digital content have been formidable, but those enterprises appear strung together by a webbing of diaphanous financial funding. One false financial move, and the entire enterprise might collapse. If we want longevity, we need libraries. After all, they have a track record that exceeds more than 1,000 years, so far. Not bad for a "technology" that many people are saying is obsolete and no longer needed.

CHAPTER 9

Depth and Ubiquity

The two remaining items in my original mordant stridulations (as some might call them) against the web have to do with its depth and the portability of books, despite the web's apparent ubiquity. By addressing these two items together, I admit a significant change in both since the publication of my "10 Reasons." More than any of the other items I address, these two changed the most dramatically and for the most part, for the better. This chapter gets at the "no there there" on the web, so to speak. Both these topics have, to some extent, been touched upon; hence, one more reason why they are partnered here.

THE WEB'S BREADTH AND DEPTH

While a case cannot now be made that the Internet is a mile wide and an inch deep, to think of it as five miles wide and a few hundred feet deep is not an unfair characterization. The web has matured a great deal in the last decade and a half, and much that was not available then, is available now. In an earlier chapter, I discussed not only the "deep web" and its contents, but also how most search engines still miss a good part of that content. Search improvements are, however, routine, and I doubt this failure will continue much longer. For example, Google just rolled out a new algorithm, Hummingbird, which does a better job of answering user inquiries.[1] The rollout was without fanfare, just a routine upgrade.

The web is rich in detail and widely varied. It's hard to think of something not yet on the web, or a topic that is not going that way soon. As mentioned earlier, both the Vatican and the Bodleian libraries will digitize 1.5 million pages of 15th century texts, books and Hebrew documents. One cannot begin to describe the value this will be to scholarly endeavors. It represents a remarkable treasure trove of materials that have been heretofore available to only a handful of scholars who study them.

This is only one of the millions of such projects of rare manuscripts, incunabula, 17th–19th century materials in science, history, literature and so on, that are available over the web. If anything, the web may be one of the deeper libraries around, not because it has more pages—that would be an easy task to accomplish—but because it has so many materials that only a few of us could see and use before the Internet made them universally available. Take, for example, the Human Genome Project and the millions of bits of DNA that have been placed on the web. It's true that much of this material is still the bailiwick of those whose lifework it is to study, but its availability to everyone with an Internet connection is without a doubt a boon to knowledge.

Futurist Ray Kurzweil argues that by 2030 (or so) we will be using technology to enhance our own minds. Only recently did one researcher control another's mind over the Internet.[2] (I'll pass over just how horrifying this is when pondered for long.) The rapid increase in computing power, combined with the information on the web, will allow us to add to our brain power via computers, thus bypassing the mind's inherent limitations.[3] Not everyone is on board with this, but I mention it here only to accentuate the vastness, power and seeming limitlessness of this thing we call the web and its multifaceted power to connect seemingly disparate things.

More down to earth are the numerous sites where individuals can learn a foreign language. Even more important than this, however, is how English is becoming the global language because, in large part, of the Internet. In 2010, for example, the majority of the world's data was, for the first time, non–English, but quickly "read" as English.[4] The reason? Computer technology has made it so very simple to read non–Roman languages that the Internet broadcasts worldwide as English. In combination with social media, the Internet makes it possible for non–English speakers to learn English and practice it with others around the world. What is more, very primitive languages that would otherwise be lost entirely are finding life, albeit in small ways, online. The Internet is not only encouraging language diversity, it is also enhancing it all over the world, from the smallest hamlet to the darkest reaches of any continent. Take that, local library!

Meanwhile, IBM's Watson, the genius computer and game star contestant is now turning its formidable prowess to the cure for cancer.[5] After taking on humans in the game show *Jeopardy!* and beating us soundly, it has now absorbed all the medical information necessary and will turn its "brain" power to curing cancer. Not everyone believes the pursuit of a solution to our cancer woes is necessarily a worthwhile endeavor. Google's CEO Larry Page recently said, "[I]f you solve cancer, you add about three years to people's life expectancy. We think of solving cancer as this huge thing that'll totally change the world. But when you really take a step back and look at it, yeah, there are many, many tragic cases of cancer, and it's very, very sad, but in the aggregate, it's not as big an advance as you might think."[6] True, perhaps, but only if you or your loved one is not suffering from it.

While not precisely the Internet, Watson has essentially downloaded all the information it could find on the subject and will now begin assembling it for possible cancer cures.[7] Further, some even think Watson might one day replace Google. While we're on the subject of medicine, we must admit Google provides a quick, easy and profoundly important way for individuals to track previously unreported side effects of commonly prescribed medications.[8] While this may not mean the difference between life and death (though it could), it may well mean the difference between a most uncomfortable reaction and none at all. Perhaps we can solve everything by "clicking" here after all.

Google Books is nothing to sneeze at, even with its pending lawsuits in Europe and possible appeals to Judge Denny Chin's late 2013 decision to declare Google's practices within the bounds of fair use." Millions of texts are available for searching, and the fact that they can be searched at all, word for word, is a real boon to researchers. Couple Google's project with the Project Gutenberg and dozens of other similar such projects, and we all have a multimillion volume library at our disposal. Although, according to a recent Rassmussen poll, users by an overwhelming margin (75 percent) prefer print to electronic, the electronic is fast becoming as ubiquitous as print, even to the point of surpassing it.[9]

Scientists now report, however, that they have successfully stored audio and text files on strands of DNA and retrieved them later with nearly perfect fidelity.[10] It's too early to say if this is the solution to all our problems, but it is a *promising* development. On a strand of DNA, scientists were able to encode an audio clip of Martin Luther King's "I Have a Dream" speech, a photograph, a photocopy of Crick and Watson's famous 1953 "double helix" scientific paper, and all 154 of Shakespeare's Sonnets. Although scientists were able to retrieve the stored DNA data with 99.99 percent accuracy, that error rate was still far higher than would be tolerated in a printed book, being equivalent to three or four typos per page.[11] While certainly groundbreaking, it should not surprise us if we think about it. Isn't this the way that God—or Nature, if you prefer—has been encoding complicated data for millennia? While there are similar successes in the biological world using the cellular walls of bacteria, the bacteria eventually died, and with it, the stored data. With this new effort, information can be stored on DNA to "sit there" for thousands of years.

This experiment confirms the 54,000 word book that Harvard scientists were able to store on DNA strands. Using the basic nature of DNA (A's, C's, G's and T's), scientists were able to fire a laser at the DNA and reveal its hidden texts. Today, this process costs so much only private labs and the Harvards of the world can afford it, but scientists think that in ten years, it will be 100 times cheaper. Said one scientist, "[By that time] it probably becomes economically viable." Surely now we can confirm what some have been saying all along: that with all these millions and millions of materials literally at our fingertips and all the storage space we need encoded literally inside of us, why do we need libraries at all?

I've been trying to say why we need them for many pages now, but I'll take few more stabs at it in this chapter, too.

For All the Vastness of the Web, Some Still Do Not Have Access

As with the other eight reasons, so with these: We need to make a few stipulations about all this vastness of materials and the likelihood of these potential prospects. First, not everyone has access to the web. Yes, it is true that tens of millions of us do, but millions more do not. Efforts are being made to close this digital divide, but it still remains.[12] It exists at various levels and among a variety of demographics. Broadband penetration is about 70 percent nationwide, with about 85 million homes having fixed broadband subscriptions, but there is also a very real financial divide that cannot be closed until public and private sectors come together. It's one thing to have the access, it is quite another to be able to use that access fully. Rather than have any more talk about the Internet replacing libraries, we need more talk about how the two work hand-in-glove, and how they must in order to close this real gap between the haves and the have-nots.

Believe it or not, there are still places where Internet broadband access does not exist in the home. We naturally think of these places as in developing countries. But even in the U.S. there is still a problem. As much as 20 percent of the U.S. population does not have access to broadband Internet service at home, according to a new Pew study.[13] Further, in another Pew Study, 15 percent do not access the Internet at all, and don't even want to.[14] If some did not have cellphone service, that figure would be closer to 30 percent. Where do these people go when they want affordable Internet service? The library, of course.

Without the library, many of these folks would not have any access, and more would not have stable access at all. Eliminate libraries, and you create an information blackout for millions. What is even more important is that the access provided by libraries is free to those individuals who cannot afford it otherwise. Don't have an iPad? There's a very good chance one is waiting for you at your local library. Don't have a laptop? Ditto. Granted, you may have to wait in line or sign up for it, but having it there and free has to be more meaningful than thinking you are among the few who cannot get access to the web, or do not have access to any web-accessible devices.

Moreover, libraries do more than just offer access to the web. They also offer access to materials that the web cannot provide, viz., millions of articles in proprietary databases, thousands of books that are not on the web and may never be for numerous reasons, job searching, résumé help, to name only a few of the many other services. This access proves vital in communities— not just communities with struggling populations but in every community, hamlet and rural township around the globe. All one has to do is go to a place where libraries are not abundant (and that territory is growing daily) to see just what is at stake, and what we stand to lose in order to understand how valuable libraries are, even in this age of hyperconnectivity.

THE WEB IS RICH AND DEEP BUT ALSO VULGAR AND RUDE

While the web is certainly rich, varied and deep, it is also silly, stupid, vulgar and shallow. Pornography was discussed earlier, as were hate sites. Countries such as Germany are pressuring Google and other search giants to curtail offensive search suggestions, such as those that attempt to predict what a user wants.[15] Even the hint of censorship sends librarians wailing into the streets, but these are attempts to create a more civil search experience. The same can be said for Prime Minister David Cameron's announcement that online pornography will be an "opt-in" for users in the UK.[16] It may not work but it's a step in right direction.

Setting pornography aside as a quick way to riches via web apps, is that all?[17] Hardly. Nonsense abounds on the web: cats, celebrities, stupid human tricks, sites with false or incorrect misinformation. A library might well have out-of-date materials, but it is the rare library that houses useless information intentionally. The web, however, is abundant in its trivia, uselessness and mindless nonsense. It's simply easier to have no restrictions at all than to have to make content-worthy decisions—pretty much the very thing that librarians have been doing with collection development since the beginning of libraries.

Librarians have recognized all along that not everything that comes out of a human head is worthy of publication or even preservation. This isn't an issue of intellectual freedom. Anyone can write or say—with some restrictions that even librarians forget about from time to time—whatever he or she wants. Nothing in the Constitution requires libraries to hold and preserve these. A kind of information free-for-all means we all lose, lose to the endless snipe hunting.

Because the web celebrates all voices, we have an information free-for-all. Anyone can publish anything, and it appears they all have. By itself, this seems like a good idea. Even though search engines do not discriminate between a Nobel Prize winner writing about evolution and an eighth grader writing about plate tectonic theory (and, frankly, it prizes them both equally), a researcher can, with time, wade through the returns and find what he's looking for. Granted, it may not be easy from time to time as many intelligent people have shown, having been duped by what they find on the web. (I submit that part of the reason for this occurring as often as it does is because we have always relied on published information being trustworthy. Untrustworthy materials either rarely made it into print or were self-published and so carried their own red-flag warnings.)

THE WEB: A HAVEN FOR SCAM ARTISTS, QUACKSALVERS AND MISCREANTS

Today, however, the matter is worse. Fake academic journals are now abundant, so much so that even scientists are struggling to separate the good from the bad.[18] This is not a new issue, but the abundance is. When University of Denver librarian Jeffrey Beall began tracking these in 2010, there were only 20 fake journals. Today, he has recorded over 4,000. Academics are recruited to fake conferences with prestigious sounding names (e.g., Entomology 2013 instead of the acclaimed and actual conference Entomology-2013). But once at the conference, when it's too late, the academics are charged a hefty fee.

Academics are using the conferences to pad résumés. According to the *New York Times* exposé, "[S]ome researchers are now raising the alarm about what they see as the proliferation of online journals that will print seemingly anything for a fee. They warn that nonexperts doing online research will have trouble distinguishing credible research from junk."[19] It is for the nonexpert—most of us—that this is such a big deal. Intelligent, well-educated individuals who are not experts in a given field will have a tough time, too, in discerning which research to trust. But it's more than even this, because the unwary or naïve can be led astray even more easily than the well-educated.

One publisher on Beall's list has more than 250 journals and charges as much as $2,700 per paper. While the director of the publishing center, Srinubabu Gedela, argues that the work is legitimate and above board, many disagree. Most of these publishers do not list their fees, and most author-academics do not know there is one until they have submitted a paper. What makes the problem all the more difficult is that many offer a 20 percent kickback on total fees to those members who will serve on the boards of these "publishing houses."

No one knows what this will do to open access (that sting notwithstanding), since some of these journals have made their way into open access databases. While open access is one possible solution to the unsustainable model of costly scholarly communication that has dominated information access for the last thirty years, if the trend of fraudulent scholarship continues, it could deflate this important trial balloon.

Proponents will laugh and say this isn't a big deal since 4,000 journals is a drop in the bucket. Besides, at least we know it's a problem and something is being done about it. Although both of those statements are true, we can't be dismissive about an information source for which it is next to impossible to ascertain the true from the false, the plausible but erroneous from the implausible yet convincing. We need to have a way of knowing which are real and which aren't.

Fake academic journals are only part of the problem of the web's being miles wide and a few feet deep. Tragedies are often the subject of instant fraud.[20] When Hurricane Sandy hit the East Coast, photos of sharks in New Jersey, a seal in a subway station, and a scuba diver in Times Square Station flooded (no pun intended) the Internet. News outlets struggled to find what was real from what was false and they weren't always successful. And even when they were, the damage had already been done. Some individuals, especially the elderly, had already been bilked of hundreds, even thousands of dollars.

Consider, too, the web's penchant for fake stem cell sites, a case that is particularly sad. For those in search of stem cells, their online treks are likely a matter of life and death for them or for a loved one. This is especially the case of parents who are searching for some outcome for their very sick children other than death, or worse, permanent institutionalization for them.[21] Parents or loved ones begin the search in earnest for a cure for a disease that has no known cure. A search of the web reveals numerous possibilities, all with credentialed scientists, or so it appears. Lamentably, what unfolds, often later, after hopes have been raised and thousands of dollars spent, are scam artists who have successfully bilked loved ones out of tens of thousands of dollars for nostrums sold by a quacksalver.

The problem is so abundant on the web that a monitor-blog was set up to combat it.[22] These sites aren't offering a near cure or even a harmless treatment. They are offering fake medicine that may be contaminated and will even harm those receiving it. Further, beyond their razzle-dazzle websites, the actual "plants" where the stem cells are harvested are often abandoned buildings with misleading addresses. The websites lure in the unsuspecting while the web owner becomes rich. Before proponents of the web scream this is an unfair charge because the problem is being addressed, I submit that without the Internet's ubiquitous exposure of them, such places would not exist. The web makes them both profitable and sustainable, much the same way once dead and forgotten hate sites have been rejuvenated by online presence. What is puzzling is that if the web existed as any other entity—say alar in apple juice, or bogus medicines sold in stores—watchdogs would be all over it. Modern sensibilities are immune to web criticism because many think we can solve everything with just a click.

Valuable medical information remains buried on the web under mountains of misinformation proffered by charlatans and quacks, relying on jillions of "hits" that repeat the same wrong information over and over again. Some physicians have even bewailed the web since patients come in thinking they have already diagnosed their illnesses and are ready to fight with their physicians about treatment.[23]

Too often, even sound medical sites showcase drug companies hawking their particular drugs and funding the hosting site for promulgation of those drugs. Further, it turns out that Google's Flu Trends algorithm vastly overstates the flu season's outbreaks contrasted with traditional methods of calculating those numbers.[24] Proponents are quick to assert that this is "only a glitch." By next flu season, all will be well. So, really, it's nothing after all. Just an overestimation, nothing to see here, keep moving. Do readers perceive a trend: Even when the Internet gets it wrong, it gets it right, too? You see, by knowing it's wrong, it is half right, or something like that.

The web also becomes an endless loop for the tragic and the awful. A news program mistakenly showed a live shot of a suspect being chased by police. Later, the suspect stumbled out of a car, tumbled down a hill, pulled out a gun and shot himself in the head.[25] The anchor attempted to get the feed pulled, but it was too late. After an abrupt commercial break, the anchor apologized to viewers. Only those who had tuned in at that moment, saw it—that is, until the clip "went viral." BuzzFeed, a website known for its "cutting-edge" social news, immediately posted the grisly shooting on YouTube where more than 1,000 viewers had posted their "likes" in less than half an hour. Although many observers excoriated the site for doing so, it did not lessen the likelihood that it will happen again.

THE WEB'S BAD IS AS DEEP AND WIDE AS ITS GOOD

The web repeats tragedies thousands of times over. Seventeen year old Rehtaeh Parsons was found by her mother after the young girl hanged herself, a victim of cyberbullying after pictures of her gang rape "went viral" and spread through her school.[26] A photograph could, of course, have been passed around in school pre-web days, but a camera would not have been present even a decade ago. In our hyperconnected world, cameraphones are everywhere and allow quick access to social media and webpostings (in fact, this is often a "selling" point). A 17 year old teenager in Ohio, Brogan Rafferty, is facing life imprisonment after he lured individuals to fake job postings via the website Craigslist. He killed the men answering the ads.[27]

After the Boston marathon bombings occurred, the social news site Reddit posted "Find Boston Bombers" thread, known as a subreddit.[28] Sounds like good civic work to use crowdsourcing to aid in the capture of the miscreants, right? It could have been had Redditt not wrongly named several people as suspects who were subsequently hounded by this same crowd. The witch hunt could have become dangerous but thankfully it did not. Reddit apologized, but how, really, does one apologize for a witch hunt? "Oops," just doesn't seem quite enough. Some complained that news outlets were also to blame, and that's true, but nothing else could spread the misinformation as quickly as the web is able to do.

It gets worse. After several videos of gruesome decapitations in Third

World countries surfaced on Facebook and then went viral, Facebook "caved" (according to some) to negative public pressure and removed the videos.[29] Facebook took six months to review its policy on decapitations. For about 36 hours, Facebook reinstituted the policy with a video of a woman in Mexico whose decapitation occurred because she cheated on her husband. Facebook argued that the "sharing" occurred because people were scandalized by it. Yet 36-hours later, they removed the decapitation video and the reinstituted policy.[30] As Cicero had it, "If we are forced, at every hour, to watch or listen to horrible events, this constant stream of ghastly impressions will deprive even the most delicate among us of all respect for humanity."[31] In less noble words, if we keep this up, we will harden ourselves against any fellow-feeling.

Bobbi Duncan did not want her father to know she was a lesbian. Facebook let him know anyway.[32] She isn't the only one, either. And while Facebook has adjusted some settings since then, the problem persists. Some will argue that it's the user's fault—a kind of blaming of the victim—and perhaps there is some truth to that. If true, however, then our choices have to be either to get online and live with it, or stay off anything that might capture our identity. It's so bad a choice it isn't even a Hobson one. Add to this the parasite websites that "look" for postings of teen pictures and videos into order to steal them and repost, making one stupid teen sexting suddenly a viral industry, and you have the makings of a brave new world gone very wrong.[33] Stricter COPPA (Children's Online Privacy Protection Act) laws that went into effect July 2013 may curb this somewhat but chances are that a workaround by those with ill intent is already in the offing.

I mention these random events, not because they are isolated incidences but because they are so numerous, all aided and abetted by the glorious, infallible web. Indeed, in many cases, it is difficult to figure how these events would have transpired without it. We have the instant gratification of being able to connect anywhere at any time, but too many of us are apparently lacking the appropriate ethical skills to tame this technology in an appropriate manner. This is not unusual, of course, when it comes to any new technology. After cars became our main mode of transportation, drunk drivers were inevitable. Clearly, we will not tolerate them the way we tolerate all sorts of madness from the web. Any attempt to rein in the web brands you as a Luddite or worse.

WEB ADDICTION WORSENS

We are wedded to this technology—and the devices we own to access it—unlike anything else. Nearly half of all business travelers would skip brushing their teeth—an exercise that not only promotes good dental health but may in fact reduce heart disease—before giving up their iPads.[34] If that wasn't bad enough, 25 percent said they would shut off the water for a day rather than shut off their iPads, while 22 percent said they'd go without electricity for a day rather than shut off Internet access, apparently willing to give up the web-accessible device the *next* day, too, lacking any way to charge them. Clearly, we moderns are crazy about our devices and lose all sense of logic about them. Consider that there are now more mobile phone subscriptions than there are people in the U.S.[35] We do not want to be anywhere without a connection to the Internet even if it means foregoing toilets and toiletries.

A few words should be said about my last complaint about the web: The web is ubiquitous but books are portable. The first instance—the web is ubiquitous—is quite true. I rarely go anywhere that I cannot find web access. Unfortunately, I often find that access is unsecure, or it will cost me something. Hence, I carry around a hotspot. I know this does not guarantee me absolute security, but it adds one additional layer of security that an open Internet does not.

As for the portability of the web, well, there is this business that you must have a fully charged, web-accessible device with you at all times, not to mention wi-fi. Some readers will laugh at this, thinking how smartphones have eliminated this criticism, but I beg to differ. Sure, one can read a *short* piece on a smartphone, but mainly only the under 30 crowd can read anything over five pages, only three if the piece being read is technical or complex in nature. I am fully prepared to accept this complaint as owing to my "advanced" age. Even so, I encounter many 20-somethings every week who ask me to "email" them a document so they can read it on a device other than their smartphones. In the fall of 2013, our students printed over 40,000 pages in *eight* days on our three printers because they did not want to read the material on their devices This 40,000 is only one place, the library. We have a half dozen other labs from which they could have printed, too. And this is the so-called "green" generation. The iPads and MacAir—or phablets—do make it easier to read longer, more complicated texts, but there again is the issue of affordability and, apparently, printing.

Even with all these devices to choose from and assuming one is able to afford them, there remains the small but annoying issue of battery life. Recharging batteries is critical, of course, to access the web via these devices. What we do on our devices and for how long (listening to music, for example, or watching a movie) makes for a longer or shorter battery charge. E-readers will mean yet a further complication. While e-readers are certainly much, much better than they were 15 years ago, they still have a way to go before they can seriously trump books in portability (and don't forget that latest Rasmussen poll that found that 75 percent of readers want a print book, not an electronic one). While we know that many users do take their iPads into the tub (see above), many of them live to regret it. When e-readers will not charge, or for whatever reason, cannot, even temporarily, bring up a purchased text, the experience is most frustrating.

While the web is both deeper and broader and has added to its ubiquity, some additional portability reasons remain for hanging onto those library cards, and the libraries from which they are issued, for at least a little while longer. We still need these bastions of freedom, of collaboration, of community—at least three things libraries offer that the web will never be able to deliver, either as richly or as fully for some time to come.

PART TWO

The second part of this book can be viewed in two ways. One way is to see it as more reasons why the Internet is no substitute for a library. The second way, and really my preferred one, are four additional things, two of which libraries encourage, and two of which they prevent, by virtue of their existence. The four are: reading, literacy, privacy and piracy.

Rapid change often causes what William Ogburn referred to as cultural lag, or "an element of culture that was in step with its environ changes and the environs are unable to keep up."[1] When that happens, pressures bear on the environment. The pressures can become too great, and so the change is rejected; or the pressures cause the change to be modified. The Internet has provided us with many such challenges or, if you prefer, opportunities, and we are witnesses to it in many areas: the social, the legal, the cultural, the intellectual, and so on. In almost every facet of our lives, especially because the Internet touches upon all aspects of our lives, we are witnesses to these changes and to the cultural lags that inevitably follow. This section presents some cultural challenges.

These changes, imposed upon us by the Internet, forces new ways of doing things that our current model cannot address. Note that I said "new way" and not a bad way, necessarily, but we all know that not every change wrought by the Internet has been for the better. Because of the "wow" factor of technology, we tend to overlook just how bad some conditions are as a result of the changes that technology brings. Some of these changes may correct themselves; others may not unless we address them. In any event, the challenges technology brings forward force us to confront them sooner rather than later. To ignore them is to do so at our cultural, social, intellectual or legal peril.

Reading and literacy, which I will take together, address what changes online reading has wrought upon us, both the good and the bad, and how it has impacted the ability of readers to read and comprehend, and how that has impacted literacy, especially among new readers. We'll look at both the current conflicts and potential ones that are likely to emerge. Have our reading habits changed? Is Google making us stupid? Are the jeremiads we hear simply the hyperventilations of a few who cannot or will not address themselves to change? Certainly Nicholas Carr, Evgeny Morozov and other experts argue that our online mania is changing us in ways that are not good, and in ways that will compromise our ability to learn, and even to know. Still other experts, like Clive Thompson, aren't so sure. It behooves us to at least examine this in some detail. It may not matter so much among adults (though that is not altogether true), but it may have a deleterious impact on children. If that is the case, then it is important we at least acknowledge the fact, should it exist, and begin thinking now what can be done to minimize these effects.

Privacy issues are a concern for anyone online. Identity theft is a multi-billion dollar problem. We know, for example, that it is now costing the country billions in lost revenues, and may cost the country as much as $21 billion over the next *half* decade in lost revenues.[2] The FTC reports that identity theft cost Americans about one and a half billion dollars annually since 2011.[3] Almost two million Americans were affected in 2011, twice the number only five years earlier. Clearly this is a significant problem, not created by the Internet alone since identities were pilfered long before the Internet emerged, but certainly it has been exacerbated to levels we never imagined before the web's advent. The question is, what are our options between those who want to shut down everything and tighten all controls, and those who, as Scott McNealy, CEO of Sun Microsystems, argued in 1999, claim our days of privacy are over?[4] Is there really no middle ground?

Next to privacy is another "p," piracy. The piracy problem, while not something created by the web, is a concern certainly made much the worse because of it. Piracy is now not only a billion dollar problem, but it also threatens to bankrupt everything from newspapers, to music, to intellectual property. Surely there is some way to make what creators create remain their property. Or, has the information-wants-to-be-free crowd won that argument, and everything created is held by all in a kind of consumerism of information? Do we understand that piracy is not just the problem of those who wish to make a buck, but all of us who wish to protect creative rights? What are the protections that exist other than copyright, and how long will copyright last in this climate of what-is-yours-is-mine mentality?

Education is also changing dramatically in light of the Internet. Some, like Thomas Friedman, want to "blow up" higher education. The MOOCs—massive open online courses—are changing even now, right under the very feet of so many tweed-coated professors, causing them to lose their balance. Further, what is the library's role in MOOCs? Are libraries prepared to aid and abet them, or are they standing in the way of them? Do libraries have a choice? Further, since many think we do not need libraries any more, what about colleges and universities? If we really can "zap" a book from here to there, why not also "zap" the best professors teaching their best topics online and be done with the exorbitant cost of a college or university education? Anyone who wants to learn something can just plug in, right? And think of the savings: no colleges, no expensive textbook costs, no salary perks for professors who teach 10 hours a week, no luxurious libraries, no parking lots, no new buildings, and no, not even any football teams. Oh, wait, on that last point I may have relegated myself to heretical status for sure. Some might well be glad to be done with colleges and universities, but God forbid we get rid of collegiate football (or baseball, or basketball...).

The Internet has shrunk our world. No longer can we remain provincial, and we shouldn't want to. Go global is the new rallying cry. The web certainly appears to be making all of us freer than ever before, but perhaps we should be sure that the cost of that "freedom" is not a slavish indifference to those very principles that keep us free indeed.

I like to think of these four things as things your library would never do to you. A library will never impede your literacy, distort your ability to read, steal your identity by exposing your private self or your creative capital, or confound your education. I do not think these things are reasons to scuttle the Internet or constrain it in any way. I do think they are reasons enough to hold off jettisoning our libraries, at least for the foreseeable future.

If we are going to replace libraries with this thing we call the Internet, let's at least wait until we address ourselves to these four prickly matters that, like so many dead skunks littering the information superhighway, give it a slightly unpleasant odor.

CHAPTER 10

Reading and Literacy

In the exuberance of our newfound treasure in technology, we may have passed over some of its latent and not so beneficial effects. Typically, the effects of a given occurrence break down into two parts: the intended or manifest effects (usually good), and the latent or unintended consequences (some good, some not). Cars have, for example, revolutionized travel for the average American, making it easy to get from place to place and allowing our fierce independence to reign. But the unintended consequences of driving are as alarming as the intended effects are appealing. Drunken driving, pollution, urban congestion, traffic gridlock, personal injury, and the skyrocketing cost of maintaining cars, not to mention geopolitical dilemmas (oil) that their upkeep has created, are but a few of the unintended consequences. For years, we ignored these unintended consequences, more or less in favor of the perceived benefits.

CONSEQUENCES: THE GOOD AND THE BAD

In a similar way, the impact of the web and its effects on reading and literacy are important matters to discuss before they become serious entanglements. I am not the first to bring this up, either. Sven Birkerts mentioned it when the web was but an infant.[1] We didn't listen then, and the problem has worsened. Many others have now come forward. Apart from the more familiar names like Bauerlein, Carr and Morozov, there are also Liu, Kress and Mackey, to mention only a few.[2] While the seriousness of this discussion will not cause us to shut down the Internet, the discussion should at least get a fair hearing. Sensible people will see these issues for the serious matters they raise; only web myrmidons will refuse to acknowledge them. Even Nietzsche,

126

whose work I find more often tedious than not, did have an important point to make about the nature of reading long before the web was born. "To be sure," he wrote, "[to be able to read well] it is necessary ... to practice reading as an *art* ... something that has been unlearned most thoroughly nowadays— [and to do this] one has almost to be a cow and ... *not* a "modern man": [and engage in] *rumination.*"[3]

ARE WE LOSING "RUMINATION" (COMPREHENSION) TO THE WEB?

To prevent readers from having a cow about this chapter, the short version regarding reading and literacy is this: We are losing rumination, or what we might call comprehension, an important characteristic feature of serious, critical reading. This is most odd to me, particularly in a time when the buzz word on college and university campuses is about critical reading and writing.

The web is jeopardizing, or at least compromising, our ability to read and comprehend (literacy). It has not enhanced our abilities in this regard, or even remained neutral to them, but constrained them in more than a passing way. The research on the subject now is far more comprehensive than it was a decade and a half ago, and more people are thinking seriously about it. Moreover, the best we can say about the web's influence on writing is that it is "not all for the worse."[4] The majority of teachers (68 percent) contend that digital tools make it more likely that students will take shortcuts with their writing. Almost half of them think it makes their writing more careless and haphazard. And the good news? The *potential* for more exposure of their writing and the chance to get more feedback makes it, well, not abysmally bad. This has to be one of the best examples of damning with faint praise that I can think of.

Clearly the most famous discussion of this topic of the internet and literacy occurred when Nicholas Carr wrote his piece in the *Atlantic* about Google making us stupid.[5] Carr began the piece with a famous line from *2001: A Space Odyssey.* Hal, the "super" computer on board the spaceship, began making its own decisions and quietly eliminating its competition. Dave, the astronaut, realized what was happening and had to "take down" Hal. Hal complained during his "lobotomy" that he could feel he was losing his grip.

Carr likened Hal's loss of grip to the way he was beginning to feel after being on the web for nearly a decade. "I can feel it, too," Carr wrote. "Over the past few years I've had an uncomfortable sense that someone, or something has been tinkering with my brain, remapping the neural circuitry, reprogramming my memory. My mind isn't going—so far as I can tell—but it's changing. I'm not thinking the way I used to think. *I can feel it most strongly when I'm reading.*"[6] Carr goes on to argue that he cannot recall as much as he used to, cannot concentrate enough on complex texts, doesn't comprehend as much as he used to, finds he has to go back and reread passages again and again, and catches himself jumping from place to place when a text is more than a few pages long. "Technology, "writes Mary Cross, "has a life of its own and mows down everything in its path."[7] Two of the things technology appears to be "mowing down" are reading and literacy. Because both are so critical to our democracy, we cannot afford to be dismissive about the symptoms we now see.

Blog Reading Slogging Us Down?

Our interests appear to be headed to blogs and away from what might be considered challenging reading. According to a recent Pew study, researchers found that about 24 percent of all American adults say they read blogs, about 11 percent on an average day.[8] On the face of it, one could argue that this turn to blog reading is only for the best, and quite possibly it is. I do not wish to make the mistake that fellow librarian Michael Gorman made a few years back when he criticized blogging as McReading.[9] But let's face it. Reading *most* (but not all blogs) does not really rise to the level of an investigative piece in the *New York Times* or the *Wall Street Journal*. Granted, some of them may, but that is not the point of blogging and to argue otherwise is to miss the point of it. Moreover, even this reading rises to the level of comprehension.

Consider Dan Fagin's attempt to alert his readers that his brother-in-law had suffered a massive heart attack. Since both of them shared the first name "Dan," Fagin made sure who he was talking about by using "Dan F" for himself and Dan D" when he referred to his brother-in-law. It didn't matter. As he put it,

> The misunderstandings pinballed crazily through cyberspace. My literary agent was the quickest on the draw, telling me she was thinking of me and glad to hear I was on the mend.... A colleague who is a magazine journalist told me she was hoping with all *her* heart that mine was OK. Another writer friend from

Seattle sent along a photo of a pastoral scene to aid my recovery. An evangelical acquaintance from eighth grade offered his fervent prayers for my salvation.[10]

And so it went. Bear in mind that all of these people are quite smart, very well-educated and putatively sophisticated readers. How could they have missed it?

Perhaps I should be glad that people are reading at all, especially young people. But as reading scores plummet or stagnate near the bottom quartile for just about all age groups, shouldn't we be thinking about what may be a strong contributing factor to this decline?[11] Some argue that the nature of the web with its snatch and grab mentality forces us to do just that: snatch and grab, diminishing our ability to comprehend and focus, and in general "mowing down" reading and literacy in the process. But others argue that the "Internet has created a new kind of reading, one that school and society should not discount."[12] Perhaps this is so, but it strikes me the same as arguing that what Rembrandt painted and what a monkey throws on a canvas are the same. If that's true, then everything is art and so nothing is. I would say the same about reading: so long as there are words, it's reading. But we know that isn't the case. We can read easy texts without difficulty routinely, but eventually it will show up when the text becomes more difficult. Like a steady diet of only one thing, a steady diet of snatch and grab reading, of 140 character tweets, of quick and dirty Facebook-postings, slowly but effectively kill our ability to read. It's beginning to make us, if not stupid, then perhaps a bit stultified?

READING SCORES ANEMIC

What makes this a difficult debate is that smart people, those who place in the upper 5 percent of all the population, always do well with most anything. They are on the web and it hasn't hurt them. Those in the intellectual stratosphere cannot be the benchmark for the rest of us. Young people in Honors, Advanced Placement and International Baccalaureate programs are not your typical, average readers. Is the web's snatch and grab mentality negatively impacting the vast middle 66 percent of us? It's still too early to tell, but the average among us are not faring well online; it may well be that even the multitalented among us aren't either, if Fagin's story is any indication.

The NAEP reading scores indicate an uptick, but only slightly higher than we were in 1992.[13] Higher is better than lower, of course, but do take into account the tens of millions of dollars spent on reading initiatives since then that have only moved us from a nationwide reading score of 217 in 1992 among eighth graders to a "whopping" 221 in 2011. If you do the math, you realize we cannot afford, literally, any more increases since this one cost a fortune! A deeper examination of these scores is not very uplifting, either, as fourth graders remained unchanged, or rather unfazed by those costly initiatives. At least one group is asking the same question about all those dollars spent on reading scores and the almost imperceptible uptick.[14]

Many factors figure into these scores, of course: from the kind of teaching each student gets, the head start these children have (i.e., whether reading was stressed in the home or if home was mere survival), how much help each child received along the way, and even how they were taught to read. The NAEP tests cannot be taught, however, and so they measure at least one level of how teachers teach reading across the nation. The answer is, not very well, even accounting for all the variables. But do teachers have a chance when every child is bombarded with texts that do not challenge, that do not aid that reader's growth? Additionally, we surely cannot discount a medium that encourages cursory scanning by its very nature, and one that focuses much more on the trivial and the ephemeral than it does on the profound and complex. What we do know is that how children learn to read, and whether or not they continue, is critical to their success.[15] We also know that by the twelfth grade, most students are not reading much of anything at all.

Anecdotally, we know that online reading is not the same as reading print. As Andrew Piper of *Slate Magazine* put it,

> Amid the seemingly endless debates today about the future of reading, there remains one salient, yet often overlooked fact: reading isn't only a matter of our brains; it's something that we do with our bodies. Reading is an integral part of our lived experience, our sense of being in the world, even if at times this can mean feeling intensely apart from it. How we hold our reading materials, how we look at them, navigate them, take notes on them, share them, play with them, even where we read them—these are the categories that have mattered most to us as readers through the long and varied history of reading. They will no doubt continue to do so in the future.[16]

Piper goes on to say, "Understanding reading at this most elementary level—at the level of person, habit, and gesture—will be essential as we continue to make choices about the kinds of reading we care about and the kind of technologies that will best embody those values." Do you see where he is—where online reading is—going? Piper believes we're headed to the elimination of print reading, and there isn't much we can do about it. I agree, despite current polls showing how much more we value printed texts than electronic ones. But he also understands that reading has been imprinted in us for the last millennia, and it will take some doing, not only to change it but to change it in such a way that we do not lose it. My worry is that we are changing how we read, changing it almost every day, and the balance of these changes is negative. It's the second part, the human and personal part that I'm sure we're not as careful about as we need to be. Some are delighted that reading is changing, but we had better watch what we hope for. We may get more than we bargained for.

IS E-READING CHANGING THE WAY WE THINK?

Yes, e-reading is changing the way we think. Nick Bilton related some of that recently when he wrote, "Last week my brain played a cruel trick on me." He was in an airport and reading the print version of *The New Yorker*. He goes on, "I became engrossed in an article and swiped my finger down the glossy page to read more. To my surprise, nothing happened. I swiped again. Nothing." He goes on to relate that he got in a taxicab and jumped out at his destination without paying. A very unhappy New York cabbie—is that a tautology?—reminded him he hadn't paid.[17] What Bilton discovered is that our brains love habit, something we all know, and it associates what we do, read, think, and remember with places, events, ideas. Memory experts have parlayed this skill in greater and more purposeful ways. They put things in a "memory palace" for recall later, creating a habit of mind, so to say, that allows them to retrieve what would appear to the uninitiated to be a superhuman amount of information.[18] We all do this to a greater or lesser degree and it helps our brains recognize what's going on. But when those "habits of mind" change too fast, too often, and too many times, well, the "palace" sort of crumbles in places, and we do things in one context that we should do in another.

The good news is that we are aware of these problems and are attempting (I hope) to address them. That they exist at all, however, means we must be far more circumspect about them and others that may arise. Ignoring them only means they will worsen and have the potential of creating a monstrous and insoluble problem. This is true of young people, especially children, our so-called digital natives. We need to be certain we are providing them with at least a reading and learning experience that matches our own, and that they are able to make the transitions between the printed and online word as are we. Early returns on this score are not, however, promising.

Physiologically speaking, there are also differences between reading online and reading the printed page. For the last millennia or so, we have been reading with the light at or over our shoulders. Now we must learn to read with the light directly in our eyes. Clearly this will take some time to adjust to, and some report readers not being able to adjust very easily. Although fonts are now adjustable, and screen resolutions far better than they were fifteen years ago, there are still some problems with the reading experience on a screen. Many discussions about the differences overlook the "impact of intangibility and volatility of the digital text on the reading process and experience."[19] This may be a difference among the older population rather than the younger, but those with visual problems, whatever their ages, still experience difficulties, or at least report that they do. It is also possible that if reading materials are made available via mobile devices, reading might actually take place since the devices are omnipresent among our nation's youth. All we know so far, however, is that students *prefer* that texts be delivered on their mobile devices; we know nothing about whether they are reading them.[20]

I disagree, however, with Abram who argues that the marginalia features of online reading are better.[21] My experience is quite the contrary, as are the experiences of my admittedly random and unscientific sample of other scholars who attest to finding it difficult. Accomplished print readers are much better at scanning a printed page than we are at scanning a website, though that, too, is likely to change.[22] It's clear now that we don't really read webpages at all anyway; we *scan* them rapidly and not even completely, and therein lies the problem. While scanning will help us locate what we're looking for, it's not easy to comprehend what we're reading when we scan, whether online or in print. But the print environment, by virtue of its ingrained way of forcing us to read, helps that habit of mind to comprehend what we scan because that's what our minds are *used* to doing. What Carr and others worry about is that the web is forcing us to scan everything, regardless of medium, only to forget it.

SCANNING, SKIPPING AND SKIMMING OUR WAY PAST LITERACY

I know I'm not alone in this, not only from my own anecdotal evidence, but also from the work of others researching online reading. Scanning in and of itself may not be a bad habit, and we all do it from time to time. Among intelligent people scanning may not be such a problem, though Carr might disagree. As above-average readers with above-average intelligence will still pick up on nuances in a text, printed or otherwise, new readers or readers who struggle anyway may find these habits of mind will only worsen their reading difficulties. What five or more years of this activity will mean for rising generations of readers is anyone's guess. I will venture to say for now, for the short term, it is not good news; web proponents will say that I worry too much and eventually it won't matter, or rather won't matter for long. But that's really an argument from silence. In any event, I hope the proponents of digital everythingism turn out to be right. This is too important a matter to get it wrong.

We're taking something of chance in all this. As Darnton points out,

> Consider the book. It has extraordinary staying power. Ever since the invention of the codex sometime close to the birth of Christ, it has proven to be a marvelous machine—great for packaging information, convenient to thumb through, comfortable to curl up with, superb for storage, and remarkably resistant to damage. It does not need to be downloaded, accessed or booted, plugged into circuits or extracted from webs. Its design makes it a delight to the eye. Its shape makes it a pleasure to hold in the hand. And its handiness has made it the basic tool of learning for thousands of years, even when it had to be unrolled to be read (in the form of a volume or scroll rather than a codex, composed of leaves connected to a binding) long before Alexander the Great founded the library of Alexandria in 332 BC.[23]

Bear in mind this is the same Darnton who is the brain trust behind the Digital Public Library of America. Darnton understands the importance of the book, its staying power, and its ability to survive. He also understands that it is a better medium for memory, at least for the time being. Even Bill Gates concedes the point, saying that "Reading off the screen is still vastly inferior to reading off paper."[24] Gates, of course, has access to the most expensive screens, the best technology and the most sophisticated technicians to make sure everything works as planned. Yet even he concedes that "when it comes to something over four or five pages, I print it out and I like to carry it around with me to annotate." So much for the sophistication of online annotative devices.

We keep kidding ourselves that with "everything at our fingertips" we no longer have to memorize anything. That's a myth that, if we persist in believing it, will come back to bite us in ways that will hurt. Good teachers will tell you that while the prevailing philosophy is "drill and kill" since it's all on the Internet, students who memorize formulas and state capitals, who learn multiplications tables and math facts, build a foundation upon which to learn more. These are the foundation for the edifice of learning. Without them, the structure will crumble. As one teacher put it, children hate eating their vegetables or going to bed early but no one is saying that's all right.[25] We adults insist upon it because we know it builds a strong foundation.

American journalist Farhad Manjoo contends that we simply do not really read online.[26] We often skim and skip through the first part of an online text (usually the first screen, perhaps the second) and then draw our own conclusions. Dan Fagin's experience also bears this out, as many of his "readers" had him nearly in the ground before he convinced them he had not been in the hospital at all. Manjoo's discovery, treated in the conclusion to this book, is both instructive and somewhat terrifying. Our online reading habits are, at best, shabby. The vast majority of us not only do not make it to the end of online texts, however long (and the longer they are, the less we read), we do not even make it halfway there!

So, is it such a big deal, skimming? We've thought so for a long time. For example, Louisa May Alcott's brother advises her, "Do not be alarmed by the number of Book [sic] which it is desirable you should read; not be induced to read with too great rapidity.... Haste in reading is a great waste of *mind* as well of *time*; of mind because it weakens the power of observation; of time because nothing in fact is accomplished."[27] Perhaps the Internet has changed all that, too?

My contention here is not that this cannot change or that it will not change soon. My point is that even as far as we have come at the end of 2013, we're still not quite there, and yet we are raising a generation of young people on what is an admittedly inferior way of reading for comprehension. Is it too much to ask that we continue to have students read printed texts in addition to the online ones they are "reading?" We know that when the transition is from print to screen it is an easy transition, but when the transition is from screen to print is considerably more difficult. Maybe it's the way our eyes trace the page versus how we scan a screen. In print, we know that our brains anticipate words by "seeing" them before they actually appear. Our eyes are not quite there yet when it comes to reading in the web-environment.

READING HARDER FOR EXPERIENCED READERS?

Bruce Friedman, a pathologist at the University of Michigan Medical School, opines, "I now have almost totally lost the ability to read and absorb a longish article on the web or in print." He complains that he skims everything now, and he has lost the ability to read a complex text like *War and Peace*.[28] Is this merely anecdotal? It could be, if the reader in question was not a pathologist at a major medical school. When sophisticated readers, readers whose life's work requires them to read carefully, find that they were until the web came along, then we must entertain the possibility that things contrary to good reading habits are going on.

I am less worried about the book disappearing than I am about those who wish the library would just go ahead and die, but more on that in Part Three. Rather, I am more worried that we are creating a generation of readers who will not be able to read well, who will find reading a bore unless it is full of razzle-dazzle clicking, and who will not only not pick up a complex text but will run from it. I fear we are raising a generation of young people who will be so print-allergic that they will disdain any work that requires extensive reading. I believe this not only does not bode well for them, it does not bode well for the salubrity of democracy. Consider that not so long ago (August 28, 2013), Twitter went viral over the death of Neil Armstrong. Does this countervail my argument that these readers do not read well? You decide: Their sadness and sorrow *was a year late*.[29]

I am aware of those who argue that young readers struggled with reading long before the web emerged. One cannot gainsay that but the web is adding yet an additional layer of reading lethargy. These same critics argue that struggling readers love to play on the web, so what better marriage can be made than to link them up with web-based reading games? No evidence has emerged so far that this approach works, even in the short term. My experience of more than thirty years' working with readers is that if they do not like reading in one context, they are more likely not to like it in another. Although most of the struggling readers I have encountered in classes suffer from much more inferior reading instruction than those only a generation prior, I have also observed that the online reading has only worsened the problem. Weak reading skills, when combined with a medium that is chock full of distractions, have only deepened their problems and worsened their difficulties.

Transliteracy is a new term that refers to the ability to read across many different platforms and media. Some critics argue now that many young people exhibit this "transliteracy" in that they "read" over multiple platforms and media and that measurement must not be one or the other but all of them in the aggregate. It sounds more like defining deviancy down or lowering the bar to make judging it easier.[30] "It is almost common knowledge," writes one school librarian, "that we have lost control of reading."[31] Whatever we call it, the fact remains that rising generations of young people are reading less competently than the generations before them, an unprecedented situation. They cannot focus on longer, more complex texts, they have a very hard time making the adjustment from school to college, and they complain that reading printed texts is too difficult. Again, this cannot all be the fault of the web alone, but the web exacerbated the already growing decline. What we do about it from this point forward is up to us.

Reading is a "multisensory activity," according to researcher Anne Mangen, and "the ways we read are constantly being molded by whatever technological innovations, devices and innovations that come around."[32] Mangen adds, "The reading process and experience of the digital text are greatly affected by the fact that we click and scroll, in contrast to the tactilely richer experience when flipping through pages in a printed book."[33] One way to confirm this theory is to observe the mere fact that when you see something memorable on a printed page, you are more likely than not to recall not only what side of the book it is on—left or right—but also whether at the top, middle or bottom of the page.

If we do this at all in an electronic text, we do not do it well. When reading in a digital text, we also suffer from what Mangen calls "attention entropy." We jump from place to place the same way we "channel surf" when we watch television. Since the experience becomes a habit of mind over time, we begin to do it in very different contexts, and soon find ourselves "clicking" about as we read, much the same way Nick Bilton above reported "swiping" the pages of his printed text to get them to change. Whether we like it or not, and whether the screen is 24 inches, 17, or only 7, our habit of mind dictates that we "change channels" every so often. While I am not arguing that one cannot enjoy a rich reading experience on an electronic screen, it is my contention that the experience may well be at a cost to memory, comprehension and even the ability to focus on what is being read.

DON'T DESPAIR: THE NEWS ISN'T ALL BAD

Of course, there is always good news. *Nil desperandum*, shall we say. According to a more recent Pew study than the one cited earlier, young adults are not only now reading more print books than before but they see ebooks not as replacements but as supplemental. The study looked specifically at 16 to 29 year olds. Seventy-five percent had read a print book during the past year. What is more, 16 to 17 year olds still rely on libraries for their reading and their research. Over half of this group consider the library "very important" or "somewhat important" to them and their families, as compared to roughly two thirds of older Americans. According to the study, "high schoolers (ages 16–17) are especially reliant on the library for their reading and research needs ... and are more likely than other age groups to have used the library in the past year, *especially to have checked out print books or received research assistance*."[34]

All of this is certainly encouraging and even contradictory to the evidence above, but when it comes to the web, all we have to do, much like the weather, is wait 24 hours. According to the most recent Pew study I could find (December 27, 2012), the number of those who had read a printed book (ages 16 and up) had declined over the previous 12 months by a whopping 72 percent. What we do not know now, however, is how long this will continue. Some indications are that print reading is losing to e-reading.[35] It is important to remember, of course, that all these Pew studies are more or less like taking the pulse of a person, taking his temperature on a particular day. Whatever the conditions, associations and environment at the time will color the outcome, but what we cannot dismiss is that while print reading lingers, ebook reading is escalating. I can say anecdotally that while students in the last three years have asked us more and more about the availability of ebooks, when they have the option, they still choose a print text (unless that text is a textbook).

This means that in the short term anyway, until this transition era is over, libraries will have to collect both print and electronic texts, and have to assist patrons in using both. This is easier said than done with declining or static budgets and shrinking staffs. Schools, too, will have to be concerned about both formats and help readers cope with the literary skills required for both, again with declining budgets and shrinking staffs. When we attempt to do everything all the time, we often end up doing them all badly. The care and concern we must take to be sure we are not leaving a generation behind (much less a child) will be critical to the success in our brave new world of digital everythingism.

Let's hope we get this right, because neither we nor those it affects, nor the survival of our democracy can afford for us to get it wrong.

CHAPTER 11

Privacy

Although my "10 Reasons" resonated with a good many people when it first appeared, others disagreed. But even the most ardent webinatic cannot get away from the one area where the web fails, and miserably: privacy. As much as we like Google, Facebook, Twitter and all the rest, getting online *at all* means you are going to be exposed, and not just a little bit, either, but quite a lot. We do everything on the web these days: pay bills, send notes, shop, book flights, read books, scan headlines, self-diagnose, subscribe to blogs, all of us, even the most vocal of critics of the web among us, do all of this and more.[1]

It doesn't matter if you go on the web only once. Once there, you are, more or less, there forever. Even for those few aliens on our planet who have not been on the web, the news is equally bad. Someone else may have put you on a site somewhere without your permission or knowledge, and even though you didn't ask to be made public, you are now no longer a private individual.

PROTECTING PRIVACY

Critics have the upper hand because, like the issue of copyright, there is in fact a law meant to protect our privacy, not only in the Constitution but also in the Privacy Act of 1974.[2] To admit the Constitution in this discussion about privacy is immediately to invite controversy. While there is no express mention of privacy in the Constitution (even in penumbras), it is apparent from the *Federalist Papers* and other writings, that privacy was implicit in the protection of private beliefs (the First Amendment), the protection of one's property (the Third Amendment) and the privacy of person or self (in both the Fourth and Fifth amendments). Some would argue (including Supreme Court Justices) that privacy is implicit in the Ninth Amendment, but other scholars balk at this. It should be remembered that Robert Bork lost his Supreme Court nomination for, among other things, summary dismissiveness of privacy in the Constitution. While I understand the arguments and agree with some and disagree with others (I am not a fan of penumbras), I think the centrality of the Constitution on the privacy of individuals makes clear that the framers were trying to protect us from government (and other) intrusions.

Even if you leave the Constitution out of it, you cannot get away from the Privacy Act of 1974 that really did mean to protect us from government intrusions, from government trying to snoop beyond what is reasonable to keep us safe from outside intruders, as well as from one another. The act, it is true, is a federal one with its focus on records held by government agencies. But it establishes an important precedent in conjunction with the constitutional amendments that there is a certain expectation of privacy that all of us have, or rather I should say, *had*. Apparently millions of us are willing to give this up to Google, Facebook, Twitter *ad infinitum* for the sake of conveniently telling one another what we had for breakfast, why someone should friend us, or why we should read book X while brushing our teeth with toothpaste Y. How, in one short decade, we went from being a country whose majority bristled at the very idea that our private matters should become public information, to one of a majority who not only think it's fine but even aid and abet the transference of painfully humiliating details made universally public, is a matter for future historians. It is as if we went on an extended vacation, and so many Heathcliffs came back as so many Holly Golightlys.

THE WEB IGNORES YOUR PRIVACY

Granted, privacy is not the same hot-button issue for everyone. The web, nevertheless, simply ignores privacy. From Mark Zuckerberg's the age of privacy is over, to Google's we deleted street data but, wait, no we didn't, privacy is now a thing of the past. Even the DVD you rented recently may well be watching you right back, as well as your iPhone. And now, ebooks have that creepy I'm-collecting-data-on-you feel about them. "For centuries," writes Alter of *Huffington Post*, "reading has largely been a solitary and private act, an intimate exchange between the reader and the word on the page. But the rise of digital books has prompted a profound shift in the way we read, transforming the activity into something measureable and quasi-public."[3]

Precisely. Even the books you read are now telling on you in a way that would, only half a dozen years ago, made you furious. Today, however, it's part and parcel of what we have become accustomed to, and the price we are willing to pay, for being online. Our reading, our buying, our watching—our everything—is now used against us, though some would say that it is used in favor of us, prompting us with similar titles, brands, appeals, merchandise. We have all become so many of life's spectators. Those who want to live their own lives don't appreciate the myriad intrusions and they are now in a decided minority. I haven't even touched upon the very sinister and frightening matter of Google glass, a new device that allows you to record everyone you see or have a conversation with.[4] While we're supposed to breathe a sigh of relief that it "doesn't do facial recognition," I think we all should realize that it can and likely will. We're also supposed to understand that it won't be distracting, just like texting and driving, I assume.

The intrusions on our privacy, by the way, are legion. Privacy intrusions occur when we surf, when we pay bills, when we look up a word in an online dictionary, when we download music, or when we do any one of one hundred other things. Every time you get online, some algorithm is recording what you're doing and why. Imagine how those Vatican residents felt after news came out that priests were downloading pornography![5] If you feel paranoid, it's only because some computer program out there is watching you. It has gotten so bad that most Americans, according to a Pew study, have given up on the idea of Internet anonymity. While most of us (86 percent) have tried to mask our digital steps, we know there is no such thing as being anonymous *and* being online.[6] And why should they bother? The National Security Agency reports that it is able to crack most encryption it encounters in emails, e-trickery, and any of the other means in which users might try to hide their identities to remain anonymous.[7] It's hard to know whether this is good, bad or indifferent news. In any event, it underscores the utter lack of privacy once one enters onto the Information Superhighway.

The television show *Person of Interest* begins each week warning viewers that our government has made a computer that watches everyone (no, it's not called PRISM, at least I don't think it is). Built with noble intentions—to prevent terrorist attacks—the computer now watches everyone and everything (sound familiar, given the recent revelations of Edward Snowden?). The show attempts to put us at rest since the creator of "the machine" uses it to catch criminals and upend misdeeds. And that's how you can tell it's television. When I see the show, I think not about the crimes it's preventing but rather about some other machine somewhere doing the same thing but with the intent of doing harm, perhaps not bodily harm but malicious intent nonetheless.

Your Privacy Is Unimportant to Us

Web privacy simply does not exit. Oh, we get, from time to time, reassurances about it from Facebook and other online social networking entities, and even Google. For example, Facebook recently went to great lengths to tell us what it is doing about teen profiles on Facebook and privacy awareness.[8] Facebook is working with attorneys general in 19 states to come up with a plan to help teens better understand how to keep matters that should be private, private. Good luck with that. Chatroulette almost failed because it could not get males to understand a simple principle that private parts are to remain, well, private.[9] Tumblr is experiencing the same sort of problems, and the jury is out whether Melissa Meyer will lock it down, or even be able to. Does anyone really think that Facebook, or any other social network or search engine, will do anything at all if it means users will go elsewhere?

"Privacy," writes *Time*'s David von Drehle, "is mostly an illusion. A useful illusion, no question about it, one that allows us to live without being paralyzed by self-consciousness. The illusion of privacy gives us room to be human, sharing intimacies and risking mistakes. But all the while, the line between private and public space is as porous as tissue paper."[10] While some level of privacy has always been the oversight of government, today's intrusions are more egregious than ever, the most recent of which from the "administration of transparency," the Obama administration.

What I find so remarkable about this utter loss of our privacy is not that it's happened but that so many hell-no-we-won't-go leftovers from the sixties would allow it without a peep. If the government makes one move to watch someone at all, the ACLU and every Woodstock "survivor" is all over the putative outrage in a nanosecond (just look at the outrage over Snowden). But let Google watch your home, have Bing record your purchases, or have Amazon tell you what to read next based on what it knows you've been reading, and no one, least of all the ACLU, bothers even so much as an "ahem." Even Eric Schmidt complains that "the lack of a delete button on the Internet is a significant issue. There is a time when erasure is a right thing."[11] Oh, and before anyone says it, don't think for a minute that deleting your web history deletes anything forever, or, again as Schmidt puts it, "The option to 'delete' data is largely an illusion—lost files, deleted e-mails, and erased text messages can be recovered with minimal effort."[12]

Privacy issues on the web are not new. The web, with every good intention (see the way to hell, paved) offers a means for preventing this. Terms of Service (TOS) appear with every website from Facebook to Twitter to Google. So, while all of us who use the web have seen these terms of service, few of us have, according to the Electronic Frontier Foundation (EFF), bothered to read them. These TOS have become so important that EFF created a special page to monitor the agreements and how they are faring in court.[13] These documents are so confusing (a main reason few of us have ever read them) that they seem as if they are written in a foreign language. They should, according to EFF, take all the "I agree" buttons away, and replace them with "I have no idea what this means" button. But one thing we can be sure of. When we click "agree," it means we agree to give up not just some of our privacy, but all of it. In fact, many call these terms of service "the biggest lie on the Internet."[14]

TERMS OF SERVICE

These terms of service are not written so much with the user in mind as an attempt to absolve the website of any culpability. It is not clear how legally binding these agreements are and whether having them stated in rambling legalese absolves the sites of culpability any more than warnings on prescription drugs or cigarette packs absolve pharmaceutical or tobacco companies from the harm their products may do. My guess is that TOS agreements are purposely written in language that is not easily comprehensible because legal privacy issues are unclear, and no website wants those legal issues to ramify against them. They define these terms in ways that seem reasonable, but actual behavior dictates how they unfold. It matters who is writing the terms of service and why. It's a pretty good guess that privacy is not high on the list simply because, in order to guarantee it, every website would have to be so tightly locked down that it could not operate very well. We may as well get over our privacy concerns because we no longer have any anyway.

Most sites make privacy seem important by incessantly reminding users that their privacy is important. But figuring out how to protect that privacy is difficult, if not impossible. Facebook, for example, has had the FTC bearing down hard on it about privacy because controlling it on that social networking site is so very difficult to understand.[15] Demanding that companies adhere to privacy restrictions is possible, however, as Apple discovered when its privacy polices did not coincide with Germany's customer privacy protection laws. In fact, Germany has the most stringent data protection laws.[16] The United Kingdom, Italy and other European countries also have strong protections. Apparently privacy on the Internet in those countries really is important.[17] We in the U.S. are too easily pleased.

It all sounds good, and Facebook COO Sheryl Sandberg assured everyone, "At Facebook, we work hard to make sure people understand how to control their information and stay safe online." Wishing doesn't make it so, and therein is the problem: How can you and your billion other "friends" stay private? Moreover, Facebook continually "updates" its information about privacy and what it does with users' postings. To remain even semiprivate, users must go in and reset their information and how they want it to be revealed. Recently, the social networking giant reminded its users that all their data is Facebook's for the taking.[18] Sure, all a user has to do is go in and make a few changes, but how many users do that? In fact, how many saw the notice, read it and understood what it meant? And does Facebook really think all those 13 year olds who signed up on Facebook (though they are, of course, prohibited) didn't really lie about their ages?

Web users also give up intellectual property rights to their posted content *in perpetuity* to any sites on which they deposit content (including comments) for the site to use as it wishes, even if that means in a for-profit manner. Amazon, Facebook and even Google have been known to use this information to sell other merchandise, or at the very least to use it to attract advertisers to the site. Not to put too fine a point on it, you agree to allow your content to work for them, as they see fit and can exploit.

Although most sites prohibit minors from using them, viewing the website's content, or posting inappropriate content involving themselves or others, no site monitors this energetically. Anthony Weiner, one among many politicians, discovered the hard way that posting inappropriate texts can be hazardous to one's political health and possibly one's marriage.[19] It cannot be said too often, and so it will be repeated again here: If any other entity played so fast and loose with our privacy, we would be howling all the way to the Supreme Court. Because it is our sacred Internet, we abide all its infelicities to gain its numerous putative riches.

It is true that there is now a movement to make TOS mean something by color-coding (or giving them grades) the contents of the sites on a webpage, but we're not there yet.[20] Others will argue that these do not apply to all sites but mainly to those that require some sort of login or registration. Furthermore, if you go online at all, you have lost your privacy to some degree. The more involved you are, the more serious and deeper the breach. In some cases, all it takes is one picture that you or someone else posts, and the damage is done.[21]

DOES PRIVACY MATTER? IF IT'S YOURS, IT DOES

In some cases, the damage can put individuals in physical danger. Consider those who, for whatever reason, wish to hide their information (divorce, abusive ex-spouses or partners or whatever). In one nanosecond, a Google search reveals all the information those individuals wish to hide.[22] Try getting it undone by Google or any other 'net entity, and you'd better not have anything else to do. Websites are generally unwilling to do anything, except in cases where the legal ramifications are serious: copyright, *child* pornography and clear libel. According to one writer, "Brin and Page both believed that if Google's algorithms determined what results were best—and long clicks indicated that the algorithms were satisfying the people who did the searching—who were they to mess with it?"[23]

In other words, you're complaining about mathematical formulae, and those cannot be wrong, biased or otherwise challenged. Further, websites like Google, Twitter, Amazon and Facebook depend on the tracking, the monitoring and the recording in order to sell ads or "long clicks." Not only does money talk in these cases but so does political clout, and Silicon Valley has a lot of it. When Google rolled out a new product that essentially read emails, Liz Figueroa, a California politician considering a run for lieutenant governor, introduced a bill that banned email advertising. She balked at the idea that what people said to one another in emails could become a target for advertising, depending on what they discussed. It didn't take long for Google to call on Al Gore to intercede.[24] The fact of the matter is that personal information is a very hot currency on the web. It makes sense, too, because if anything on the web is to be monetized, it will have to be your private information, likes and dislikes.[25] If commercial companies cannot use personal information, then all those billions in advertising dollars suddenly disappear.

Consider Google Earth that lets users zoom in on various homes, or

Google Street View to locate various city amenities. But both also showed skimpy-clothed sunbathing, especially teens. Furthermore, Google also collected personal information off unrestricted wi-fis as the cars went about various cities—Google Street view data supposedly deleted by Google turned out not to have been after all.[26] Anyone who now believes that privacy concerns have been addressed is drinking Google's "do no harm" Kool-Aid.

WHERE ARE ALL THE HIPPIES WHEN YOU NEED THEM?!

What astounds about all these privacy breaches is how complacent the American public remains. We do not seem to care any more, though, as I said earlier, only two decades ago we would have been all pitchforks and burning torches if anyone or anything had attempted to invade our privacy in ways only half as obtrusive. Indeed, look how we have responded to the revelations of Edward Snowden. We are quick to complain almost daily about "Big Brother" in the form of government watching us (when in fact in many cases it is protecting us), but raise not so much as a syllable about these websites and the manner in which they ransack every aspect of our private lives for their benefit.

At the risk of sounding like a kooky conspiracy theorist, bear in mind these are the intrusions into our privacy by web-based sites we know about. Take Google Now service. The service amalgamates what it knows about your search history, your calendar, your email, your web searches, services you've signed on to, and then shows you what it considers to be relevant information about what you are doing and where you happen to be.[27] One cannot discount that such a service may well be useful to some, but once the information is on the web, if Google can capture it, so can anyone else. But search engines do not have to be this way, as Disconnect, a new search engine that does not track searches, is trying to show.[28] There are untold numbers of intrusions we do not know about, or that have not yet been uncovered by some enterprising investigative journalist—oh, wait, we've replaced all of them with bloggers. Never mind.

Even granting that the government is trying to keep us safe, how much intrusion is too much? After 9/11 government officials promised that technology and its associated innovations would make us safer. And so, before all the rubble cleared, surveillance cameras, big data, and watching eyes began in earnest.[29] Should we celebrate Assange and Snowden? Would that we could but their effect appears to be more towards making all information free and less making any of us safer or more private. The reach is now everywhere, when we book a flight, fill a prescription, visit the doctor, or read a book. Government, Google, Facebook, Twitter and online stores literally everywhere are all tracking us for what each one believes is a good reason: to protect, to share information, to make us safer, to make life easier and, let's be honest, to make themselves indispensable.

The problem inherent in all of these cases of intrusion is that the data collected, the videos recorded, the blood pressures taken and recorded are put in so-called "safe places." But we all know that any website is hackable, so nowhere is this information safe from prying eyes. Nothing prevents anyone close to it from selling it, looking at it or associating any of it with you, or using it to stalk you or your family, or otherwise cyberbullying you in some way. Brogan Rafferty was the 17 year old Ohioan who placed fake job ads on Craigslist in order to murder those who applied for them.[30] The young man received life imprisonment but that does not bring back the three dead men, nor does it erase the tragedy of men desperately looking for work and searching whatever leads they could find. Doubtless, someone explained to them that the Internet made this all the easier!

We would like to think that all of this is merely a matter of a new technology finding its way, its place, but the fact of the matter is that none of it is likely to change, and more than likely it will worsen, since, after all, it already has with each passing year of new and better technology. Privacy expert Charles Morgan makes this poignantly apparent in a simple analogy. "If we legislate a five-mile-an-hour speed limit, 41,000 people would live next year," he points out, but "the lifestyle that we enjoy would be severely changed. You can put sort of that same analogy in the flow of information. If you totally stop it, we're going to suffer a lot."[31] In other words, like it or not, we're willing to sacrifice some for the good of the majority, and we just all hope we're not next. It's Utilitarianism run amok. Of course, some might argue that slowing down traffic to a standstill is not the equivalent of tightening up privacy laws to prevent fraud, identity theft, stalking, child pornography and the rest. In the end, too many powerful people have too much to lose if we try to make changes now.

That should not, however, prevent us from demanding the privacy we deserve. "[Privacy] to my mind should operate on a sliding scale," writes David Meyer, "under the individual's control: total privacy from those who want to research information for themselves or communicate in confidence with others, through partial privacy for those willing to exchange personal data for convenient services, down to zero privacy for those who want to strut their stuff in public."[32] Meyer goes on to argue that we are losing even a semblance of privacy with each intrusion, and this threat of privacy loss is far more dangerous than any terrorist threat.

Privacy Is Difficult but Not Impossible

Before anyone hyperventilates, let me hasten to add that when properly locked down and properly encrypted, data are only hackable by the exceedingly well-informed and competent. Unencrypted data are often hacked by some 15 year old computer geek who lives down the street, but that's our brave new world. Data can be breached regularly, and too many times it turns out to be a careless act that exposes it.[33] The really frightening thing is that it happens not just to so-called mom and pop startups, but to the giants of the information safe-guarding industry. It even happens at the Department of Defense and the IRS. This is what Morozov is getting at when he talks about "technological solutionism." We think we can do anything with technology, and we think that with the right data and the right technology we can solve any problem. But we forget that problems like privacy remain unresolved at best, ignored at worst, since the ribbon cutting opened the information highway. If anything, privacy matters are worse. O'Harrow sums up the problem best:

> One big problem with the data industry is the *inevitable* mistakes. The authors of the 1974 Privacy Act knew this. More and more, as the country turns to ChoicePoint [a data security industry giant] and its competitors to screen and assess individuals, the consequences of those mistakes are going to loom ever larger. Forget the old adage, "If you've done nothing wrong, you have nothing to hide." If recent history serves as a guide, the innocent ... are going to be routinely caught up in these digital dragnets, right alongside those who have been accurately targeted. ChoicePoint acknowledges as much. The company gets up to fifty complaints a month from individuals about credit and background reports. But it often blames county clerks, data contractors, and others for providing bad information that leads to bad decisions.[34]

So every company passes the buck to every other company, and soon we have a sizable mess on our hands. At what point do we determine that privacy is too much violated? When we do, what, if anything, will we do about it? By then the genie will be out of the bottle and so far gone that no one can lure it back. Meanwhile, whatever anyone wants to know about us, our homes, our incomes, our wealth, our health, our children and so on, will be open for anyone to snoop about and use however they determine to use it. Once it's online, it's easy for *anyone* to access. "The more control we gain of information, thanks to Google," writes Randall Stross in *Planet Google,* "the more we also experience a nagging worry about loss of control of information most dear to us."[35]

We lose this control because we are unwilling to give up the convenience of information at our fingertips. We rely on companies to "scrub data" and "anonymize" it, taking out anything that might refer to us, or to where we live, or our social security numbers. We also hold out hope that the identity of individuals is lost completely in the aggregation of data. Of course, it is in the public relating of it. But *until* then, until it gets to that point, many eyes and hands are on that data. We are left to the good natures of those who deal with this data that they will not let it out. All too often these days, however, we understand only too well and too quickly how misplaced that trust has been. All it takes is one disgruntled individual who out of spite takes advantage of his access to your information. When we lose privacy, we're losing one of the most important community builders, one of the truly important ties that bind.[36]

If truth be told, we are our own worst enemies. We give up this information easily and without forethought. Our children, whether they are 9 or 39, give out information about themselves and their families, where they live and where they go to school. We and they do it because, if it's not done, access to the all-powerful Oz-net is prohibited, and none of us want that. Everyone is looking at our personal data: government, commercial ventures, the SEC, the IRS and a host of anonymous, nefarious individuals, all hoping to cash in on it in some manner.[37]

HYSTERICAL HYPERBOLE?

Think this is hyperbole? Our phones, including our smartphones, now, are dialed without our permission. Emails arrive from individuals we have never heard of. We are harassed by various prompts to buy this or that thing since we liked another. Our cars tell us where to drive and how, even parallel park for us. Cameras follow us everywhere. Just twenty years ago, we would never have thought of shredding papers. Today we have to because we know our identity can be taken from our trash. Thanks to the lucrative identity theft business, even the shredding can be filched and pieced back together again. We lose our privacy through commonplace events, the eavesdropping on our back decks, our personal medical records sent to Washington "for the betterment of all," a tsunami of advertising and even our genetic codes. In *Database Nation*, the author contends that we are losing the little privacy we have left and likens it to the loss of identity and privacy in George Orwell's *1984*. In that future, totalitarianism sacrificed privacy to allow a revision of history as it was being recorded. "Over the next 50 years," writes the author of *Database Nation,* "we will see new kinds of threats to privacy that don't find their roots in totalitarianism, but in capitalism, the free market, advanced by technology, and the unbridled exchange of electronic information."[38] The sad fact of the matter is that it isn't just what we do on the web that erodes our privacy, but the technological innovations that come along help us lose what privacy we have left faster and more comprehensively.

Contrast the colossal loss of privacy with what your library has done to *protect* it. It never gives out your name, your address, or any information about you. You never get a suggestion about what to read unless you *ask someone*, and your checkout records are shredded and burned three months after you turn in your books. Libraries have a responsibility to uphold the Family Educational Rights and Privacy Act (FERPA), even at the college level. Libraries take the matter of privacy seriously, and while some would argue that ALA's stance on the Patriot Act was both grandstanding and political, it is within the keeping of libraries' longstanding commitment to safeguard the right of privacy of the individual.[39]

So, do we want to jettison the one information access that protects our rights as much as they possibly can, protected the way you would protect it, or do we want to make the web our only option and give up *all* our privacy? America has always prided itself on providing choices for its citizens, but now it appears we're hell-bent on making the Internet our only choice for anything. And what a dubious choice it is turning out to be: have information at your fingertips but give up all hope of being a private person. Yes, of course, the web is great for many things, but it isn't the panacea for everything and we should quit trying to make it so. It certainly is not a panacea for your privacy because it never tried to be.

In fact, the web has brazenly exploited our privacy for its own ends, and in ways from which we may never recover.

CHAPTER 12

Piracy

Like most of the issues discussed here, piracy is not a new problem, nor is it an exclusive one to the web. In fact, it has been going on long before the web was even a thought. Webster's defines it as "attacking or robbing ships at sea" or "an act of robbery on the high seas." The definition alone places its age at hundreds if not thousands of years old. "The first law to establish exclusive rights, a monopoly in copyright, dates back to 1557, when Elizabeth I squelched counterfeiters' use of the new technology, the printing press, to manufacture fraudulent documents for everything, including Royal charters."[1] Now, of course, the term "piracy" refers to any act, on land or sea, in which one makes something his that belongs to another. Piracy is complicated and space reserved for it here can only scratch the surface. In fact, the topic is so complex that whole books are devoted to it.[2] Surely, a topic this old, and around for this long, can't be the fault of the web, right?

Yes and no. No, piracy isn't the fault of the web but like most things the web touches, it makes them better or worse—in this case, the latter. The maritime piracy off the Somali coast is no laughing matter, and continues even at this writing, giving at least a patina of truth to the initial definition of robbery on the high seas. Sadly, that piracy not only involves loss of property and life, but also sex trafficking and more. It is a mad, mad world we live in.

Piracy is a poor relative to copyright by virtue of the fact that the latter precipitates the former. For those who are guilty of piracy, copyright either doesn't exit or it simply does not apply to them; hence, this not really a matter of copyright so much as a matter of ethical nescience. Copyright, as we saw, is in place to protect intellectual property, and its existence creates its own set of issues. But piracy, while typically a violation of copyright, is deeper and broader than that. Piracy is more a defiant act symbolic of the belief that no intellectual property belongs to any one person but to "all the people." Creators create, true, but they create for others to consume, and customers, pirates seem to be saying, can do whatever they please with the creations, including and especially, making their own income from them. Why bother to create when you can sell or repackage what someone else has done? It's just sitting out there, on the web, just waiting for someone to make use of it, or so it would appear, goes the line of reasoning.

Piracy comes in many flavors, so to say, and so we'll sample a few of them: music, movies and books. We'll also visit another "p" particularly prominent in this discussion: plagiarism. Space does not admit a full ventilation of these subjects so they will be treated summarily. Of course, if you believe proponents of the web, piracy is in fact dead with respect to it. Spotify, Rdio, and Netflix have made piracy moot, at least that is what Norwegian researchers at Ipsos report. Piracy has fallen dramatically in Norway.[3] But we all know that piracy isn't dead, or, if it's ailing at all, it's worse than a head cold.

MUSIC PIRACY

Ever since Napster, piracy and music have gone almost hand in glove. You remember Napster, right? Briefly, Napster was a file-to-file sharing site that allowed users to share files, mostly audio, with one another. Most of the music was encoded in MP3 files. It seemed like a good idea at the time. You heard some new, good music, and shared it with others. But wait, who was buying all this music? Well, as it turned out, not very many people. Soon, thousands of music files were flying back and forth through cyberspace and very few paid for the very many. College students flocked to it and quickly began trading copyrighted music that few had paid for. Napster, unsurprisingly, ran into copyright infringement problems and eventually lost; a take down was ordered. It came back briefly as an Internet music store only to be bought out. Others followed, such as Grokster and Gnutella, to name a few, but those, too, fell afoul of copyright infringement, being seen as pirated music sites like Napster.[4]

It's unfair to say the web created the piracy problem but more than fair to say that the web made it very easy to commit. Without the web, piracy all but disappears. After the lawsuit and the failures of copycats, the Napster-like problems went away and the web had learned a valuable lesson, right?

If only. Not everyone agrees that the web has much of anything to do with the problem of music piracy in specific or piracy in general. For example, two professors, Oberholzer-Gee and Strumpf, one from Harvard, the other from the University of North Carolina, wrote a paper that ostensibly proved that with respect to music, file sharing had little impact on music sales.[5] In fact, they were more than a little pointed in their conclusions:

> We find that file sharing has no statistically significant effect on the purchases of the average album in our sample. Moreover, the estimates are of rather modest size when compared to the drastic reduction in sales in the music industry. At most, file sharing can explain a tiny fraction of this decline....
>
> If we are correct in arguing that downloading has little effect on the production of music, then file sharing probably increases aggregate welfare. Shifts from sales to downloads are simply transfers between firms and consumers. And while we have argued that the file sharing imposes little dynamic cost in terms of future production, it has considerably increased the consumption of recorded music. File sharing lowers the price and allows an apparently large pool of individuals to enjoy music. The sheer magnitude of this activity, the billions of tracks which are downloaded each year, suggests the added social welfare from file sharing is likely to be quite high.[6]

So, in other words, piracy is actually good for social welfare, good for music because it increases the number of listeners, leaving the music industry unharmed. I am particularly drawn to the line, "File sharing lowers the price and allows an apparently large pool of individuals to enjoy music." It's almost like saying that the addition of cocaine to Coca-Cola dramatically increased the desire of consumers to want more, or that widespread rioting dramatically increases the number of would-be shoppers at local stores. The 2004 paper caused quite a stir. The music industry balked at it, of course, but the paper had been thoroughly peer-reviewed. It proved unassailable, or so its authors thought. And it sent the music industry into a quandary over why music sales had hit the proverbial rock bottom. Were artists just as bad as we over–40 thought they were or was it something else?

Several challenges came to the Oberholzer-Gee and Strumpf contention, but too many challenges came from the music industry, and none of them had been peer-reviewed, although apparently few knew of the peer-review hiccups with which we in academe are all too familiar. Some argued that the authors merely proved that music was now abundantly available and that there were now tens of thousands of digitally available songs.[7] Others felt they had not proved their point but only confirmed the obvious: More digital music had been recorded and downloaded.

In 2009, however, the authors revisited their famous (or infamous, depending on your perspective) study, and some argue they changed their tune a bit. "File-sharing technology," they write,

> considerably weakened copyright protection, first of music and software and increasingly of movies, games, and books. The policy discussion surrounding file sharing has largely focused on the legality of the new technology and the question whether or not declining sales in music are due to file sharing.... Copyright exists to encourage innovation and the creation of new works; in other words to promote social welfare.... Sales displacement is a necessary but not a sufficient condition for harm to occur.[8]

While the authors are now willing to admit that "the empirical evidence on sales displacement is mixed," and "we do not have yet a full understanding of the mechanisms by which file sharing may have altered the incentives to produce entertainment," they fall short of overturning their original conclusions, only that file sharing could have a negative impact. Consultants for the Capgemini for the Value Recognition Strategy did a study in 2007 for the UK record industry and found that the file sharing impact was responsible for at least a 20 percent drop in sales, not an insignificant amount.[9]

So what do we make of this? Without question file sharing and the iTunes Store have contributed to the problem of piracy, and the overall impact has not been altogether positive for the music industry, especially for struggling musicians. Granted, the idea behind the iTunes Store was to create a system in which intellectual property rights could be protected and digital music enjoyed by everyone (and Apple would have another revenue stream). By 2004, the Apple iTunes Store had sold 200 million songs, a trend that increased every year until 2009 (the change came when the price rose from 99 cents to $1.29 and higher), but the sales were for *songs*, not albums. The ease of sharing music (or anything else, for that matter) made the transfer of it all the more likely, and at least some of the time without payment. The other curious fact was that many of the "big name" bands weren't available for download. When the Beatles famously gave in to Apple iTunes, the illegal downloads of their music increased.[10]

But of course the Beatles do fine in any market. Who hasn't fared as well are just about all other artists. Music is a complicated sales market in which even gold and platinum winners do not necessarily "make out like bandits." Nearly every young person at one time or another thinks he or she is the next big thing, whether or not they can carry a tune. Clearly the change the web has wrought in music has been gigantic, helping Apple and others who benefit most directly, but not necessarily artists, music stores, or anyone else.

Sure, any band can now get an audience by putting its music on the web but very, very few bands get much else. Hardly any of these "free music" bands make enough money to make a living, even to eke out a poverty-stricken one. The music business, like many other fine arts based businesses, has always been a tough vocation, but the web has made it even tougher while holding out the carrot of "golden" opportunity.

Music piracy is not likely to be "solved" any time soon. What happens to the music industry in the meantime is anyone's guess. For example, we know that music stores will cease to exist, as most already have. Further, we also know that "album" sales (in whatever form they take or will take) are also going the way of all flesh. If you want a song for free, you are likely to be able to find it somewhere, although it may not be the artist you want. It's also unclear how long entities like iTunes will endure over time. It's all about change, of course, so surely some enterprising 13 year old will come up with a way to share music much more easily and freely.

Capitalism is the worst form of economic theory, except for all the rest, but I'm not sure this is the way we want to deal with all intellectual property, not just music. If you're an enterprising musician, you can put your music online, but don't expect to make much money even if it's very, very good.

Do we want a medium that makes everything that is yours mine, and everything mine, yours? Yes, apparently we do. The web has played us a siren song, and we have fallen victim to its seemingly sonorous melodies, so much so that we give up just about anything to be sure it can still exist easily. No cost is too much, or so it would seem so at this juncture.

Movie Piracy

Piracy has also hurt the movie industry, already near collapse from the advent of VHS tapes. What has made it so much more of an issue is the presence of the web and the ease with which we can share movies. China has always been a problem for the movie (and book, and music, and really anything that is copyright protected) industry. A cell phone can make a recording of a movie and within minutes of that movie's release, it will appear online and be for sale somewhere in China, however poor the quality.

It isn't just the Chinese who are making copies of copies, although they have some of the highest levels of piracy. It's also anyone with a cell phone, though I could have written any young male, as that appears to be the pattern.[11] And the only people making money? "In the United States, as piracy lowers the value of media, technology companies have essentially managed to set the price of music and video, and tried to do the same for books. No matter what something costs to make, Amazon and iTunes try to sell it for as little as possible, since they make money in other ways."[12] In other words, it doesn't matter to those who are reselling the product or even making it for free. How much something costs isn't an issue. In the U.S. anyway, we have a very different view of how this works. European markets try to protect what they create. Here we tend to sell it to the lowest bidder and then wonder why the quality is so thin and the substance so lacking. It may not be robust economic theory, but you get what you pay for.

The movie industry struggles with how to deal with the cost of piracy. The Motion Picture Association of America estimates the cost of piracy to the movie industry at about $20.5 billion annually.[13] Not many people think this is an accurate number, and some even go so far as to place it closer to less than a billion, as if that makes it no longer a problem. But it is very difficult to get this sort of hard number on the cost of movie piracy. How much would someone pay for a pirated movie if they couldn't get it elsewhere? Some wouldn't pay anything, some might pay the full price, but ascertaining that number is not as easy as it appears.[14]

In any event, whether the number is $20 billion, $58 billion for all online piracy (as some have claimed), or even $250 billion as one study recently revealed, it's a safe bet that it costs something, and it is hurting industries to some extent.[15] Strumpf, however, argues that "a dollar less in film spending actually has a larger impact since it impacts other parts of the economy. If file sharing leads to less spending on films, consumers have more money to spend, which will completely offset these effects. There is no multiplier effect."[16] While no doubt true, that does not mean they will spend that additional money on anything that will help those who depend on the movie industry for their livelihoods. If file sharing is the absolute, then perhaps we all need to brush up on our coding.

So the movie industry, like the music one, is left with trying to figure out what to do: sue and risk making consumers angry, or reduce the price and therefore all the salaries associated with making movies, so the cost can remain low. It would not hurt for A-list celebrities to make less than their usual eight figure salaries, but I doubt that approach is any sort of solution to count on. Other approaches are along the lines of ATM-like machines that charge for downloading.[17]

Europeans are taking the matter of piracy much more seriously than the U.S. since the problem is so much more widespread, but they are also choosing to protect intellectual content over the convenience of the web. It's not going to be easy, that's a given, and the jury is still out on how their efforts will unfold and what level of success they will have. But they are making the effort. Yes, I know: The web is infallible, and, I don't think for a minute that the web can be controlled easily. If we put our collective minds to it, however, I am certain we could come up with a workable solution. The problem is that any workable solution would mean shackling the web in some way, and that, at least for now, is the worst form of heresy.

Foreign governments, for better and often for worse, have been manipulating Google, Microsoft and others to bow to their wills if they want access, and of course those companies cannot turn up their noses at potential customers, now can they? Europe provides an alternative to kowtowing to the web and all its latent and manifest consequences. Where is it written that whatever imbroglios the web creates we must quickly ignore or work around because it is the absolute? We have adapted every other technology or innovation more or less to fit us as much as we possibly can. With the web, we seem to have resigned ourselves to becoming the tools of our tools, as Thoreau had it. Or is it, as Thomas Friedman said, that the world is flat, and we must flatten ourselves and everything in it to adapt?[18] The Internet may well have made it possible for Third World nations to step up to the global market but it's unclear if that has been as big a boon to them or us as it first seemed.

PIRACY AND SOFTWARE

In our modern age, piracy is most often linked to software, and no wonder. The effort of tens of thousands of lines of code and an equal number of man-hours to create them has to be protected somehow. If not, how could one make certain that what he or she creates will be protected as soon as it is released? Johns relates the story of NEC piracy that users only found out about when they tried to execute their warranties, warranties that were written very similarly to NEC's own.[19] (The story in brief: What began, seemingly, as a routine intellectual property theft in places legendary for such things, China and Taiwan, turned out to be a complete fake facsimile of the entire NEC company. The fabricators even distributed in its name entire product lines. It was all but impossible to tell the fake company from the real one, the fake warranties from the valid ones.) And the piracy proved a very good one. The pirate multinational signed agreements with more than four dozen businesses all over the Pacific Rim. When the piracy was revealed in 2006, it had the effect we often see on the web. On the one hand, many now understood that they could as easily have fake NEC chips, screens or keyboards as they could have real ones. On the other hand, many cheered that a giant corporation had been bested at its own game by a more flexible, albeit outlaw corporation. They even came up with a new name for it: "brandjacking."

What the NEC story reveals, told in depth by Johns, is just how Wild West the web really is. This story of a colossal identity theft of a corporation, rather than being jeered at by computer geeks, is being applauded by them. It shouldn't come as a surprise since many hackers are applauded as well. They are "taking it to the man" or "becoming the new Robin Hood." And it all seems like fun and games until either someone goes to jail or one of the hackers is himself hacked. Then it isn't so funny. Still the weberati continue to this day to argue over what intellectual property is and find themselves conflicted about what constitutes intellectual property and whether it can be legitimately *owned*.[20] Until they come to a unified (or what for them will constitute a unified) view, piracy on the web will continue or go unabated.

Why should anyone care? Counterfeit software is used as malware to conduct cybertheft. According to a recent study commissioned by Microsoft, cybertheft in 2011 was a $115 billion business. Forty-two percent of all packaged software in 2011 was pirated. Consumers will spend about 1.5 billion hours trying to clean up the messes counterfeit software wreaks.[21] One example should illustrate the breadth and depth of the problem. In January of 2013, the U.S. dismantled the most significant case of pirated software. U.S. Immigration and Customs Enforcement (ICE) broke up an international piracy operation run by two Chinese men, Xiang Li, 35, and Chun Yan Li, 33, of Chengdu, China.[22] The two were charged with selling $100 million worth of pirated software. The two ran their operations from a website, Crack99.com, that offered pirated software. This kind of pervasiveness and this kind of ease made simple and profitable by the click, click, click of the web, means anyone who uses a computer is at risk.

It isn't just cybertheft, but also cyberattacks and cyberwarfare. Cyberattacks are now a problem for everyone, including universities.[23] Experts say the attacks are "increasing exponentially" and are now outstripping the ability of colleges and universities to thwart them. Using higher education's own philosophy against it, cyberattackers prey upon the free and open exchange of information on campuses, exploiting them for whatever they can find.

Cyberwarfare is yet another problem as governments try to outwit one another and sabotage their systems. The problem is growing, too, and remains dangerous in the extreme. Even the very act of it often encourages those who are attacked to close more loopholes and redirect their efforts to repelling future attacks, making the world yet more unsafe.[24] The problem has become so dangerous that *Washington Post* writer Robert J. Samuelson now contends, "If I could, I would repeal the Internet. It is the technological marvel of the age, but it is not—as most people imagine—a symbol of progress. Just the opposite. We would be better off without it."[25]

Cyberattacks also apply to libraries, not only their systems, but any software brought into the library on flashdrives. Instead of putting money toward better services, libraries will be spending it on cybertheft protection. The problem has grown to such a far-reaching extent that antivirus pioneer Evgeny Kaspersky fears the "Net will soon become a war zone, a platform for professional attacks on critical infrastructure."[26] His views are a chilling insight to our future, arguing that "this war [against pirates] can't be won; it only has perpetrators and victims. Out there, all we can do is prevent everything from spinning out of control. Only two things could solve this for good, and both of them are undesirable: to ban computers—or people." And remember how the world is flat? The top two regions in the world of programmed viruses are, no surprise here given the above example, China and Latin America, with Russia coming in at number three. So, while the flattened world did allow these regions to become part of the global market, the lion's share of their activity turns out to be pirated and counterfeited software.

Should anyone think that this is less an issue now because PC production is about half what it used to be, don't get too comfortable. Smartphones, tablets, laptops and phablets are all just PCs on a different scale. And, of course, we're already seeing the damage that can be done by those seeking to do mischief. Phreaking has been around a long time, defined as the hacking into any phone communication system, mainly to get free calls, but the term is less prominent now because phreaking is simply hacking and hacking is now abundant everywhere. Hacking into any computer system, just for fun or to create havoc, occurs with such regularity that many think it is just part of "doing business" on the web, but it's more than that. The Swiss cheese look of so much code begs the invitation at any level. By relying on the web as a chief tool of information access and sharing, we open ourselves up to the loss of just about everything we hold dear outside of family.

The web community, however, emerged out of this hacker mentality, more or less, so the emergence of this problem should not surprise us. Some put the origin at MIT, and that is in part true, but a good case can be made where home computers became a staple: Palo Alto.[27] Thus renegade clubs or groups were developed for the sole purpose of bypassing capitalism in some way, or as appeals to those wanting to steer clear of the conventional and the traditional. Stewart Brand's *The Whole Earth Catalog*, among others, became a kind of bible for these groups. The language of it all had a very sixties patina about it, calling for putting an end to monopolies or for making long distance phone calls free. The fertile ground produced much good, of course, and much of what we enjoy in technology today. The hacker mentality also matured into today's groups like Anonymous, a cadre that wreaks havoc on computers by illegally breaking into them to overturn, stymie or otherwise halt what they view, in their infallible wisdom, to be all that is right. Anonymous is nondiscriminating politically, hacking into North Korean, Ugandan, and Israeli sites. While they are now attacking issues that resonate with a modern public—to overturn antihomosexual bills, to oust Kim Jong-Eun, or to protest anything Israel does—make no mistake about it: the group is actively engaged in illegal activities. We all enjoy a Robin Hood until he attacks *our* bank account. And of course he will, eventually; it is who he is.

No one disputes that software piracy is a big problem or that it hurts consumers and developers. Microsoft may be the leader among software companies whose software has been pirated. This is not a surprise since Windows is the dominant operating system. In April of last year, Microsoft submitted half a million takedown requests to Google.[28] That's an enormous number of requests for pirated software and should be enough to raise anyone's eyebrows, right?

Not exactly. Not everyone agrees that pirated software is a terrible thing after all. After agreeing with the above statements, one technology historian and blogger on technology writes, "It may seem counterintuitive, but piracy has actually saved more software than it has destroyed. Already, pirates have spared tens of thousands of programs from extinction, proving themselves the unintentional stewards of our digital culture."[29] In this view of things, pirates get software, dicker with it, hack it and modify it and send it on its way, better, stronger and now free. Further, he writes, "Libraries everywhere would be devoid of Homer, Beowulf, and even the Bible without unauthorized duplication," a point that is misleading because it conflates two different historical periods as if they were one, creating a kind of confused anachronism. Homer, Beowulf and the Bible were not bound by copyright (and only specific translations of them are today) and so could not really be pirated. But such sentiments—and they are not rare on the web—serve to indicate the kind of thinking that goes into piracy. It's not a bad thing really, goes the argument. In the long run it will help make a better world for all technology. It's sort of like defending the intruder who steals your television because he dusts the entertainment center before leaving.

So, the picture on pirated software is this: It's a sizable problem, an expensive one, it occurs frequently, and wreaks havoc on victims but offers rich rewards on the perpetrators, so long as they are not caught: a high risk but high reward outcome. Meanwhile, not everyone within the web community thinks it's a good idea to go after these pirates; and most, as we shall see below, are allergic even to the thought of punitive legislation.

Books and Piracy

Ever since Napster, piracy has been around, and, like a bad virus, continues to sicken just about anything related to computers. Books, too, have caught the sniffles. Granted, pirated books have been around a long, long time before the web. Countries with no copyright laws, or even those with modest ones, have not always been very respectful of U.S. copyright laws. Just about any book that has seen the light of day will appear on a newsstand somewhere in China, but as we have seen over and over again throughout this book, the web makes everything easier, quicker and more pandemic. That includes good things as well as bad. Once books make their way into digital formats, pirates unfurl their sails and the race, so to speak, is on.

As bad as piracy is, one cannot make a strong case that it is financially as harmful for publishers as it is for both the music and motion picture industry, but it does hurt. The jury is decidedly on the side who say that it does impact sales. For every three or four studies that say it does not hurt sales (and, of course, the team of Oberholzer-Gee and Strumpf is one of those making such a claim), there are more that say it does and have the data to prove it.[30] Piracy may help little known authors *some*, but the digital content of all authors gets financially compromised. Further, publishers are far more diligent about takedown notices, and some, such as Simon & Schuster, are beginning to release data about pirated sales to their authors, a move unlikely to have been made if it didn't matter very much.[31]

It only makes sense that once books made their way into the digital format, materials would get handed around. As long as books were in paper, creating a pirated copy was cumbersome and expensive, but, of course, still done. Today, however, anyone can "publish" a book, and many are doing so. What is hard to extrapolate from data about book piracy is just how many of the sales are compromised by pirating, and how many of the number of "B-list" authors are despairing and turning to self-publishing. Both have an impact. Many "B-list" authors (and some A-listers) are tired of books going to publishers who do almost nothing in marketing, make back only their investment, and then let the book die without any effort to reprint. Meanwhile, the author who worked to bring the book to fruition has made a pittance. Consequently, many authors have resorted to what was once considered the bane of all serious publishing: self-publishing. Not at all the vanity publishing of the 20th century, self-publishing is far more upscale than it once was, but its rise increases the likelihood of piracy as well, because the format is electronic and therefore easily reproduced.

As we saw with music, and to an extent with movies, some see book piracy as its salvation. After all, computer geeks everywhere who united and declared that "information wants to be free" have aided and abetted piracy by ignoring copyright. Piracy is here because

> For some, it's the only practical way they can access content, either because the item is not available any other way or it costs far more than they can afford. And for others, it's a protection against the evil hegemony of the film, music and book industries. Piracy is never going away. The genie is out of the bottle and there is no way to stuff it back in again.... [W]e need to face facts. Piracy's here. It's staying. We can't stop it. So we need to find inventive and attractive ways to work around it. We need to accept that this brave new connected and tech savvy world we live in has different rules and different limitations to the one we were born into and grew up in.[32]

It's hard to figure how we got to the point when paying full price is for schmucks. If you don't want to pay for something, you don't have to. Or when you cannot get something easily and legally, get it unlawfully. Or when you have an axe to grind against some capitalist organization, do your own thing! And, finally, of course, there is the we-must-bow-to-the-demands-of-technology argument. I wonder how long industry would last if we were all to approach it in this manner? Can we end piracy? Probably not, but we can make it too expensive to commit, something we apparently aren't ready to do.

It isn't from a lack of trying. There are a myriad of bills and laws that have been put forward over the years, some of which were covered in the chapter on copyright. With respect to piracy in specific, only one needs concern us: Stop Online Piracy Act, or SOPA, for short.

The SOPA, known in Congress as H.R. 3261, was introduced by Republican Representative Lamar Smith of Texas on October 26, 2011. The bill's purpose, as its title states, is to encourage "prosperity, creativity, entrepreneurship, and innovation by combating the theft of U.S. property...."[33] The bill seeks to end online piracy and stop the reproduction of counterfeit goods. The idea behind the bill, so it appears, is to close the loop that the web opened by providing a more effective and stringent means to stop online piracy.

To say few like the bill is an understatement, and that includes many librarians and library associations. The SOPA led to one of the largest online protests but that isn't saying a lot since it is, after all, easy to get a few million on your side about an issue that the community finds repugnant to begin with (and at least 50 percent didn't really read it before signing off on it). The opponents of SOPA dragged out the old bugbear of free speech and objected to the bill's provisions to shut down domains. Some argue, too, that the bill does not provide enough exemptions and that it is counter to some of those same exemptions outlined in the Digital Millennium Copyright Act (DMCA). In addition to librarians' concerns about free speech, there is also the fear that SOPA will expose libraries to litigation.

While it would be an easy fix to apply to SOPA the same exemptions as DMCA, the fear about libraries and ligations is unwarranted. Libraries have been exempt from these since the 1976 Copyright Act, and these exemptions have been strengthened, not weakened, by the Supreme Court in two recent cases involving copyright: the Georgia State University Reserves case, as well as the *HathiTrust* case.[34] To dismiss SOPA solely on the exemptions is on the hysterical side. The web community dismissed SOPA because it runs counter to its motivations to make everything free (except the companies that host the web and make money from it). For example, the cyber security bill, Cyber Intelligence Sharing and Protection Act (CISPA), which had a few technology companies on its side, ran afoul of the web community, sparking widespread protests and shutdowns.[35]

Is there anything to worry about? If one abides by copyright, no.[36] Takedown notices will occur, but if people abide by them, there isn't anything to worry about. Will so-called evil people make money? Of course they will, and that includes Google and other web-based entities, but building a policy based on the politics of envy is worse than worrying about whether all of us can have access to everything, regardless of copyright. If we take away creators' incentive to create, we'll lose the backbone of democratic capitalism. We can always tinker with the laws to make copyright and piracy restrictions better, but once we discard them, it will take something just short of war to get them back.

The simple fact of the matter is that the information-wants-to-be-free crowd will never allow any bill that regulates information so that people have to pay for it. First Amendment absolutists (and this includes just about every librarian in the world, and all of the American Library Association) will make the perfect the enemy of the good by arguing that restriction of any word or thought is bad for the free world (and pornographers, pedophiles, hate-mongers, et al., everywhere, are thanking God, or rather Google and ALA, for believing this). Meanwhile, intellectual property and creativity are roadkill on the Information Superhighway. Some will argue that this is a defense aimed at those not willing to innovate in the face of the web's brave new world. We hear that routinely when something is difficult to do, or when the web runs (briefly) into a bit of a roadblock (see, for example, Google Book Search and its disregard for copyright). We're told to get with the program, start to innovate, this is the new normal, if you're not with us you're against us, and we will bury you.

Nice approach that, and one that when encountered in any other context but the web is seen for what it is: bullying. The culture of the web is doing much to degrade what we have taken millennia to build. I'd hate to see our intellectual heritage go without at least a small fight.

PLAGIARISM

It cannot be doubted that the web has given us more plagiarism than we ever had before. And no wonder, seeing as how it is, after all, so very easy. While no one can deny that the web is chiefly responsible for the rise in intellectual theft, and among even the best and the brightest, we cannot dismiss the role that human nature plays in this. In a recent study, researchers found that there is such a thing as the "cheater's high."[37] The authors conclude that although people expect to feel worse after over-reporting their performance on cognitive tasks, they actually feel better about it, at least until they are caught. We might feel bad, but we feel worse about getting caught—and not so much that we are actually guilty. Even so, plagiarism on the web is rampant. As mentioned in an earlier chapter, Coursera, a MOOC platform, is struggling mightily with the problem. Unfortunately, there does not appear to be any quick way to prevent this since any kind of cutting and pasting can be done so easily and so quickly it is almost undetectable. Many colleges and universities have turned to plagiarism detection systems like Turnitin to help slow down the onslaught.

Herewith, then, are yet more reasons why the Internet is no substitute for a library, or should not be. Is piracy and plagiarism so important that we are unwilling, if only for a moment, to consider our options but with some restrictions? Oh, there, I said the r-word, but indulge this lengthy quotation to consider what one of the greatest innovators of all time said with respect to restrictions:

> ... [W]hich of us has ever heard talk of art as other than the realm of freedom? This sort of heresy is uniformly widespread because it is imagined that art is outside the bounds of ordinary activity. Well, in art as in everything else, one can build only upon a resisting foundation: whatever constantly gives way to pressure, constantly renders movement impossible.
>
> My freedom thus consists in moving about within the narrow frame that I have assigned myself for each one of my undertakings.
>
> I shall go even further: *my freedom will be so much the greater and more meaningful the more narrowly I limit my field of action and the more I surround myself with obstacles. Whatever diminishes constraint, diminishes strength. The more constraints one imposes, the more one frees one of the chains that shackle the spirit.*
>
> *The more art is controlled, limited, worked over, the more it is free.*[38]

Not to put too fine a point on it, but the most innovative musician in modern times, Stravinsky (above), felt that he was never more free than when he was restricted by rules. Remove the rules, all the resistance, and nothing is left, according to him, but the abyss, the loss of real freedom, the endgame to creativity. Could it be that we have created a similar situation by insisting on a kind of theoretical freedom that in reality is unknown? At the risk of sounding overly philosophical, perhaps Stravinsky is right, that creativity needs rules and restrictions to make it free, within the rules, or as he puts it, the more *controlled, limited, worked over, the more it is free*. Stravinsky isn't the only one either, when it comes to this idea of bounded freedom. Wasn't it Defoe's domesticated goats that, when left with seemingly endless boundaries, were so wild that they were indistinguishable from those that roamed untethered?

Suffice it to say that there is a middle way here between, on the one hand, laws so severe no information can be shared, and a complete usurpation of them so that no one owns any intellectual property at all. All we have to do is have the will to find that middle way and then insist upon it.

PART THREE

The last part of this book tackles the future of libraries, and what that may be. Chapter 13 looks at current conditions, Chapter 14 uses a strategizing template (in this case TEMPLES: technology, economy, markets, politics, laws, ethics and society) to supply an educated guess and sees a negative future and a positive one. Depending on whether you see the glass half full or half empty, both a negative future and a positive one emerge. I chose this approach because this particular strategizing tool looks at current conditions better than the more familiar SWOTS analysis, at least as far as libraries go. Once the conditions are sized up, it is not much of a stretch to envision what the future might bring under those circumstances. In the end, everything is guesses, but useful ones, I hope.

It's become something of a cliché now to talk about the future of libraries, and on two counts. The first is a bit of a wag's cliché: Future? What future? The Internet has made them obsolete, and thus all the carping that follows, ranging from "they're toast" to "they're a 15th century invention in a 21st century world." Some readers may think I exaggerate, but only recently, Miami Mayor Carlos Gimenez said in response to the library cutbacks there, "People have said that the age of libraries is probably ending."[1] If some readers think this applies only to public libraries, let me remind them of the trend so far: First school libraries began to disappear; now it's public ones. Do you need to guess which will be third? The second cliché about the future of libraries comes from the lips of librarians and runs something like this: "Oh, yes, we need to change and we will, we are." Honestly, not much has changed so far. And we librarians aren't exactly the best people to raise this question about our future with. When M. G. Seigler dared to think aloud on the subject of the end of libraries, a hailstorm of negative comments, threats and wailings followed.[2] We have to do better than this. Thinking that the future of libraries looks bleaker than ever before isn't the same as saying the earth is flat.

It is very unlikely that libraries will cease to exist immediately. It is also extremely unlikely that they can continue along the same lines they have for the last millennium and not find themselves in obsolescence. Changes are already upon us, and librarians need to embrace them and adapt their libraries instead of trying to make the changes fall in line with 19th century [sic] librarianship.

Libraries *do* have a future, that's the good news, but that's just about all the good news. They have a future but it may be a scant one unless we act quickly and decisively. Our future largely depends on us. We know we need to change but are we willing to make those important changes? Look, for example, at our buildings. With the exception of a few dozen, the cliché is right: we are a 15th century invention trying to make a go of it in a 21st century tech-savvy world. The building I work in was built in 1968. In that year, U.S. businesses spent *zero* dollars on automation. By 1995, U.S. businesses were spending *one billion annually*. But that's nothing compared to today's costs. In 2012, information technology costs businesses more than *3 trillion dollars*.[3] Although it is true that more and more businesses are questioning their return on investment in technology, it doesn't appear that this spending frenzy—because that's what it is—will slow down much in the near future.

This is important because information that was once the bailiwick of the library is now the bailiwick of any entity with web-accessible devices. Businesses, unlike libraries, have seemingly endless budgets to acquire these devices. The niche that libraries must fill will be those places where information is needed but cannot be accessed easily by those who want it. It must also be a niche in which the information obtained is the right kind at the right time. Librarians, always respectful of privacy and intellectual property rights, strike me as the perfect purveyors to fill this niche. Are we up to it?

I don't mean, are we capable of doing it. Unquestionably, we are. I'm not so sure, however, we're willing to let go of some truly outdated ways of doing things in order to present ourselves as the logical choice. Take, for example, our web presence to date. Even our most important clientele, faculty and students, tell us we're *the last place* they look to find information, and one reason is that our portals are so uninspiring.[4]

The fact of the matter is that we're still using tools in our toolbox created for a past in which information was exclusively the bailiwick of librarians, housed in a bastion of bricks and mortar. It isn't any more, and we need to let go of the idea that we are gatekeepers of much beyond what most people can access from their laptops, iPads, phablets or whatever other devices emerge in the near term. One would think that librarians would be used to this since we have always dealt with format change, but today's technology has changed so rapidly it has outstripped even our ability to keep up with it. Instead of planning for a format, we need to plan for delivery systems, both those we know and those we can only imagine, and it won't be easy. When the first phone moved from a land line to a unit the size of a shoebox, it looked laughably cumbersome. Who among us thought it would become the single most important device, now only slightly larger than a credit card, from which our users access everything? Did any one of us think that it would happen *this* fast, in less than three decades? And now that we're used to them, they, too, will go the way of all bits and bytes as we prepare for the *next* delivery system.

So, first, we need to get rid of some of these tools that are holding us back and move to other ways of doing what we do so well: put people and ideas together to create yet something else new and exciting. How we do that going forward will depend on how innovative we wish to be, and how much risk we're willing to take. Librarians, as a group, are risk-averse. We like the ebb and flow, the smooth flux of life, but in a decent and orderly manner, don't you see?

How can we possibly plan for a future that we cannot now even describe? Earlier I mentioned the use of DNA to record audio and text files. That may well be the answer to the bandwidth and storage problems. But then again, it might not be. What we do know is that most of the technology we use now will not be used in the same way or to the same degree—or even at all—in the coming decades. We don't need to plan so much for the next Big Thing as we need to position ourselves for *whatever* comes our way. Our focus should be on the output of knowledge, not so much on what the data are inputted on.

Our puzzling future will also include some low-tech devices, and knowing which ones to keep and which ones to discard will become important. As we look at some of the changes already underway and can catch a glimpse of those on the way, will we be up to the challenge to change and adapt quickly? Heretofore, we have had decades to adapt. Going into the future, it appears we may have, if we're lucky, only *months* to make the necessary adaptations. While we may well be able to keep the façade of most of our buildings, we need to be ready to change much of what is inside them now if we hope to be here in twenty or thirty years.

That's really our challenge. Can we marshal ourselves and our resources in such a way to make these needed changes, keeping the best of what we have and know works well, while also embracing new technologies appropriately? Some will doubtless think this statement contradictory, given all the billingsgate I have hurled at the web, but I don't see it that way. My *furor scribendi* about the web has been directed that way because too many people using it (and some associated with it) think that's all we need to replace libraries. My contention here has been that *we need both because both serve very different, but equally important, purposes.* And furthermore, that there is a place in the world for libraries if libraries are willing to change and if individuals are willing to accommodate them. If not, it will be a battle that libraries will lose, but so will everyone else who has ever used a library.

Author David Nasaw gets it right in his book *The Patriarch*, a book about Joe Kennedy, Sr. The first sentence of his acknowledgments underscores what we may be losing: "No work of history is possible," he writes, "without archivists and librarians."[5] It isn't only history but papers one must write for this or that report, this or that business, or finding this or that job. Eliminate the library as an intellectual entity and you may well be eliminating all that is left to preserve a well-informed electorate, to preserve our culture and to augment our intellectual history. Bear in mind that Nasaw has at his fingertips access to the most technologically advanced information, yet he knows where he must turn: to librarians and archivists.

"We've gone from a world in which there is too little information," writes author Neil Gaiman,

> in which information is scarce, to a world in which there is too much information, and most of it is untrue or irrelevant.... We've gone from looking at a desert, in which a librarian had to walk in the desert for you and come back with a lump of gold, to a forest, to this huge jungle in which what you want is one apple. And at that point, the librarian can walk into the jungle and come back with the apple. So I think from that point of view, the time of librarians, and the time of libraries—they definitely haven't gone anywhere.[6]

The good news is that libraries are so far thriving, even though they rely more on place in contradistinction to the web which relies on really no space. That may seem counterintuitive, but millions of Americans rely on libraries for jobs, news, social media, access to the web and more. According to the American Library Association, almost 70 percent of Americans use their public libraries, with seven in ten libraries reporting an uptick in usage of some kind over the previous year. Just over 90 percent of all libraries provide job information for patrons, with 73 percent helping patrons fill out applications, create résumés or complete some other job-related function. Try Googling that, especially if you don't have Internet access to begin with! Libraries use social media to connect with patrons, have ebooks for them to "check out," and provide various kinds of other technology-related access and help patrons find what they want quickly and easily.

The movement in academic libraries is much the same. After close to a million dollar renovation to the main floor of our 45 year old building, the library I work in has seen an increase in just about every offering. Student usage is up more than 30 percent, traffic in our building up almost 40 percent. Our reference services have also increased a whopping 50 percent. We expected some increase since we moved from being open 90 hours weekly to 24/5 (our data revealed we could not even pay students to come to the building after 7 on Friday, or Saturday before noon or after 6). But even adjusting for this, our increase in foot traffic has been nothing short of remarkable: almost 28,000 in one month alone, one fourth our *annual* total before the changes. If you build it right, they will in fact come, and in hordes. Part of the increased traffic is the more welcoming space we created. The main floor is more open, and there are numerous rooms for group study. We also have added other tools for students to use and advertised what we can do for students better than we had in the past.

Such changes will go only so far, however. Academic libraries, including this one, are looking at other ways to increase services while holding down costs. Data curation, staff reassignments, digital preservation, and cross training are a few of the many options libraries are examining carefully.[7] Academic libraries will have to use frugality as the benchmark to creating their future. Trying to manage it all will take a great deal of imagination and even more luck. Working more closely together will be the key to our future success, not only as we plan our future but also as we share our resources with one another.

Libraries have always been collaborative organizational structures, if not from the beginning, then certainly over the last fifty or more years. In this new age of technology, economic realities and the rest will mean that we'll have to rely on one another on a much more aggressive scale. We will have to embrace technology fully, but dictate to it what we need, not have it dictate to us what we can do. If we do the latter, we will surely be replaced over time. If libraries attempt to make information access their key role, they will be replaced by a better, faster, more ubiquitous web-based service of some kind. If we emphasize what we have always done—preservation of the cultural heritage of our nation and its interpretation—then we will have insinuated ourselves into the future in a manner that cannot be replaced by mere machines, no matter how smart they are or become. This cultural heritage means not only information access but also social and civic engagement, a place where citizens can join together to accomplish whatever goals they have set for themselves and their communities. It means *knowledge*, not just information.

Archives will continue to hold and preserve tens of thousands of documents that are one-of-a-kind, documents about areas, regions or histories that cannot possibly be found anywhere else. While the book may take on a kind of artform as it is replaced by electronic versions, it will still remain as a primary source in the short term. One cannot discount, however, how important such books may become when, in twenty or thirty years, they stand as the only reminder of the paperbound age.[8]

Finding information is the easy part, and any search engine can do this faster and better than a librarian, but what a search engine cannot produce is a place for people to work together and a way to find out what all these data mean. We hear a great deal about "Big Data," as if this will solve all our problems. But "Big Data" is nothing more than millions and millions—no, make that trillions and trillions—of information points for someone else to massage into a meaningful representation of something useful.

Big Data may tell us a lot, but the raw way in which it comes to us tells us next to nothing until it has been marshaled into something worthwhile. Big Data is everything ... now if we only knew what it means! I believe this is but one niche that libraries can fill: a convenient space for cooperative work for helping others understand what all the data means. Can't you do that online or in chat rooms? We haven't so far, and apparently there is something in our makeup that needs, requires, face-to-face confabulation. Our so-called tech-savvy students repeatedly say that even with all the MOOCs and online hybrids, if the course is a difficult one, they want it face-to-face.[9] In other words, if it's something they have to struggle with, they want to be able to interact easily and repeatedly.

The same is true, I think, of the work that goes on in libraries. While the footprint may shrink some, we humans still like making eye contact, at least for now. And until Apple, or Google, or the Internet makes *that* obsolete, libraries will remain not only useful, but absolutely essential to our intellectual creativity, into whatever form it might evolve.

CHAPTER 13

You Are Here

Having spent the last couple of hundred pages in a consistory of complaints about Google, the Internet, digitization, e-books, and all the rest, while praising libraries, librarians and what they do, my jeremiad against the web must sound a lot like this lamentation:

> Oh, false and all too human thoughts—I see things turned out differently from what I hoped. Because now that anyone is free to [post online whatever] they wish, they often disregard that which is best and instead [Google] merely for the sake of entertainment, what would best be forgotten, or, better still, *erased*.... And even when they [Google] something worthwhile they twist it and corrupt it to the point where it would be much better to do without such [searching], rather than having a thousand [hits] spreading falsehoods over the whole world.[1]

Is this from the comment section on Amazon books, or some other DIY ebook creation? No, rather it's a letter from Niccolò Perotti (the necessary changes having been made), writing to Francesco Guarnerio, about twenty years after Gutenberg's press. While Perotti looked forward with hope to the new invention, it didn't pan out that way, at least not so far as he foresaw it. And to be honest, Gutenberg did bring an end to the beautifully illuminated manuscripts that are now worth hundreds of thousands of dollars. Will my lament turn out as pointless as Perotti's?

Perhaps. My intent, however, is not to disparage new technology for the sake of disparaging it, or to give the impression that it is worthless, the *bête noire* of our civilization. Rather, I call attention to the fact that we, especially those of us in libraries, are letting technology dictate our future, rather than using technology to create a proud one. Further, to the fact that as marvelous as our technology is, it still isn't ready to replace libraries, and if we let it, we will be sorely regretful later. If we continue to allow technology to dictate our future, the future of libraries is a bleak one. If we choose to use technology to create our future, we may have a more promising one ahead of us.

Before that possible future, however, where are we right now? What are the trends in librarianship in key areas, in staffing, patrons/users, collections, and space/building? Looking at where we are now may help us understand better where we might be headed if technology dictates our future, or if we use it to create one. We hear a great deal of noise now about our future, but let's not be deaf to the signals, too, which are also present.

STAFFING

There is a famous passage in a play most of us know by heart, having read it first in the ninth grade, that speaks to us, or at least should, on our future. The play is *Julius Caesar*, and the scene is the one in which Brutus and Cassius discuss their individual fates. Brutus worries that Caesar will turn the Roman republic into a monarchy, and Cassius plays this fear.

> Men at some time are masters of their fates:
> The fault, dear Brutus, is not in our stars,
> But in ourselves, that we are underlings.[2]

At least one part of the problem with our present, and it has been alluded to more than once in these pages already, is who we are. We librarians, as a group, are slow to change, and slower still to embrace change even when it is inevitably upon us. Part of our difficulty is in our own self-preservation instinct, and in that we are no different from any other profession. A plan to do away with my job or yours should be met with at least some little resistance if we're doing anything worthwhile at all. But librarians' resistance to change is deeper than that. It may not be all that different from any other profession, but it gives the appearance of being more rigid, brittle. It has been said that the prognosis for American health care is grim owing to cost, access and quality. The same could be said about the future of libraries.

One major reason for the resistance to change is a point alluded to above: the greying of our profession. The *Monthly Labor Review* contends that by 2019, almost 60 percent of us will be 65, a mere five years from now. Our job growth is also slower than average for all occupations.[3] We are, at best, a senior profession, and our replacements are not keeping up with our retirements. It's better than it has been, thanks in part to the Laura Bush 21st Century Librarian program. Without that, no one would be around even to turn out the lights in ten years. Even with it, we are having trouble replacing those taking retirement. While there are those outside our profession who are dubious of both the education and the subsequent degree, we cannot give them the only say.[4] When some *within* the profession (a chief librarian, for example) express a reluctance to hire librarians, however (choosing instead Ph.D.'s for example), the situation can be said to be in deep trouble.[5] Library education will have to change. Once the succeeding generation of librarians takes over, our resistance to change should diminish. Until then, the resistance to change will remain palpable.

Going forward, we will have to improve what we define as "satisfactory service." How we view that as we move into the future will be of critical importance. Bear in mind that the Internet does not shrug its shoulders, get testy or act superior when providing information. If our value-added feature over the web is human service, it must improve in all areas. Our service record, while largely good, can stand to be reminded of what makes it weak. Certainly our acceptance of what constitutes success is one problem, as we have defined it, at least when it comes to reference service, as answering correctly 55 percent of our inquiries.[6] We must improve this in the future, and must improve it in all forms of the reference encounter.[7] This is much easier said than done, simply because it's much easier to correct the defects of a machine—write new code that eliminates the bug—than it is to remove deep-seated antipathies that have been acquired over years of public service.

Although identified in a book written now more than twenty-five years ago, these "sins of service" are all too much with us still.[8] If we are to carve out a niche in the future, our present must remediate its service record. If we cannot remediate this part, we will not have much of a future and will have no one to blame but ourselves. The sins of service that remain areas for amelioration are apathy, the brush-off, coldness, condescension, robotism, rule book and runaround. These are obvious enough failings without delineating them.

Contrast what appears to be, at times, our hideboundism inherent in our service, to the forward-looking mien of companies like Google, Twitter and even Yahoo. Already their technicians are not so much thinking of integrating computers into our daily lives, but already doing so, all with an idea to make things easier, faster, stronger, more seamless and more convenient (or so we are to believe). Voice recognition technology is already much improved over what it was last year, and wearable technology is fast becoming the next big thing however horrifying, Google glasses may be.[9] Libraries simply cannot compete against this kind of brainpower, and will have to find their niche in the future, providing access but also providing much, much more than just access.

Library staff must approach patrons with value-added service uppermost on their minds. Some models for the future of service are really adaptations of ones that we have, in some ways, been doing all along. They are also models some of us bristle at but our hackles may no longer be an option for us if we hope to reach our clientele.

For example, the business or customer model has been bruited about in professional pages but is very much despised by some in our profession. This is really nothing more than the client-centered model of the middle eighties.[10] Libraries have always been very much patron-oriented. What forces this particular model as one to examine more closely going into our future is whether we have examined it thoroughly enough to see what benefits it offers. Almost no one in libraries, especially academic ones, likes to think of patrons as clients, or even consumers, but this may well be nothing more than the profession leftward lean. Patrons are consumers, and so that makes them, whether we like it or not, customers of a type.

In the vademecum on the subject, *The Client-Centered Academic Library*, Martell provides us with a part we have missed: "In theory, the academic library is sensitive and responsive to the changing client needs for information. In practice, the library is relatively insensitive and unresponsive to these needs. This posture is not an error of omission but reflects both the predominant image of the library's proper operational role and organization structured to foster and shield that image."[11]

We cannot compete with supplying better, faster or more "cutting-edge" access. What we can do, however, and better than our technological savants, is provide accommodating spaces in which all of this, and more, can take place. Those spaces, however, will not look the way they have for the last two hundred years. They, too, will need to take on a more proactive look and feel, designed for the here and now, but also adaptable for the future. Assessment will be instrumental in circumscribing what this process should be and how it should unfold.

We need library leaders who are ready to respond to ever-changing patron needs, fearless about making decisions, all the while protecting what is good about the last hundred years but ready to embrace what the next few decades will present. Our planning should not be 10 to 15 years out, but only three to five, with an ever-ready mindset to drop what isn't working and embrace what *might*. Because we still live in a transitional age made up of patrons who are eager for technology, eager for collaborative spaces and, yes, still eager for print, we will need leaders who can make decisions that satisfy all these users, and still have an eye for the future.[12]

We've known for some time that there is "no one best way" in organizational development, but we still have a tendency to hold out for a best solution, or one right answer to every question.[13] Now, and going into our uncertain future, it will be necessary for library leaders to live with a degree of uncertainty, forging ahead and making the changes as they go along, as needs dictate. How do we break out of the bureaucratic mindsets that have dominated librarianship for the last fifty to a hundred years? By forcing ourselves to make bold decisions and try many new approaches, adjusting and adapting as each situation requires.

Whether tenure for academic librarians can continue under these conditions is questionable. It isn't that tenure is inherently bad, but it does force a kind of straitjacket on the library for reasons that are inherent in the tenure process itself. The library of the future will be filled with so much uncertainty that placing librarians on a six-year tenure track for jobs that may not exist at the end of the probationary period does not appear either possible or fair. Furthermore, tenure is not exactly a flexible or nimble model when it comes to change. Having said that, if librarians take on more responsibilities in the future as they must, whatever *status* is granted to teaching faculty should be granted to them. Some form of security will remain, most probably in the form of multiyear contracts of one, three and five years.

Librarians today remain deskbound, an unlikely scenario in coming years. This will mean going to where students are in computer or writing labs, even dorms, as students write their papers. Embedded librarians are becoming more common and will likely be a commonplace feature in coming years. While current library tutorials are class-bound, the multiple, brief online tutorials that now occur will likely become more commonplace, too. This has at least two advantages. First, it frees up librarians from having to teach scores of the same library research courses over and over again. Second, it allows students to access the material over and over again, as they need it, not when librarians are able to deliver it. Further, librarians will also be involved more in teaching subject-specific information literacy *courses*, not classes.

These courses will include the ability to teach and manipulate technology, to deploy various forms of media, and to be able to instruct others in all of these. Some have referred to this new librarian model as "eBrarians," but we need a more clever strategy to define what librarians will do in the future before we need yet another clever name.[14] Librarians who can do all the traditional things librarians have done well, and also these many new things, while remaining flexible, will have positioned themselves for the future, regardless of what they are called.

Library deans or directors will need to be at the vanguard of these transformations in the future. While change has been slow in academic libraries overall, the rate of change will need to step up to meet the speed with which the change in access is occurring. This will mean providing more bandwidth for patrons and offering more spaces for various kinds of research that may not dovetail all that well, or even at all, with traditional means. This does not mean changing spaces and staffing for the sake of change, but it does mean changing spaces and staffing to meet the growing demands of new areas. Library deans or directors will also need to lead the way in helping the library to acquire more open access to scholarly materials whenever they can. It's very unlikely that open access will move quickly enough to cover every area of acquisition in libraries and make a serious difference but whenever open access is available and can be matched to current demands it should be pursued.

Finding the right mix of librarians' flexibility, skill sets and familiarity with technology combined in a space that is inviting to college-aged adults in an age of skyrocketing costs is not, of course, going to be easy.

PATRONS

Mobile environments, present now, will dominate our future in some form, as will social networking in some manner because our patrons demand it. Most libraries have some form of mobile access now—perhaps even a mobile app—but not as many have embraced social networking fully. In some ways, this may have been because we understood the nature of this arrangement better than others. New studies reveal that the use of social media may be a poor academic strategy.[15] The study done by the Miriam Hospital's Center for Behavioral and Preventive Strategy focused on young women. It found that freshmen women spent up to 12 hours engaged in some form of social media. The study also found a link between the extensive use of social media and lower GPAs. Obviously, libraries do not need to be encouraging something that may be a predictor of failure, but limited use of social media to encourage academic study and research is in order.

By 2012 there were more than six billion cellphones in existence worldwide, and we're closing in on more than two billion personal computers, laptops and phablets. More than 800 million of us have registered on Facebook, and 1.5 trillion or more messages are being sent annually.[16] Not to put too fine a point on it, but many of these users, for better or for worse, are employing social networks as their discovery tools. Are we librarians?

Which social networks libraries should pursue is anyone's guess. In March of 2013, for example, for the first time ever, Facebook lost visitors, and not just a few thousand but *millions*, about nine million per month in the UK and two million per month in the U.S.[17] Younger social network users are using something else, Twitter especially, and Tumblr.[18] Facebook is working furiously to expand its services and offer more reasons to continue, so it cannot be counted out. Whatever its individual fate, ignoring social networking trends altogether would be a strategy aiming for inconsequence for libraries.

The MOOCs, massive open online courses, and their delivery over a number of platforms like Udacity, Coursera, and MiTx have turned the pursuit of a college degree upside-down. Many of these students, if matriculated anywhere, may not have done so at a college in the city in which they reside. Since this has not been the traditional way that academic libraries have served non-matriculated students in the past, changes will need to occur. At the beginning of the year MOOCs took off like a rocket from a launching pad. Unfortunately, too many of them looked like they had been launched from North Korea, as they soon crashed and burned after takeoff. Coursera, for example, is rife with plagiarism. Some universities, such as Duke, have scaled back their MOOC plans. And the old bugbear of the web in general, intellectual property rights, is now raising its fearsome head.[19]

Then there is the whole "technology hype cycle" phenomenon.[20] When technological marvels appear, successful ones will have a hype that catapults them to unprecedented levels of expectation. That particular technological marvel will, the hype says, solve everything, do everything, complete everything. Typically what follows is a slough of despond. Or, as Wood has it, a trough of disillusionment. If the technology is successful, a much smaller incline of enlightenment ensues and a plateau of productivity is reached. It is instructive to remember that this occurs with nearly all new technology. Many unsuccessful ones, however, when they plunge into the trough of despond, never really climb back out. Some, too, climb out and then are replaced altogether. Consider, for example, that PCs, we are told, are dead.[21]

Have MOOCs entered their downward trend? Perhaps, but something else will likely replace them. Indeed, Khan Academy appears to be doing this already, although it isn't exactly a MOOC, just MOOC-like. Former hedge fund manager Sal Khan began by creating brief videos on important topics in mathematics and science. Topics on algebra, calculus and other similar subjects are available over YouTube.[22] To date, Khan offers about 2,000 videos that have attracted more than two million students.

Libraries positioned to deliver materials to students in MOOCs will be ready for this future. Of course, traditional colleges and universities will remain but if MOOCs are successful, many fewer small colleges and universities will survive. The combination of serving a traditional population and an unconventional one will help to solidify the primacy of libraries in the future. Our future will be made up of those users we have always served, and, for lack of a better word, "know-mads" or individuals who learn wherever they are but are not wedded to doing so in a linear fashion. Know-mads move in and out of the higher education scene. As one observer wrote,

> Forward thinking institutions and their partners have been [providing online education] for years, as a natural extension of existing provision. Rather than see it as an either/or choice—replacing one education model with another—we now have different ways of learning suited to different types of students. Offering a highly flexible model, online education is particularly beneficial for people who need to fit study around family commitments or who want to continue to work while they learn.[23]

Currently, libraries adopt new technology carefully and deliberately, and that is not a bad thing at all. Going forward, however, we'll have to adapt more quickly. Having said that, we'll need to do better with respect to how we instruct patrons in their use. For example, according to recent studies of first year students in 2011, 60 percent of them did not evaluate the quality or the reliability of the information they found (hence, Googling everything), and three-quarters of first year students did not know how to find scholarly materials (peer-reviewed, for example). Integrating materials into a cogent presentation or paper is beyond almost half of them.[24]

We might think that this would be a perfect opportunity for academic librarians to step in and show their worth, but we're not, or we haven't so far. Our approach to information literacy is indifferent and unimaginative. The future for us means having to try any number of different venues and approaches, not wedding ourselves to any one in particular, and being ready to change them when required.

Is this just hype and hyperbole?

Think about it for a minute. Rising populations of students in K–12 are already growing up in educational contexts *without* libraries. Many K–12 schools have media centers, if they have any "library" space at all, and most of these are equipped with everything *but books*. In New York City, the transition away from librarians is accelerating. In 2008 there were almost 400 certified librarians in the city schools. Today, there are 333 and not all of them are working as librarians. The reason? "[A]dvancements in technology, shifts in teaching practices, and the addition of classroom libraries have made librarians not as necessary as they once were," city officials argue.[25] The problem of vanishing libraries and librarians is reaching critical proportions in the United Kingdom. Library officials there predict that there will be 1,000 library closures by 2016.[26] If true, this would bring to closure one fourth of all UK libraries since 2009.

Young people in these and other schools will matriculate into academic institutions but without the habit of going to libraries for research. Furthermore, these students will have many fewer institutions to matriculate into, according to experts.[27] Of the 4,500 or so institutions of higher education, experts point to only about 500 that appear immune to financial difficulties in the coming 25 to 50 years. If true, this means that the majority will close or merge, or be replaced with what some are calling "niche" institutions. Furthermore, the cost of going to college is higher than it ever has been before, with the average student completing undergraduate degrees owing more than $20,000, and some with $40,000 (and a few, much more) as they begin their work lives. As one critic puts it, setting costs aside:

> [T]he real story of American higher-education bubble has little to do with individual students and their debts or employment problems. The most important part of the college bubble story—one we will soon be hearing much more about—concerns the impending financial collapse of numerous private colleges and universities and the likely shrinkage of many public ones. And when that bubble bursts, it will end a system of higher education that, for all its history, has been steeped in a culture of exclusivity. Then we'll see the birth of something entirely new as we accept one central and unavoidable fact: The college classroom is about to go virtual.[28]

In other words, the cost and debt aside, what is really going to put pressure on colleges and universities is the ability students will have to access their education outside of the traditional four-year residential institution.

Should all of this come to pass, our clientele, our patrons or our customers—call them whatever you wish—will be more than a little different from what libraries and librarians have served in the past. Being prepared for these eventualities will mean the difference not only between success and failure but also between a present and a future.

COLLECTIONS

We librarians have been a bit slow in reshaping our buildings and in reshaping our catalogs. We are also slow in dispensing with unused and out-dated collections. Much of what we can provide access to can be offered via proprietary databases that are web-accessible. In an age of scarcity, we still want to do everything that we've always done, however, and we expect our institutions simply to provide us more money to fund both the old and the new. Heaven forbid we give up something that isn't being used, used by only a fraction of our patrons, or has simply been here or been done that way since libraries began. This is unrealistic and such sentiments will be our undoing. Are we sleeping through life's waiting room, as an old Sufi saying has it, unawake to the changes in the world around us? I hope not.

One area in which libraries can create future collections will be found in the expansion of institutional repositories (IR). Academic libraries can be—should be—integral to constructing these substantial information assets on their campuses, and really *must* be in the future if library collections are to be sustained. As such, IRs are the intellectual digital footprint of a campus, becoming the digital locus which the energy of the campus resides. These repositories are the digital archive of scholarly papers, works in progress and so-called "grey litera-ture" or technical ephemera. Even small campuses can provide important infor-mation that would not otherwise be available without the existence of IRs.

While some see IRs as potentially competing with traditional publish-ing, IRs are really complements to traditional publishing. The IRs are more like storehouses of materials that may or may not rise to the level of books or of bookmaking, or peer-reviewed articles, though some already do. The value of IRs both to the intellectual community and to libraries should be obvious. They stand as key ingredients to the collaboration of that academic community's members with each other, as well as to the outside world. (For more on collaboration see: http://miracle.si.umich.edu/.)

In order for IRs to succeed, however, some form of open access will also have to catch on. Open access has already been ventilated earlier so only a few brief remarks are needed here. Many IRs offer content through open access already but open access will be required for the future of libraries and especially academic ones. The current serial purchase model for libraries is, as we all know, unsustainable. The cost of many electronic serials, and aggregate databases containing them, exceeds the high five-figures, and some have even surpassed six figures. No library or institution of higher education can afford to continue paying such exorbitant fees. Open access provides a way wherein first-rate content can be shared and at a fraction of the cost. Open access has been slow but it is likely to pick up in the coming years since library budgets continue to remain stagnant or are declining.

Expect, however, that publishers will go kicking and screaming into the open access future. For many publishers, serials are a healthy cash cow and they will only let go of that revenue stream if it can be replaced with another similar healthy one. What is more likely to happen is that libraries will simply quit buying as many serials, forcing the hand of publishers to offer a new model. If librarians allow publishers to set both the tone and the agenda of the new model, any hope of savings will be lost, if not initially then surely long-term. Just look at what has happened with ebook models. Everyone knows that it does not cost $9.99 (or more) to "print" an ebook. Furthermore, that price may have been subjected to some price-fixing by Apple for certain, Amazon possibly.[29] And yet this is where we are because we allowed others to make those important decisions for us. While librarians are not to blame by any stretch of the imagination, we have not done nearly enough to force the hand of those who supply our content. It isn't all that easy, but we should do a better job of it going into the future.

The library is electronic now and will be ineluctably more so in the future. Even if the majority of us agreed with all the criticisms made here— and that is probably not the case—it would not matter. This is going to be our future, and we must plan accordingly or be left behind. What libraries of the future must do is make sure such access is not any more complicated than access made by the patron without the library.

For example, when ebooks first arrived on the scene for libraries, their circulation was cumbersome, ridiculously configured and unnecessarily complex. Sure, ebooks were in their infancy and only needed to age. But the aging process was slow and provided for very little improvement. The iPad emerged and everything changed. Only then did ebooks begin to come alive and make a great deal of sense for libraries. Chapter 8 discussed some of the current models for ebook delivery. Ebooks may not look the way they do now in five or more years, yet they will remain important.

Add to this yet another difficulty: The competition for resources, fierce now, is sure to be fiercer in the future. Those institutions that can find ways to create new revenue while holding down costs will compete more successfully than those with more expensive models. Libraries have for too long been the financial black holes at institutions, costing small and large fortunes but not creating much in the form of a revenue stream. Partnerships with other departments and libraries will be important going forward. It should not come as too much of a surprise if the future brings with it a centralized library for a host of institutions of higher education. Since much of what will be offered will be electronic, why would states want to duplicate those resources at ten, twenty and even (as in my own state) fifty institutions? Creating one large library-like facility that would deploy librarians to various locations for on-site help would be more cost effective (though not necessarily better) than the current model. If not this, then centrally located library facilities that would address the needs of that region are not out of the realm of possibility. Here's a for instance:

In my state, South Carolina, there are 55 public and private institutions of higher education. The state has three recognized areas: the Upstate, the Midlands and the Low Country, or, geographically speaking, piedmont, midlands and coastal zone. It would not surprise me if in the future, three mega-library regions were developed to handle all the higher educational library services of the state, assuming the state cannot reduce the number of colleges, universities and the like.[30] These are not unlike the so-called "super libraries" that have appeared in the UK.[31] The same could also be envisioned for Tennessee, another state in which I have worked.

Already school libraries have vanished, and public libraries are on life support.[32] If academic libraries think they are immune, they had best reconsider. At least this approach would salvage library services from extinction. Again, this isn't necessarily the best case scenario for librarianship; it is the one, however, that current trends—the lack of public funding, the constant return-on-investment refrain, and the incessant pressure that technology brings to bear on the work of libraries—appear to be forecasting.

In the meanwhile, some libraries will begin either to create their own content or find more suitably managed content for the future, most likely in some form of open access, mentioned above. It isn't because they will necessarily want to: it's because they *have* to. In a study comparing investment in public and academic libraries, academic libraries are coming up on the short end of the budget stick in just about every category.[33]

SPACES AND BUILDINGS

First of all, the traditional library isn't dead yet, as the University of Chicago's Joe and Rika Mansueto Library proves.[34] An $82 million dollar venture, the library has room for 3.5 million volumes, but the volumes are retrieved by an automated (robotic) system in about 10 minutes. Opened in 2011, the library preserves the traditional while making way for the future. Mansueto is the exception to the rule, however. The future library will provide less space for books and more spaces for group study, in addition to newer, faster and more complex technologies, a move that brings some to tears.[35] The physical footprint of the library will shrink accordingly. Some libraries will outsource all their cataloging, while others will opt for a hybrid model. The only consistent cataloging to be done in the future will focus on archival materials not found anywhere else. Cross-training for librarians will also be critically important. Mention was made earlier about the need for librarians with the ability to code going into the future, but for all librarians, it will be necessary to bring a wide diversity of skill sets to the table. A librarian who can manage systems, work the reference desk, teach classes in a subject specific area or general education course, and make cataloging changes will have a far better chance of not only securing a job but keeping it.

The look of traditional libraries will not be very much with us in our future. Changes in the allocation of spaces are inevitable. While often more associated with public libraries, the idea of "makerspaces" even in academic libraries is not out of the realm of possibility in the future. We hear a great deal about this in the professional literature: Makerspaces are places where patrons can come together to create whatever it is they want to create and have the tools at hand to do just that. In other words, these are libraries less about books and much more about social gathering places for creativity of all kinds. They are about the creation of information and less about access to it, though that is needed if one is to create successfully. They aren't about knowledge consumption so much as they are about knowledge creation.[36] This sort of debate will go on because right now, no one really knows what the library is *going* to be, we just know that there is a very high probability that it *will not* be what it always has been: a very large space for books and reading. This saddens some of us as we believe that reading remains the key to knowledge and everything else. Take this away from people, or deemphasize it, and the future is going to look bleak. An uneducated populace cannot really function as a democracy.

Change is never easy. Consider the following examples with respect to changing traditional library buildings: the New York Public Library, the Harvard Library and the Bodleian Libraries at Oxford in the United Kingdom. These are offered as examples of the difficulty of change, not to pass any judgment on the decision to change itself.

The controversy surrounding the New York Public Library and its planned changes, billed as a battle between the futurists and "bookish loyalists" has been ongoing, truculent on both sides, and unsettling. The rollout of the planned changes that critics said would turn the venerated building into a "Twitter-friendly aviary" and a "palace of presentism," and would move tens of thousands of books below ground, created a firestorm of controversy. But moving the books was only half the problem; replacing them with computers proved the other half, and no one, especially the NYPL, looks to be winners in this controversy.[37] The fight, which has been going on since the announcement of the *renovation* is now mired in court, as a group of scholars and preservationists have sued the library to hold up the planned $300 million dollar renovation.[38] By late summer of 2013, the president of the library announced that the library would unveil a new design that would preserve much of the old.[39]

Harvard, the nation's largest academic library, is trying to combine the best of both the old and the new worlds, but again, not without controversy.[40] The Harvard plan was widely reported on and much discussed after it appeared. Feelings ran high on both sides of the transition, those in favor of it, and those very much opposed. While the plan did move the library more toward a digital-friendly environment, complaints about planned staff reductions flooded the press.[41] The transition ended in a stalemate, with proponents calling for the change and a movement toward progress, opponents calling it a sellout and a disappointment. The point of discussing the transition here is merely to point out that the road ahead will be a most rocky one for all involved: administrators, librarians, and patrons.

Finally, change occurred in one of the oldest libraries in the world, the stately Bodleian Libraries, and very small changes at that. Since 2000, six new libraries have been built and 19 smaller libraries have been consolidated into larger units. Opponents complain that the Bodleian Libraries will go "from well-staffed and browsable libraries into a series of flagship book depositories, clean, cheap and faceless."[42] On the other side are those who see the former libraries as "a perilous firetrap" while millions of other books "were stored at huge expense in salt mines in Cheshire." Technology aside, which frankly did not seem to be an issue in this case, many more individuals viewed it as consumerism over the attempts to make the libraries more inviting as badges and t-shirts that read "ask me" singled out staff from patrons. Suffice it to say that change—any change—going forward will be greeted with both supporters and critics, both groups of which will remain quite vocal. Meanwhile, the struggle to prevent the library from getting lost amid the hue and cry from both sides will be formidable.

One thing our spaces may lack in the future, sadly, is print books. We must face the prospect of the bookless library because it's already being pressed upon us. Jason Merkoski (who built the first Amazon Kindle, by the way) is right when he contends, "In 20 years, the space of one generation, print books will be as rare as vinyl LPs. You'll still be able to find them in artsy hipster stores [did he mean libraries?], but that's about it."[43] He is also right when he goes on to say that we have made a "proverbial pact with the devil in digitizing our words" because Big Brother "won't be a politician but an ad man."

Merkoski, along with others, however, helped usher in this new e-future, and so here we are reaping the harvest what he and many others sowed. In September 2013, over one million volumes were removed from various University of Saskatchewan libraries to make way for the coming digital/electronic age.[44] Officials there say the move has come in response to a 42 percent drop in circulation over the last decade. This is hardly new. Librarian Fred Heath of the University of Texas at Austin announced the removal of about 90,000 volumes from that library almost a decade ago.[45]

Bookless libraries are evolving but some are being created from the beginning. For example, the Applied Engineering and Technology (AET) Library at the University of Texas, San Antonio, has been bookless for more than a few years. Apparently, it is thriving, if we can believe the press surrounding it.[46] The library accomplishes its service to about 2,000 students and faculty weekly with articles and ebook databases, and has been doing so since it opened in 2010. For students without e-readers or computers, the library provides both. In the fall of 2013, San Antonio will also host the nation's first bookless public library, BibliTech.[47] The library is patterned after the Apple retail stores and is the brainchild of Judge Nelson Wolff who became inspired after reading Walter Issacson's *Steve Jobs*. The only other bookless library, not also an engineering library, is Drexel's Library Learning Terrace.[48] By the time this book sees the light of printed (or virtual) day, others will have emerged. But not everyone is in agreement that bookless libraries are here now, or coming soon.[49]

CONCLUSION

This is where we are today. We see on the horizon the need to adapt quickly and well. But can we? Some argue the change needed in libraries is a kind of change libraries are unable to make.[50] These critics argue that libraries (public and academic) can offer many services, but the backbone of their existence has been lending books and that is now being rapidly replaced by tablets, Kindle Fires, iPhones and iPads. Further, more and more people are buying these devices for this very thing. Additionally, buying books for your e-reader device is so much easier than driving to your library, parking the car, going in and looking for the book, finding it isn't there, or has been misplaced, then having to drive back home, in the rain, angry and disappointed, or so the scenario is often drawn. Furthermore we are already in the middle of bookstore closures, which are like mini-libraries anyway, so how is it possible for libraries, so similar to bookstores in the traditional sense, to get away unscathed? Is there any hope for libraries? Well, when you put it like that...

Those who think libraries are already growing extinct are a small, vocal group that is rapidly increasing in numbers. They have the advantage of what technology has wrought in every area related to libraries—books, magazines, search engines, information access—helping their arguments along. Our reasoning that we offer just the same kind of access as Google et al., only free, doesn't resonate so much in an age when return on investment is so critical to maintaining a service, even a very, very good one. If we are to win this debate, we're going to have to come up with better and stronger arguments.

We are, however, sometimes our own worst enemies. We have been trying for the last five years to make our online catalogs mimic search engines to little effect, mainly because it is costly, but also because we want the kitchen sink in these searches when our users are fine with just a glass of water. Our catalogs still stink, or as some librarian critics put it, our "catalogs still suck" or suffer from "suckitude."[51] Further, our solutions—to make everything free, *and* to become all things to all mankind—are so far untenable. Finally, we've given little evidence that we are capable of making that change quickly or well.

The last chapter will offer two roads to our future, one that is bleak, another more positive. These two roads are only representative of what is ahead of us, not of course the only two available. What it comes down to is our willingness to fight for what is good and right about traditional libraries, and take that nucleus into the future, with all the changes that it will require.

CHAPTER 14

Are Libraries Obsolete
After All? Two Scenarios

An unattributed Latin saying goes like this: "If you are wise about uncertainty, beware lest things become certain."[1] I do not think one can survey the current landscape and come away with anything less than uneasiness about the future for libraries, not because of anything inherently wrong with them, but because current trends and outside forces are pushing us headlong in a direction that does not have our best interests at heart. So, let's be prudent, as prudent as we can be, and tell the unvarnished truth about two possible future scenarios, one that looks at the landscape as if all the trends were against us, and the other, more optimistically.

HERE COME THE SCRYERS

In answer to the quip of this chapter title, "are libraries obsolete after all?" I think I can answer with both an emphatic no but also a realistic yes, unless we do something quickly.

I'm not trying to be witty or diffident. I'm answering this question in both the short and the long terms. In the long term—in about twenty years, if not before—I fear the answer must be an unequivocal yes, that libraries (really all of them, but academic ones specifically since they are the center of this book's focus) are headed to obsolescence unless we—"we" meaning librarians—act more decisively for our profession. Without decisive action on our part, the technologies will be in place by then that will simply make libraries, as we know them today, pass away into something akin to Hamlet, in which "sith nor the exterior nor the inward man resembles that it was." I'm not saying that technology is the devil, but I remind readers that the first Apple computer made by Wozniak and Jobs in the latter's parents' basement cost $666. Just saying.

Libraries are changing so rapidly, so quickly, that in the short fifteen years since I wrote the article that launched two books, the future obsolescence of libraries appears all but inevitable unless we are willing to change our course in some dramatic ways. The good news is that this is beginning to occur. The bad news is that it may not be happening fast enough or in enough places to change the current and growing opinion that libraries are obsolete.

Granting the pessimism that events will continue against libraries, there are some qualifications that provide for a more optimistic outlook. That is why the answer must also be no. Certainly, in the short term, say over the next seven to fifteen years, libraries will remain largely the way they are now. Partly this is a product of the protean nature of technologies. So many of them rush upon the scene, and about half never make it before the technology hypecycle overtakes them.

Those that do survive will have an impact on libraries, sometimes minor, sometimes profound. Libraries will then make changes at the periphery until eventually those changes make a substantial difference at the very heart of what we do. The projection that about 50 percent of all universities and colleges will fail by 2020 also looms large. At the risk of repeating the obvious, if colleges and universities fail, so also will academic libraries.

The fierce financial pressures on colleges and universities that are forcing them to cut costs while trying to stay alive, combined with online courses that will eventuate into online degrees, will result in not a few academic libraries giving way to complete and utter change. Since almost no one thinks the current college degree scenario is financially sustainable with so many graduates owing $20,000 or more, a major higher education change is in the offing.

Failing colleges and universities, plus the few that remain scrambling to curtail costs and make college affordable, will combine with the pressure of technologies to eventually change the library milieu radically. The very conservative nature of librarianship toward change will also cause it to respond all too slowly, making the need for a replacement all the more necessary. Still, even granting all this, there are a few things that can throw a wrench in the pessimistic scryer's projections, and that scenario will comprise my most optimistic future prediction.

TEMPLES, A CRYSTAL BALL?

What has governed my thinking on whether or not libraries are obsolete in our technologically astute future follows along the lines of an environmental analysis. We're all familiar with SWOTS and how that works, but I have looked at other, somewhat newer approaches that help one view the world in which we now live. Around 1960, when SWOTS was gaining its momentum, we humans totaled about 3 billion people on the planet. Since then we've more than doubled that number to just over 7 billion. By 2020 we could easily number 10 billion more. For better or for worse, we do *everything* faster these days.

It struck me that something newer, more attuned to our times was needed. I think I have found that in TEMPLES, an environmental scan that looks at the following: technology, economy, markets, politics, laws, ethics, and society.[2] A few words about how each works will help readers follow my thinking.

What new ***technologies*** exist now or are emerging that either influence what libraries will do, or are *replacing* what libraries are already doing? If a service existed that we did as the "only game in town," is there now a service, available only through libraries, or is it now economically available to anyone?

The ***economy*** refers to financial instabilities that impact libraries. Are there federal, state, or local economic pressures that will impact how the library works, or how it can work? Are there institutional economic pressures either from the lack of tuition-driven funding or the downturn in state allocations that are pushing the library to make decisions very different from the ones it once made? Can the library change or neutralize these pressures? If no, what constitutes an appropriate response?

Markets are really the marketplace, and in this case the questions to ask are what marketplace events have transpired that allow a competitor of library service to emerge and challenge successfully what libraries are doing? For example, are OPACs no longer needed because free discovery tools make them obsolete? Why are surveys telling us that the library's portal is, if chosen at all, chosen as the last place students look for information? Where are they going that is so much better and why are they going there instead of coming to us?

The ***political*** climate obtrudes almost daily, and especially in the public and private context for academic libraries. What are its pressures? The important point to make here is that the library cannot afford to alienate *any* political group. After all, money from any one group spends as well and as easily as money from any other.[3] Librarians may want to "make a statement," or support a particular ideology.[4] This is fine for individuals, but doing so as a library, or in the name of the library (and it is *very* hard to separate the two), will spell early and quick doom, for just as soon as you side with one ascending political party, it will be replaced by another, leaving you stranded. For example, many of my colleagues rail against Republicans only to look shocked when Republicans defund them.

What are the *laws* or regulations that impact libraries at either the state, local, or federal level? What pressures do they put on libraries, and how can the library address them? Has the library adopted them as it should?

Ethics refers more to how libraries conduct their business, but it also refers to how well known this is to the library's clientele. Copyright and privacy issues are two that fall into this category. What are libraries doing to publicize how they treat these issues and secure their clientele?

Finally, *society* refers to how demographic features have changed that make a significant impact on the library's mission, goal, and vision statements. Shouldn't the knowledge that we add billions of bits of data daily to the storehouse of information impinge upon our thinking? Shouldn't the fact that we now have a generation that is "growing up digital" change the way we deliver services or how we make available our collections?

Using the TEMPLES approach, herewith are two possible futures:

Scenario I: Yes, Libraries Are Obsolete, or Soon Will Be

TECHNOLOGY

Nowadays, we can do whatever we want without interacting with anyone else, or only interacting with them virtually. Governments rise or fall online, and freedom is broadened or severely circumscribed, but all of it happens online at astonishing speeds. When Eric Schmidt was CEO of Google, he set out a 300 year plan to fulfill its mission.[5] For better or for worse—and Google has done a good deal of both—with about 280 years to go, does anyone really believe it will really take 280 more years to complete?

Despite the web's array of useless playthings, some of its offerings are most beneficial. Coming wearable technologies will help us track things like blood pressure and glucose levels and even prevent heart attacks and possibly seizures of all kinds with all of their pre-warnings. The convenience of doing everything online and in your pajamas (or less) appeals to a growing majority of individuals.

Much of what the rising generation is doing in their daily lives, they are doing via technology. They will grow up thinking that all the really significant things they have to do, they can or should be able to do with an app, or some form of technology. Some colleagues will say that they still have to go to school and college, but that, too, is rapidly heading toward an online life. Even in K–12, some students are able to get through virtual school without ever showing up in a red-brick building, and I don't mean just homeschoolers, though they now number in the millions. Getting a GED is now more commonly done online than in a face-to-face context. If the rising generations have to go elsewhere to do something in person, it will probably not be high on their list of things to do, and they will avoid it if they can. If we are going to reach these young people, we'll need to be there online, too, but what can we offer that will not already be available elsewhere, and what will override the inconvenience of coming to a certain location in order to do it?

Technology is enabling everything that libraries do now, or will do in the future, to be done online. For example, open access, which I highly favor and believe is a must if academic libraries are to survive into the next decade, will not need a bricks and mortar library to support it (e.g., Digital Public Library of America [DPLA], HathiTrust), just substantial funding from various sources to keep it going. Funding sources are drying up quickly, even with the backing of billionaire George Soros.[6] Without them, open access cannot work; and without open access, the skyrocketing price of serialized information cannot endure. In other words, libraries appear to be damned if they do, and damned if they don't by technology. Currently open access journals are only the tiniest percentage of all journals (less than 10 percent), but they are proliferating, and many libraries are turning to that option. If open access proves wildly successful, why would we need libraries? Wouldn't that information be available to anyone through a web-accessible device?

ECONOMY

If technology is unconvincing, add to this our lackluster economy, especially as it concerns libraries. For just over *three* decades, the trend in library funding, regardless of the library (academic, public or special), has been down, and sometimes precipitously so. Academic library funding, to remind, has nosedived since 1982, when the average funding came in at 3.7 percent of education and general (E & G), to 2 percent at the end of 2010, and it's *still* declining.[7] Even if nothing else had changed, this alone forces many of our clientele to look elsewhere for access to scholarly information. And so they have.[8]

Some will want to argue that libraries and librarians will be needed in the future more than ever to help patrons sort things out, and I would agree that this is true in the short term. But in the longer term, as more and more materials become full text, and searching algorithms prove more and more robust (e.g., Google's Hummingbird), and as more and more dollars are shifted away from libraries, the need for librarian intervention will grow less and less, at least in the minds of those paying for it. Bear in mind that this is not the case today. Libraries in the dawn or midday of our technological age are very much needed. Libraries offer that wonderful environment in which collaboration can take place easily and well among a wide diversity of individuals whom you can meet face-to-face.[9] But will this always be the case?

Let me give you a for instance.

MARKETS

It's 2033 and our hypothetical young person has grown up digital throughout her life. Every paper she wrote in high school she researched via online materials, either Google, Google Scholar, or some other online facsimile. Now she's ready for college but her choice of college is limited because more than half have closed. She can choose to do her entire degree online. If she wishes a hybrid model, she can choose to enroll in several MOOCs or MOOC-like courses. If she wants interaction with others, she can Skype (or use some form of this in future, whatever it's called) all without ever leaving her parents' basement.

But for the sake of argument, let's say she chooses one of the few remaining residential universities over an exclusively online degree program. Once she arrives on campus she finds that the former library building is now the technology center. The library is gone because costs needed to be cut, and Lord knows, no university, no matter how much it struggles, is going to cut any athletic team (even though they are one of the main reasons costs have risen so dramatically).[10] Chances are that any libraryesque unit in 2033 will be housed with IT so that staff can keep everything running and up-to-date. In any event, our fictitious student has access to all the materials in the HathiTrust, the DPLA and a half dozen other sources that have since emerged, and none of these have to be accessed through a library portal.

Copyright has been replaced entirely with something on the order of open access, tepid enforcement, or both.[11] In any event, everything our 2033 student needs is online somewhere, through some nonlibrary portal. At what point in the process does the librarian become critical, necessary or even helpful? Today, we are desperately needed because we provide access to all these copyrighted materials at a fraction of the unaffordable cost it would be to an individual. Our need is made all the more necessary because most courses are still acroamatic, or lecture-bound, so students are already on the campus (but find the research process tortuous). But by 2033, or thereabouts, will this still be the case if information-wants to be free, really is, and a web portal is all that's needed?

POLITICS

By 2033, all of these changes will have occurred and students will never come into a building called the library because there won't be one. Politicians will have argued libraries out of existence owing to scarce dollars. They are too costly, everything really is on the Internet and, what's more important, what isn't doesn't matter. In fact, many politicians already are arguing us out of existence, as we have seen. Materials that libraries might have provided exclusively will already be freely available online or made accessible through a marketplace competitor, making the politicians' case actually resonate with tax-conscious voters. The only requirement will be some sort of web-accessible device that today comes in the form of a laptop or an iPad, but in our future scenario will be in some other form, sleeker, faster, and more powerful.

LAWS

With the push of the information-wants-to-be-free movement, the coming future will witness the end of copyright as we know it. No longer will there need to be a concern for protecting copyrighted information because that law will have changed so dramatically (or have been rescinded) that it won't matter. Intellectual property rights will also vanish in our future. Initially, scholarship will decline some as those who created our knowledge base retire, quit writing, or go into some other work. But the vacuum this creates will be short-lived as, remember, all of us are scholars. We'll crowdsource everything so the authorship of our new scholarly communication will not be in one person's name alone, but in the name of humanity. What's more, it will be free to anyone who wants it. We'll all know it's a work in progress, so errors will corrected as we go along. There will be no real need to get it right as that will happen, eventually.

ETHICS

The ethics of what will be our main source of information doesn't have what one would call a stellar track record. The web gives wide berth to peccadilloes because it abhors quality control. We are coming to accept this today. In the future, we will not give it so much as a second thought. Today, we brand everyone who dares raise even a small voice against the web as a crank, a dolt, a doddering Luddite. In the future, those voices will be silent altogether. Let me give you a current example of the ethics of information today.

The Internet is much better than its early infancy, but it still remains a source that requires collaboration from elsewhere. Part of this is the nature of the World Wide Web. It allows anyone to say anything, however outrageous, silly, racist, hurtful or stupid. But, of course, no one would resort to online chatter to prove anything, right? Remaining clear of chattering sites is a no-brainer. The trouble is, however, that even supposedly serious sites have some of these same chattering problems. While not the exclusive fault of the web, these chattering concerns contribute significantly to the rush to judgment, the rush to get there "first."

No one wants to fund a study that proves nothing, though one might be hard-pressed to prove that the itch to fund such studies has subsided. Research fraud is nothing new, but in the last decade, it has escalated tremendously, especially in the sciences. China, for example, makes no bones about requiring its researchers to produce significant, positive results, first. Surely this rush had something to do with the fact that 13 scientists were singled out for fraud in one month in 2007.[12] Would that it were only China! The U.S. has had its own share of fraud or slipshod research, too.[13]

While not exactly the fault of the web, certainly the need to get out there first has something to do with it. The pressure to produce something significant, something quickly and something immediately publishable has everything to do with why the web is making libraries obsolete. Libraries give rise to images of doddering white-haired men and women double-bent over accountant's lamps with stacks of paper and a jillion books, and, oh, don't forget the cobwebs! The web gives rise to images of success, rocket fast movement, and youth, not that any of those things have anything to do with veracity or sound research.

Speed trumps ethics in the future. It's just too quaint to think that libraries like the Library of Congress or the Library of Alexandria housed anything but the merest of information. Every two days, humans produce as much digital content as we did of any kind since the dawn of civilization until 2003. That, according to experts, is about five exabytes of information.[14] (We'll set aside for the moment that at least three and a half of those exabytes are cats, stupid human tricks, and baby pictures.) Libraries simply cannot compete with what technology can deliver quickly, easily, seamlessly, and doesn't have to be right today so long as it's right *eventually*. So again, what is the need for a library that really used to house all that knowledge that no one else could afford? Knowledge takes too long, and our clients want information. Why will we need catalogers and reference librarians when everything will be full-text searchable by super-smart algorithms that will conduct reference interviews the way they are supposed to be conducted, without human bias and fatigue?

SOCIETY

Society has shifted toward information access that increasingly does not favor libraries. We have seen this happen in at least two areas now, and it's beginning to happen in yet a third. Magazines went viral, so to say, and now only the fittest survive and those are online. Sure, a few here and there, usually journals of opinion, can still be had in paper, but we all know that the digital writing is on the wall. *Newsweek* went all digital in 2013, its last printed issue in December of 2012. It cut its staff to the bone and pretty much closed up shop. A print magazine that was for nearly a century the mainstay of every American home is now but a memory.[15] *Time* magazine continues to publish, but its managing editor, Richard Stengel, grants that printing a magazine "is the most expensive single thing [to do] to chop down trees, and put ink on paper and then put it on a truck and deliver it to your house."[16]

Newspapers, as have been alluded to already, are struggling to stay afloat.

Dozens have already shut down, and even the biggest, the *New York Times*, is headed in that direction. Only recently, did Jeff Bezos of Amazon fame buy the *Washington Post*.[17] With magazines and newspapers already gone, or nearly so, and ebooks pushing monographs in the same direction, in the future, everything that's important will be online. What isn't, society won't care about. Yes, it's still unclear how all of this will be paid for—even online ads are not a sure thing anymore—but we are still heading toward that cliff, or precipice, or the edge of utopia, depending on your view. Further, we're not sure what will happen with investigative reporting when all the reporters are, well, you and me. But it's happening without these questions being answered, and that trend, that movement, isn't exactly the best news for a culture and a profession whose *raison d'être* depended on dead trees.

Can everything end up free, paid for only by ads or something like them? Apparently so, if you believe Chris Anderson of *Wired Magazine*, who spends scores of pages explaining how everything from cars, to health care, to stocks, to a university education can eventually be free. Perhaps it will finally come down to this (http://www.humanadspace.com/home/) wherein we all offer our foreheads for adspace. Although the site looks a bit like something out of *The Onion*, a parody magazine, apparently it is a place where not-so-permanent tattoos can be placed strategically on one's person. Never say never. Of course, what most are *really* counting on is some sort of transfer of wealth in a way that takes from those few who have it and transfers it to those who do not. Some would call this a form of socialism, but I don't want to descend into the political. The transfer would have to come all at once, and from many of those who are now the major stockholders of online companies. In a way, they'd be taking it from themselves and giving it to ... themselves, or to their companies. I don't pretend to understand how all this is to work, and I'm a bit suspicious when the plans are this indefinite. Suffice it to say that I am more than a little doubtful about everything, or even most things, becoming free, and that goes for knowledge.

But some scenario in which once very expensive journals and books are meted out to libraries at exorbitant prices, turns into a plan that allows a more financially sustainable approach, appears to me inevitable, simply because no one can afford the current arrangement. If this does not happen, nothing in libraries will survive for long as most will simply "settle" for whatever they can find online.

What will become available online will be quite a bit of "stuff," too, as we move from an Internet created by people, to one created by machines themselves or, into what is sometimes referred to as the "internet of things" (IoT). The reason why this is important to our discussion is that the original Internet, according to dictionaries defining the phrase, was created by people, and in this new phase it will be one in which data will be created by the things themselves, so to say. Another way of looking at it is that everyday physical objects (people, places, signs, grocery bags—you name it) will be able to identify themselves digitally by using codes, sensors, or some unique identifier. Once we have moved into this realm, sometimes called "ubiquitous computing," the Internet will be all-encompassing, indeed.

Some of this technology is already here, as, for example, when your copy machine tells you the toner is low or the paper is empty by a connection over the web. The reason why this is important is that it frees humans from having to do all this work and eliminates our propensity for human error. How this will work for or against libraries is anyone's guess, but I can foresee many applications, most of them eliminating the need for librarian intervention. We are still a few years from this, and it will only work if adoption occurs everywhere and not in random, isolated places. Still, it is but one more piece of the puzzle in which a future scenario does not include libraries or librarians.

The evidence appears to be mounting against libraries and librarians. Is there a scenario in which both survive? I think there is, and so herewith one in which librarians aren't replaced, and libraries aren't obsolete after all.

Scenario II: No, Libraries Are Not Obsolete, and Never Will Be

Is there a way forward in which things don't turn out so technologically biased? I can think of a few cases in which the tech revolution begins to unravel. I know that I am nearly alone in this belief, but if you think about it, isn't this the way that every futuristic science fiction movie ends anyway? Everything is moving along oh so swimmingly, and then, suddenly, something happens, some little thing, a pebble, a one letter code, an infinitesimally small strand of DNA, and all the world is suddenly making its final swirl, its final spiral down the proverbial drain. Whether it's dinosaurs in *Jurassic Park*, zombies in *World War Z*, aliens in *After Earth*, or a human from Mars in *Stranger in a Strange Land*, all sci-fi adventures begin well only to end in a war with machines or with some other man-made thing that goes haywire. So are there a few "haywire" scenarios we can imagine that actually favor the survival of libraries?

TECHNOLOGY

While it may appear silly in the extreme, there are a few scenarios in which technology isn't *über Alles* in our inevitable future. If that turns out to be the case, then all bets are off with respect to the obsolescent libraries. Under what conditions could we find libraries thriving alongside robust technologies?

I think there are at least three. It is very unlikely that any one of those would be enough to slow the great push to all things digital. But together they may well be enough because they are inherent in the Internet that is already present, and may cause an unraveling from within. Let's call this trilogy Infrastructure, Hactivists, and Privacy Issues. No one of these can sink the web alone, but together, they may well create conditions that might slow down the growth of the Internet the world over.

Infrastructure. In order for the Internet to be all things to all people *and* replace libraries after all, it will have to become more stable. Currently, we do everything on essentially one super highway with one lane, from solving complicated mathematical problems to stupid dog and human tricks, to a glut of pornography, baby pictures and Google Books. People shop online, but they also watch television and movies, stream music and read books. The current structure of the web isn't sufficient to keep adding more and more *ad infinitum*. This isn't a matter of needing "more tubes"; it is a real matter of needing more lanes for all the traffic. The notion of "unlimited" bandwidth is simply a way for web hosting companies to attract potential customers. While we are not currently at any real limits, we are closing in on a saturation point that may make the silly supersede the serious.

Some universities and colleges are already restricting bandwidth so students will not use it all up on nonacademic pastimes. More institutions have made trade-offs, no longer hosting their own email but encouraging students and faculty to use free services like Google's gmail. K–12 schools, especially, are having a tough time making sure they have the needed bandwidth for their own students, and few of them are really planning for the future. With more media-like tools and devices becoming available, this could grow into a critical problem very quickly.

The library isn't immune to this, either, since it hosts a good portion of bandwidth that the universities and colleges require. Unfettered access to the web, often available through library portals, creates extra online demands. Add to these needs the growing requirements of online access to courses, the number of databases that now stream videos and music, and you have the makings of the proverbial perfect storm. When many or most things must be accessed online, even a half day of downtime creates insufferable angst; just imagine what *days* offline might do. Online redundancy helps, of course, but it also adds to rising costs, something no institution can afford to be too casual about today. Since bandwidth is often a product of where you are geographically and the provisions for it through some company, the likelihood of creating greater divisions between the haves and the have-nots seems more and more unavoidable. It makes for an intriguing screenplay, doesn't it: a future time in which bandwidth goes to the highest bidders and so some communities are isolated? Uprisings occur, and there will be blood, to quote a famous cinematic line. If Mervin Kelly's 1951 augury comes true and future networks become more akin to the nervous systems of humans, then those without access to it could become a mite testy.[18]

Don't get me wrong. I'm not making a case that the Internet itself cannot bear these burdens but that individual providers—colleges, universities, school systems, for example—might not be able to provide enough bandwidth for their clientele. The only way I can imagine a case in which the whole of the Internet might become troublesome is when everyone—all billions and billions of us (to ape the late Carl Sagan for a moment)—attempt to make all this information-wants-to-be-free work at once, from all our devices. Yes, I am treating this in a jocoserious manner, but the prospect of something similar occurring is at least possible.

Bandwidth isn't the only problem. We have hardware problems as well. Only recently has the issue of "going green" been discussed in connection with IT issues. Indeed, for too long, it has been the "grey side of information and communication technologies."[19] We have created these machines and their hardware with little regard to where they go when they reach obsolescence. Since many of the new technologies have so-called built-in obsolescence (it is meant to go out of date), this is rapidly becoming a serious matter. Writes Plepys, "Clearly, [hardware] has a potential to decouple economic growth from environmental degradation. However, without considering potential rebound effects of increased [hardware) consumption, the environmental implications can quickly become detrimental."[20] Sadly, they did and they are. While Plepys does not want this matter to hinder innovation, he saw the desperate need in 2002 to support those technologies that promote sustainable economic growth. Again, while it isn't likely that this issue alone will cause pause among anyone, it remains a serious enough issue for us to address. But any optimism at this point is clearly Pollyannaish. When "greens" rush to some summit, a gathering of Wall Street moguls, or call on Occupy Wall Street anarchists over some real or imagined insult, almost none of them show up without their environmentally unfriendly iPhones or other web-accessible devices. If this group cannot get exercised about the matter, it is very unlikely anyone else will.

Then there is the bigger problem of things like ebooks and their delivery. While not really a fault of the Internet, the issue is now a problem *because* of the Internet. Ebooks, as an idea separate from their delivery, are a boon. Having 24/7 access would appear to be a plus factor. But then we move into the reading problems, the literacy problems, and the not-reading-below-the-scroll problems—and they are no longer an unconditional good.

For libraries they are, *inter alia*, as Clifford Lynch called them, "Faustian"[21]:

> Sadly, ebooks have not only failed to deliver on much of their promise, they have become a vast lost opportunity. They are becoming a weapon capable of considerable social damage: a Faustian technology that seduces with convenience, particularly for those who consume a great many books, but offers little else while extracting a corrosive toll on our social institutions and norms.

Lynch is quick to point out that this is less a technology problem and more one having to do with the rights holders and how they have chosen to apply the technology. I remind readers in passing that whether one holds technology or publishers to blame, we didn't discuss this issue before web access became ubiquitous. In the end, we don't buy ebooks like we once did paper ones. We buy licenses, and a continued adherence to this model could well sink, or at least put a hole in the bulwark we call the future.

Ebooks, like other problems listed in this chapter, are resolvable. The question is whether there exists enough will on the part of librarians to force a change in their favor, or whether the strength of the uniform façade of publishing will prevail. How we solve this problem will determine whether the library of the future continues on a trajectory toward obsolescence, or on one that puts the primary focus on libraries' ability to deliver information in whatever format it appears. The charge that libraries reduce publishers' sales by offering ebooks for circulation is similar to what we heard when libraries provided serials to patrons. Serials publishers increased the cost to libraries to account for the decreased sales. It appears the circulation of ebooks is headed in the same direction.

It should be noted, however, that at least a small part of the problem with ebooks exists because of the late Steve Jobs (the lawsuit pending against Apple with respect to price-fixing), a child of the web and father of all things digital. His desire to control books in the same manner he did music led us to this untenable impasse. Over and over again we run into technology that we can in fact deploy; rarely do we give much consideration to the idea of whether we *should* deploy it. It's only much later, when swamped with vast ethical and even moral issues, that we begin to consider thinking seriously about them. Certainly the social impact of technology, mentioned above and *passim* in this book, should have been a fair warning. Now that we are faced with more intractable problems, we may give it a first thought, that is, if it isn't too late.

Ernest Cassirer summed this up quite nicely in his pivotal "Form and Technology," written now more than 75 years ago. Technology, he argued, doesn't ask what is, but what can be, and we have certainly been, depending on your point of view, its victims or its beneficiaries. If truth be told, we're both. Cassirer goes on to formulate a "philosophy of technology," a mere scintilla of which is very worth repeating at length:

> If we judge the significance of the individual areas of human culture primarily by their actual effectiveness, if we determine the value of these areas according to the impact of their direct accomplishments, there can hardly be any doubt that technology claims the first place in the construction of contemporary culture. Likewise, no matter whether we reproach or praise, exalt or damn this "primacy of technology," its pure actuality seems beyond question.... Yet even if we think it impossible to constrain or stop this course of things, a final question remains.... [The] mind reconciles itself with its fate and becomes free.... From the clarity and certainty of seeing follows a new strength, a power or efficacy, a strength with which the mind strikes back against every external determination, against the mere fatality of matter and effects of things. Insofar as the mind considers the powers that seem to determine it externally, this consideration already contains a characteristic turning back and turning inward.... Instead of exploring the depths of effects, it returns to itself and, by means of this concentration, achieves a new strength and depth.[22]

At this point, we can only hope so.

Hacktivists. I'm using this term here in the widest and most general manner. I use it to refer to anyone or any group that seeks, for whatever reason, to upset or make nearly impossible access to the World Wide Web for whatever reason. This includes denials of service, certain targeted sites or places, and any government that seeks to undermine access to the unfettered web by its citizens.

Those of us living in the United States may smile at this for various reasons, but perhaps we should be a little less smug and a great deal more circumspect. The ability to hack any site is too common for us to be so arrogantly dismissive. In the last few years, we have seen many attempts and an increasing number of successes as hactivists of every description target for disruption any site of their choosing. Often these attempts have political designs. It should be of more than passing concern that China, as mentioned earlier, continues to rank first in the number of hacktivists seeking unlawful entry into sites (41 percent of all attacks, according to experts). These denials of service range from the minor to the grand, from single individual websites to the United States Department of Defense. More recently, these attacks have come as distributed denials of service (DDoS) in which a number of hacktivists gather together for the sake of bringing down a system.

In a concerted effort, a group of hacktivists in Iran targeted a number of U.S. banks in 2013.[23] They successfully disrupted business in Bank of America, Citigroup, Wells Fargo, U.S. Bancorp and PNC. Another group attacked WordPress and PayPal.[24] These attacks occurred for a variety of reasons, not all of them comprehensible to laypersons. In any event, they had a target and zeroed in on it. Of course, in every case they were eventually repelled. As I write these words in late 2013, a denial of service has occurred at the *New York Times*, coming on the heels of one that occurred in May of 2013. Bear in mind that one of the largest such attacks was the work of a 16 year old in London.[25]

It isn't just banks or corporations either. It's also you and I. Consider, for example, that in March of 2013, the single largest public attack occurred because an antispam group called Spamhaus wanted to make a point, to attract attention to itself, or simply to be a nuisance, in which case it was eminently successful. In any event, it did gain ignominy as Internet service around the world slowed. Sites like the BBC, the *New York Times* and Netflix all slowed down noticeably.[26] In April of 2013, the financial site Schwab went down after two successive and fierce DDoS attacks. Small banks and credit unions have been targeted in 2013, not to mention entire governments.

Furthermore, not all are denials of service; some are telephony denials of service (TDoS). The TDoS attacks, because they target VoIP (Voice over Internet Protocol) systems that require different and perhaps more complex security, are also easier targets for hackers. What is more distressing about these attacks, however, is that because they attack phone lines, they can end up clogging emergency calls for ambulance, police or fire.

So the question that rivets the mind is, will there come a day when these attacks cannot be repelled? Right now the answer has to be no. The system upon which the Internet was built relied mainly on the goodwill of others and so has left many avenues open for those who mean to do harm, interrupt service, or otherwise tamper with information in some manner. No one is arguing that the ability of hackers to hack will grow less, only that the problems will become more and more formidable. While librarians remain in what we think are fairly safe locations with little information that hackers might want, it is a naïve thought. Our information may be too commonplace to be attractive, but our access to personal identities, while limited, is nevertheless substantial enough to attract miscreants. Because our systems are on balance less secure than sites that are already being hacked into easily, those personal identities are pretty much there for the taking.

Taking out power grids or disrupting the water supply may make for good storylines in thriller movies, but unfortunately they aren't that far off from what can already be done. Some have dismissed the idea that these are real possibilities for hackers in the future but have dismissed them with less than reassuring promises that are couched in words like "probably" or "not very likely."[27] As I write this chapter, the headlines are filled with stories about Edward Snowden, the high school dropout with high-level security who decided to throw a wrench in the safety of the country to make a statement about privacy. Since hackers like a challenge, and because people like Snowden are hardly rare, our online future appears not only very unsure, but also very risky.

I haven't even mentioned the problems that may emerge when too few people own too much information access. Will they try to monetize it the way they are now? Will it happen in a different way, one in which only the privileged few can have access to it?

Privacy. Having just mentioned Snowden, now is as good a time as any to mention the last area of weakness in technology for the future. Privacy, which we all pretty much gave up when we ordered that first tie or pair of shoes or book online, is becoming a little more important moving forward. I make a distinction here between what a given public company can know about me and put online, and what my government can know and follow. Privacy is not an absolute any more than freedom of speech is (and yes, I know some of my colleagues disagree with this assertion). There must be limits, conditions and qualifications to just about everything we do, and that is particularly true about our online lives. By going online, however, I should not give up *all* my privacy to websites. Octogenarian Nat Hentoff, once a voice for the absolutist view of the First Amendment, is now a fierce voice for absolute privacy.[28] Hentoff makes salient points about privacy but perhaps goes a bit too far with respect to what government should have a right to do. Absolute privacy cannot be extended online, and should not be extended to those engaging in criminal activity. We cannot have it both ways: a safe country free of those seeking to do harm, and *absolute* privacy for all citizens.

Having said that, we really must do a better job of protecting the privacy of casual online users, or, in other words, most of us. Lawrence Lessig is right when he says that we need to rewrite or redo or reconstruct the Internet to give us both better privacy and more security. It appears we *can* have this, if only we're willing to make it so. Or, as Lessig puts it, "Because the fact is that there is technology that could be deployed that would give many the confidence that none of us have now. 'Trust us,' does not compute. But trust and verify, with high-quality encryption, could."[29] He goes on to argue that we don't have it now because of our own stupidity. We simply let others make the decisions we should be making ourselves, not unlike what I have been arguing that we librarians have been and sometimes are now doing with the march of technology: We are letting it march all over us.

Let us use the technology to do what we must, but also employ it in the service of privacy to citizens as well. As mentioned in the chapter on privacy, social networking sites, which account for the vast majority of casual online users, are perhaps the worst violators of online privacy. We must demand better, and then leave if those sites will not meet our standards. Likewise, online ordering. Laws should protect users from having their information sold, and the penalties exacted for violators must be stringent enough to dissuade repeat offenders as well as others who might be tempted to follow suit.

It might not be enough. We are so smart with our technology that we may be able to watch what you think, literally.[30] As brain research ramps up, and we get closer and closer to mapping the human brain, it appears that we can also decode thought, making it possible to find out what a person has thought or said to him or herself. According to Nita Farahany of Duke University, "What we thought of as this zone of privacy can be breached." Oh joy!

If we cannot get a firm grip on privacy going forward, the use of technology *could* diminish some, or at least be slowed down, as more and more people are aware of the intrusions and become fed up with them. As I write these words, already tens of thousands of younger users are leaving Facebook.

No, it isn't because of security reasons, and no, it isn't the millions that were reported in late spring of 2013.[31] Rather younger users are notorious for jumping on that which is popular (and also where their parents have not yet signed on). Online use is changing, and the recent events of Julian Assange and Edward Snowden have at least brought to light what Lessig and others warned about years ago, and what CEO of Sun Microsystems mocked us with, his you-have-no-privacy-get-over-it comment. But we should have privacy, and we must demand that it be more robust in the future.

ECONOMY

For the foreseeable future, the economy will remain unfavorable to libraries. State spending differs, and while some states have seen a slight uptick, most have seen none at all, or an outright decline. This is unfavorable to libraries because libraries, often expensive financial black holes, are targeted for cutting, if not first, then second of all. Most colleges and universities, in whatever state they are located, have seen deep spending cuts over the last decade. While education is always much talked about but often shortchanged, public colleges and universities have seen dramatic drops in state support. In my own state, as South Carolina support for public education has been anemic, over the last two decades it has dropped precipitously, and has the dubious distinction of leading all other states in cuts to higher education. The byline here is that we were once state supported and now are state tolerated. Students now have more college debt than ever before, and many are now reconsidering a college education because it is too expensive and results in too much debt with which to begin a career. This could lead to lower levels of college attainment in the near future.[32]

One obvious consequence of all of these cuts is decreased library allocations. Libraries cost a lot but generate very little revenue. Yes, what we purchase is for the entire university population and, let's face it, for the communities in which these libraries are located. But if the materials did not cost so much, were not held by so many proprietary restrictions, these costs would go down. In states from the West Coast to the East, from the North to the South, all have seen the bloody edge of the budget cutting knife.[33]

Academic librarians have been clever enough—but have we been too clever by half?—to help diminish some of these draconian cuts so that students and faculty do not notice them much. But those days are over, and if cuts continue, then the staple of research materials that libraries buy, whether in paper or electronic format, will be noticeably diminished. While it is unlikely libraries will ever get back to good economic times, pushing things like open access may well make the economic bite come with smaller teeth.

MARKETS

Like the economy, so also the market has been unkind to libraries and will continue to be so into the near term. While I write this, there is considerable feel-goodism regarding libraries within many library circles. But too much of this strikes me as whistling in the dark. I agree with all the points being made: we live in a completely different age, in a new learning context; while no longer so much about books, we're now about collaboration; we are becoming more sustainable, and also more resilient.

The fact of the matter is that our clientele, from young children to older adults, simply are going places other than libraries for access to information. The good news is that they are still reading books, both print and electronic, still visiting libraries, and still finding them extremely important (more on this below, *Society*).[34] All of that is very encouraging and should not be dismissed, but we should not make more of this than is here. We are "important" to young people. We now must become so integral to their lives that they will happily pay for library upkeep from now on.

Markets are now filled with competitors, and not just Google. Young people are able to go online and ask questions of Ask.com, of course, but now they are able to take advantage of reference experts all over the country, not just their local libraries. Further, they are also able to access almost anything they want from any number of several hundred thousand websites. For example, whether their bent runs from the contemporary to the erudite, they are likely to find what they want, even down to the Loeb classics or original manuscripts of the 13th century.

After Google is successful in closing its various lawsuits, more online books will be available. We librarians simply have to admit it, as much as it may pain us to do, those non-library discovery tools on the web are far, far superior to any OPAC. On-demand printing makes just about any text available to anyone who wants a printed copy and is willing to pay for it. While the print-on-demand costs are currently very high, over time those costs will go down. If rising generations of young people who text instead of talk, *Tumblr* instead of make new friends, and play games instead of run out of doors, have as an option going to a library or going online, is it really any wonder to anyone which they will do? I sincerely hope they will make the effort to go to a library. That is my strong desire. To make that desire a reality we will have to change the way we view our work, our service and our clientele.

One area we can improve in, however, is value-added services. Providing open clean spaces for reflection, thought, collaboration and more will attract new patrons. While it will cost more money initially, it may well save us in the future. Even though young people are willing to study just about anywhere there is noise, a quiet place for reflection still resonates with many. Furthermore, they love studying with others, and libraries provide all the amenities to do just that. Renovation after renovation of old libraries, and newly constructed ones, proves again and again, that if you build it well, they will come, and they will come in hordes.

Information consumption, if added together, is now measured in exabytes, one of which is equal to one quintillion bytes, according to experts. In 2013, about two exabytes are being exchanged each month, with experts predicting that by the end of the decade, it will surpass 13 a month. Of course, when you filter out the pornography, hate speech, rumors, celebrity nonsense, and all the rest, it may not be quite so much as all that. Even so, it will remain enormous.

Only a library is currently equipped to handle the fact-from-fiction that this glut of information will require. In order for us to be "better informed," as almost anyone writing about this topic seems to take for granted, someone or something will be needed to help tease out what is useful and what is not. Librarians are trained to do that, and that should be one of the value-added features we showcase regularly. We need to do more to market this about ourselves so we're not the only ones who know it.

We'll also need to reallocate scarce funds toward these new initiatives while leaving behind the tried and true from previous decades. More money will have to be spent on technology, access, electronic texts and so on if we are to attract new users. Our collaborative spaces must be attractive, offer multiple amenities, and serve users where they are if we are to continue to be successful in the future. Cloud-based ILS offer us much to consider.

Is there anything more in markets to make us hopeful? I think so. Because so many of these technology companies are startups, or startup types, they have to earn their place, or they won't make it. Librarians must also adopt the best technology available, not just the new for its own sake. Had libraries been forced to justify their position all this time instead of relying on what will be viewed by some as "intellectual welfare" (as opposed to intellectual capital), might we be better positioned today? Well, shoulda, woulda, coulda, as one First Lady put it. Still, it's worth pondering. One of our biggest and best attributes, the analysis of information, is one that cannot so far be replaced by the web. It's time we accentuated this more.

POLITICS

Thinking about politics will keep you awake at night. On the one hand, libraries of any kind aren't on anyone's hit list to close. From that point of view we're as American as apple pie. On the other hand, when budgets are tight and tempers grow short, libraries are going to be one of the first, if not the first, place to get cut. Only the arts are likely to precede us. Clearly, the political climate is an ill-wind that hails against us.

Before anyone charges me with wanting to silence us politically, let me hasten to say that political expression is, of course, a constitutional right and one that I wholeheartedly endorse. But ideas have consequences, and if we carve out a niche that is strongly opposed to ruling parties, we have only ourselves to blame when those parties are in power (and ruling parties are, after all, much like the weather: just wait a bit and they will change). It would be better for us to remain politically neutral, but it may be too late for that now.

Until the economy improves substantially, there does not appear to be any significant relief for funding in the near term for any library, regardless of its location.[35] After many years of putting off getting our fiscal health in order as a country, we are now paying for our liberality in spades. Sadly, too, the situation in many states is so critical (see Detroit, Michigan, for example) that even programs for those who need it most are being curtailed or otherwise compromised.[36] Even in a strong economically viable state like Virginia, libraries or library-related state-supported consortia are being cut.

This dismal fiscal state of affairs is particularly distressing since library use continues to escalate, and it does so in especially weak economic times. As more and more people lose their jobs and cannot find work, they turn to libraries for access to job postings, applications, résumé writing and even retooling. But even as they do this, their libraries are being underfunded. This is, unfortunately for libraries, the "new normal." By remaining politically neutral, we take away any political party's animus against us. By remaining politically partisan, we give at least one political party a very good reason to shut our doors.

LAWS

The good news on the legal front is that there are few laws anywhere that militate against libraries. With the possible exception of those laws created in countries where freedom does not ring, legislation for libraries is strong. Libraries, at least as an ideal, are still held in high esteem, even revered. But esteem reverence plus five bucks, will get you a cup of coffee at Starbucks. Unfortunately, follow-through funding is rarely present.

Public library legislative days are commonplace in many states. Only recently (in the last decade) have academic libraries joined in these efforts. While it is a good gesture, much more needs to be done on campuses with the administration, and at the legislative level.

ETHICS

Ethical concerns have always been held in high regard by libraries, and their adherence to laws with specific reference to them, for example, copyright, has always remained sound and admirable. We are, however, on the cusp of change with respect to copyright, or so many think, but those changes can only be brought about by Congress. Libraries will do well not to get caught up in the information-wants-to-be-free mania by breaking contracts, broaching or even pushing the limits of copyright. Policies and procedures will need to be kept intact, at least with respect to contracts and copyright. It's fine if libraries want to push for open access and a change in copyright, but making those changes ad hoc may not be the way to go. Libraries have to be politically careful about what they decide to engage in because their funding, whether at the state or federal level or both, depends on the political goodwill *of both parties*. Encouraging initiatives that alienate half or more of your political capital will only result in funding curtailments that will have a much longer and further reaching negative outcome.

SOCIETY

Are there societal issues that impinge upon our obsolescing libraries? A few come to mind, though they are, perhaps, less societal, and more problems that occur within society. Let's begin with the physical issues.

While not precisely a scenario gone wild, some problems remain with humans using machines for long periods of time. David Schenk's *Data Smog* chronicles much of the negative effects of information overload on all of us who use it regularly.[37] It isn't anything to dismiss lightly, either, and all of us have felt it. Not only is it the proverbial alienation that Robert Putnam (*Bowling Alone*) and others have discussed, but real physical issues. I am not dismissing the alienation arguments, but these are far more familiar to readers.

Less familiar are cardiovascular stresses amplified by the frustration from using any technology, no matter how well it is made or how well it works. The frustration adds to our stress, but it also causes us to take it out on others. How many readers haven't secretly wanted to hurl some machine—a laptop, a desktop, and iPad—out the window for the sheer joy of seeing it break? Furthermore, how many of us, even when we're not using any technology, have wanted to snatch an iPhone out of someone's hand who should be driving, going through a grocery line, or being quiet in a movie (or even a church) instead of talking, texting or surfing. Yes, everyday living with technology has its own inherent frustrations, but technology has not only added to them, it has magnified them.

Add to these the toll the machines take on our vision. Staring at machines over time will result in a number of vision-related health issues, the smallest of which may be poor vision. But prolonged use also causes headaches, eyestrain and other similar vision problems. These health concerns in turn lead to our overall confusion that Nicholas Carr has chronicled so well in *The Shallows*.[38] Some may want to think his argument is all stuff and nonsense, but I suspect those who protest too vigorously against it are protesting what they know only too well. The mental confusion or fatigue or whatever it is one wishes to call it, causes us to remember less, read more haphazardly, and think less clearly. In fact, at least one group of researchers in Tel Aviv has recognized this unintended consequence as "computer mediated communication" (CMC).[39] The study found that some psychosis is evident in otherwise normal individuals after prolonged use of the Internet, and especially social networking sites. Individuals who spend most or even much of their time interacting in cyberspace find it difficult to interact in person. The study is by no means conclusive, but it has the advantage of being a confirmation of common sense.

Perhaps more distressing is the loss of memory that appears to be a significant feature of long-term Internet use.[40] In Cohen's study, participants typed factoids into a computer, one group knowing they would be erased, another group knowing they would be able to come back to them. The group that knew they would be erased "were significantly more likely to remember the information if they thought they would not be able to find it later." Participants did not make any real effort to remember items they thought they could go back to. While much more work needs to be done, clearly something is amiss. We all know young people who have grown up on a calculator who cannot do simple math in their heads or make change at a register when the register doesn't tell them how much to give back (or when you add a penny after the fact and they have to calculate the change in their heads).

Critics are sure to cackle at this, but I think the growing evidence about our loss of memory and diminution of associated cognitive tasks are being confirmed daily by overreliance on technology. What we do not know is the long-term effects of this overreliance. Will some sort of evolution occur that will allow us to make these adaptations with few consequences, or will we leave behind a whole generation of young people in the wake of our "progress?"

The issue of eyestrain may seem laughable to some in the sense that it occurs only among certain groups who would have had problems anyway. But as Carr points out, it's a bigger deal than we may think. In my earlier book I did make mention of saccades, the jerky eye movements we make when we read. I pointed out then that early research showed that we all do this differently, depending on what is being read and by whom. Carr points out that in 2006, Jakob Nielsen, a design consultant on web pages, conducted an eye-tracking study of web users.[41] He had 232 people wear a small camera that tracked eye movements as they read. What he discovered was somewhat astonishing for those of us who care about reading. Hardly anyone, according to Nielsen, read web pages in the same systematic way they read books. The majority skipped down the page in a manner that resembled the letter F. Nielsen concluded that the F stood for "fast," and told web page owners that this was the manner in which users read their important content. In other words, rapidly.

In case some think that this research was merely a sort of fits and starts problem with people merely "adjusting" to a new reading environment, Farhad Manjoo reported on newer research that proves even less encouraging.[42] Manjoo reported on research done by Chad Schwartz of *Chartbeat*. Schwartz looked at how people read *Slate*, a very popular online magazine. What Schwartz found out, Manjoo sums up nicely: "So here's the story: Only a small number of you are reading all the way through articles on the Web. I've long suspected this, because so many smart-alecks jump to the comments to make points that get mentioned later in the piece." Manjoo goes on to point out that Schwartz's research shows that when we read on the web *we cannot stay focused*, or as Manjoo puts it, "The more I type, the more of you tune out." And it isn't just Manjoo, and it isn't just *Slate*. When we read on the web, very few of us make it more than halfway.

Think about that for just a minute: Less that 50 percent make it after the first scroll, and even fewer to the first jump to another screen. The good news, if you can call it that, is that nearly *all* web visitors see all the videos and all the pictures. Now there's some great news. Think of how easy it would be to influence what people take away about a scandal with just pictures or videos? While I write this, the Obama administration is wading knee-deep though a myriad of scandals. If you were inclined to paint him in a poor light, you would insert a picture that does just that. Conversely, if you want readers to take away a good impression, or if you want them to view the scandal as unimportant, you insert a completely different photo or video.

It's more than just a casual nescience of reading, too. *Popular Science* announced in September of 2013 it was shutting off its comments section.[43] Although very much in favor of technology and intellectual engagement, the comments will now be closed because trolls and spambots have taken over and make it now impossible to carry on an intelligent discussion about science, or anything else for that matter. Writes LeBarre, the online content editor, "even the fractious minority wields enough power to skew a reader's perception of a story." Individuals disgruntled about one thing or everything tend to spoil it for the rest of us, as one bad apple destroys the barrel, as it were. Anonymity creates incivility, apparently. We're able to demonize our mothers, our lovers, our friends—in short, everyone, so long as they don't know it's us. Writes Maria Konnikova, psychologist and best-selling author at the University of Columbia,

> Whether online, on the phone, by telegraph, or in person, we are governed by the same basic principles. The medium may change, but people do not. The question instead is whether the outliers, the trolls and the flamers, will hold outsized influence—and the answer seems to be that, even protected by the shade of anonymity, a god will often make himself known with a stray, accidental bark. Then, hopefully, he will be treated accordingly.[44]

Konnikova is much more optimistic than I am about the eventual survival of online civility. In the years that I have been watching it, it has only grown worse and shows no signs of alleviation, remediation, or even mediation. It's the flame-throwers' way or the highway.

Some will argue that this is the fault of readers and not the web. I disagree.

If the medium is the message as McLuhan held, then the web is the medium, and it controls the message. As bad as all this is, I do not see it as a particularly awful problem among intelligent *adults*. Manjoo is quick to point out that he is guilty of this fast skimming himself. But what about those we are trying to teach? And more importantly, what about those who are in high school, or middle school, or kindergarten? What hope have we of teaching them how to read when they are growing up with a medium that encourages skimming, jumping about, and scattershot reading, if at all, and eagerly looking for a picture or video to explain it? And what are we to make of those whose entire educational reading experience is looking at pictures or watching videos?

Schenk also points out that the smog of information leads us to make poorer decisions, not better ones. So, is "Big Data" too big? Quite possibly. It may be far too big for us to make any real sense of it, or to extrapolate what we need from it to draw a sensible conclusion. Neither Schenk nor I would argue we want less data, but sometimes, the whole glut of it leaves us in a miasma of "stuff" that we might well be better off with less of. As has been pointed out before in this book, the whole concept of the Internet and seeking and getting all the "right" data leads us to a false sense that we can conquer everything. That is, that with enough data we'll not only make the right decision, we can make the right one *no matter what the problem*.[45] We are poised, with our fingers already on the return key, to think we can solve every ill the world can offer with the panacea of "enter" and waiting for the results.

Gary Small, a professor of psychiatry at UCLA and director of the Memory and Aging Center, studies the physiological and neurological effects of digital media on our brains.[46] He believes, as do others that what the web is doing is changing our brains. He contends that the explosion of digital technology "profoundly alter[s] our brains." As we use all our devices—laptops, smartphones, search engines and so others yet to come, the activity stimulates certain areas of our brains, creating new neural pathways. This sounds good, right? But wait. According to Small, it does this at the expense of weakening or even destroying other brain structures on which we must rely. It changes what we think, how we think, and even how we communicate what we are thinking. He found that even an hour a day stimulates our brains in ways we don't yet understand completely. How many of us spend only one hour a day with technology? And the question now is, at what expense? While it may not matter for old and nearly retired librarians like me, what is it doing to our children and grandchildren? We can kid ourselves and say nothing now, and make fun of those who raise questions like this as so many stupid Luddites. But in the same way that the use of calculators has all but eliminated the ability of younger people to do even small arithmetical calculations in their heads, so we may come to find that a steady stream of early and unbroken digital stimulation may create among the young an inability to think independently, critically, or even logically, to say nothing of their reading skills.

Even students understand this about themselves. Although many "snapshot" studies must be viewed with only passing interest, a recent one shows that students know only too well they are "digitally distracted."[47] In a study of six colleges, 80 percent of them said they used their devices during class an average of 11 times every day. They admit this is distracting, leads to confusion about class work or its content, and impacts their grades. But that's only the good news. The bad news is that 90 percent of them would throw a fit if anyone tried to limit or otherwise constrain their use of these devices whenever they want to use them. Of course, they all still expect to make A's.

Finally, Schenk, Carr and Putnam all warn against the self-centeredness that the web seems to infuse in all of us. Wait, some of you are saying. Just look at the outpouring of help we were able to muster against all sorts of disasters. Unfortunately, that altruism lasts for only one or two clicks. Sometimes that is enough to solve a small problem. But all too often, once the clicking has stopped, so does everything else. How many long-term givers does the web engender? It's hard to say for sure, but we know that it is a hotbed for fake charities or scam artists. Beyond this, however, we also know that the Internet has a tendency to help us get more of, well, ourselves. With a search string and a click, we can wrap ourselves up in a tight cocoon of self-centeredness and sameness while shutting out the rest of the world.

How to Prevent Library Obsolescence

Can any of this actually slow down the adoption of all things Google (or whatever noun you wish to insert)? No, not really. They are, however, factors that could hamper its continued escalation toward library obsolescence. We cannot count on these things. If there is a future for libraries, it must be a proactive one we create. Below are some ways we can vouchsafe our future.

I leave off this list the larger fact that libraries and reading are still the most fundamental part of what we do.[48] Without them, much of what we have created worth preserving, worth saving, has come from their existence in some small hamlet in some remote part of our country. In that place, a young person reads a book, gets lost in fantasy, is caught up by science, or sails away to some foreign land, all within the confines of his mind. Libraries light those fires, like so many beacons, all across this great land of ours. Now is not the time to let them fall into obsolescence.

- Librarians need to do a better job telling the world what it is we do and why we do it
- Librarians need to be more service-minded, and we need to do a better job of controlling costs
- Librarians need to be better risk-takers by changing our environment
- Librarians need to adapt technologies to services, not services to technology
- Librarians need to help our patrons help us by demanding our services. If we fall into obsolescence, we'll never come back
- Library leaders are needed who will treat technology as the library's plaything instead of the other way around
- Full-service libraries are vital to our democracy
- Full-service libraries are bridges between the haves and the have-nots
- Full-service libraries are vital to creativity and collaboration
- Full-service libraries are vital to our intellectual and cultural lives
- Full-service libraries are essential for the survival of our democracy, for any democracy that values freedom of speech, free expression and the exchange of ideas. Because, in the end, ideas have consequences, and the only way to augment the consequences of good ideas while minimizing the consequence of awful ones, is the one bastion where the interchange of ideas is commonplace: libraries.

Epilogue: Reviving the Spirit of Andrew Carnegie

A much shorter version of this appeared in Against the Grain *in 2011*

Occasionally, readers or critics will ask me what is it I expect from the Internet. I make accusations and lodge complaints, but never offer any constructive criticism. So, herewith, my answer to those who want to know what the web could do.

Readers old enough to remember Andrew Carnegie will stare with wonderment at this epilogue's title: Reviving the spirit of Andrew Carnegie?! they'll ask, incredulous. Isn't that like saluting Gordon Gekko?

I can't untangle the robber-baron fact and fiction regarding Mr. Carnegie but that isn't the reason for invoking his name. Rather, I invoke his name for the spirit of philanthropy for which he is rightly famous—especially and particularly his magnanimity to libraries. As an academic librarian, I can only admire his eleemosynary genius. And here's why.

Our nation's libraries, as I have argued through this book—really, all of them—are at risk. Without a new Carnegie, and soon, we may lose them entirely.

Our nation's K–12 libraries have all but disappeared. Nationwide, public libraries, when not cutting hours or having their funding cut entirely, are closing their doors. School libraries are either gone completely, renamed media centers or replaced entirely by electronic devices and access, making the need for a "room" as such, unnecessary, or so we are told. And our academic libraries are shrinking before vanishing altogether. The web makes libraries unnecessary. It is making them obsolete. These are mantras we librarians hear regularly. Library materials have "all" been digitized. "Everything is on the Internet!" we are told with encouraging smiles. And now library buildings are in the crosshairs of technology. The plod of progress, the promise of technology threaten all libraries, including New York City's grandest, where "Patience" and "Fortitude"—the library lions—sit in appropriate but regal silence, a synecdoche for all our national intellectual storehouses. Well, on behalf of all libraries, it's time—maybe past time—to give those lions a little roar.

Google notwithstanding, good, reliable, information is only scantily present on the Web. The bulk of trustworthy information resides only in aggregated databases, some of which cost as much as cars, literally, and so are affordable only to libraries. While striving to be green, libraries still depend on the printed word. Moving to an electronic format exclusively (which some libraries have tried) has been unsuccessful so far.

Oh, I hear the clucking of tongues from here. I'm *laudator temporis acti*, some will say, an adulator of the (library) past because it's old; not a virtual, but a full-blooded, Luddite. My argument in these pages isn't, however, either-or: either libraries or the web. It's a both-and argument. Of course the web is valuable and its usefulness extensible. We need its convenience, its fingertip accessibility, and its "everyman"-ishness. But for whatever else it is, it just isn't ready to replace libraries now, and I think it never will.

The web has been around only a little over a decade yet some are calling, have been calling, for it to replace libraries. Yet in every hamlet in this country, libraries have been the community centers of creativity, drawing together the rich and the poor, entrepreneurs and literary hopefuls, amateur technicians and would-be rocket-scientists, all rubbing shoulders, all learning together. And they have done this for mere millennia. If the web is to be the library's replacement can we at least wait for it to reach adolescence?

While we're waiting for the Internet to mature, let's revive the spirit of Andrew Carnegie by calling on today's technology titans to help save, for at least one more generation, those buildings that educated the young and the old, the black and the white, the rich and the poor, *for centuries*. Let's call upon these numerous parvenus to use their newfound billions to create a foundation for libraries with a new set of three Rs for our nation: renovate, repair or replace. Many others will be needed if libraries are to remain, but calling on technology giants first would serve as the perfect beau geste for their eager digital-everythingism that push our nation's libraries to the edge of extinction.

The folk singer of my youth, Joni Mitchell, once famously sang that you don't know what you've got till it's gone. Maybe libraries are démodé, obsolete, or soon will be. But if we can revive the spirit of Carnegie for one more generation, we may find that libraries are better than attending the "University of Google" exclusively. We may discover "Web-only" doesn't build community, risks alienation and intellectual myopia, fosters misinformation and may doom the rising generation of readers to a snatch-and-grab mentality that sinks their literacy while destroying their reading comprehension. We may learn that virtual "crowdsourcing" has its place, but is no substitute for looking one another in the eye and sharing, if only briefly, in face-to-face togetherness and collaborative knowing.

Do we think libraries unnecessary today because all our ideas are only 140 characters long? I hope not. If that's all our culture were then it might not deserve something as grand as a library after all. No, I believe our culture is more significant than that and too big to fit in a mobile device—nor should it. It needs room to spread out because it captures the whole of our civilization and everyone in it. Some say it takes a village to raise a child. If true, then surely it takes more than a text or two, more than a bit or a byte, to preserve a culture as grand as our own.

Someday we may be ready to jettison the Patience and Fortitude of our ancestors. When we do, let's be sure we choose an equal worthy of the giant it postures to replace. For now, it isn't the Internet, and I am certain, if we are willing to act, it never will be.

Chapter Notes

Chapter 1

1. Callimachus flourished circa 200 BC; hence, two millennia.

2. Mark Y. Herring, "10 Reasons Why the Internet Is No Substitute for a Library," *American Libraries* (April 2001) 76–78. http://www.americanlibrariesmagazine.org/article/10-reasons-why-internet-no-substitute-library. Accessed July 2013.

3. For interested parties, the poster is still available. The link is here: http://bit.ly/dnSqk5.

4. The documents referred to are Nicholas Carr, "Is Google Making Us Stupid?" *The Atlantic* (July/August 2008). http://www.theatlantic.com/magazine/archive/2008/07/is-google-making-us-stupid/306868/. Accessed March 2013. Carr followed this up with a longer argument in *The Shallows: What the Internet Is Doing to Our Brains* (New York: Norton, 2010). Bauerlein is best known for his *Dumbest Generation: How the Digital Age Stupefies Young Americans and Jeopardizes Our Future (Or Don't Trust Anyone Under 30)* (New York: Jeremy P. Tarcher/Penguin, 2008). Birkerts' book is *The Gutenberg Elegies: The Fate of Reading in the Electronic Age* (London: Faber and Faber, 1994).

5. This is the same point that David Weinberger makes in his book, *Too Big to Know: Rethinking Knowledge Now That the Facts Aren't the Facts, Experts Are Everywhere, and the Smartest Person in the Room Is the Room* (New York: Basic Books, 2011), 4.

6. Alvin Toffler, *Future Shock* (New York: Random House, 1970), 312. Also quoted in David Weinberger, *Too Big to Know*, 6–7.

7. Weinberger, p. xii.

8. Roger Kimball, *The Fortunes of Permanence: Culture and Anarchy in the Age of Amnesia* (South Bend, IN: St. Augustine's Press, 2012), 36.

9. Clive Thompson, *Smarter Than You Think: How Technology Is Changing Our Minds for the Better* (New York: Penguin Press, 2013), 6.

10. Weinberger, xi.

11. Evgeny Morozov, *The Net Delusion: The Dark Side of Internet Freedom* (New York: Public Affairs, 2011), 69.

12. Aldous Huxley, *Brave New World* (New York: Perennial Classics, 1998), 219. Also quoted in Kimball, 27.

13. Bradford Lee Eden, *Innovative Redesign and Reorganization of Library Technical Services: Paths for the Future and Case Studies* (West Point, CT: Libraries Unlimited, 2004), 36.

14. John Budd, *The Changing Academic Library: Operations, Culture, Environment* (Chicago: Association of College and Research Libraries, 2012), 106, 108.

15. Budd, 30.

16. The idea that "trusting the people" figures largely into the argument of many who favor the Internet. See, for example, Jeff Jarvis, *What Would Google Do?* (New York: HarperCollins, 2009), 82–84.

17. Jarvis argues in favor of the first part

of this sentence—we are talking to more people than ever before, p. 51. But Robert Putnam makes the case for the latter half of this sentence throughout his *Bowling Alone: The Collapse and Revival of the American Community* (New York: Simon & Schuster, 2000).

18. It's told many places but Jarvis tells it admirably on pages 48–49.

19. Plato, *The Republic: The Arts in Education*, Book III.

20. Robert Theobald, "The Healing Century: Why Change Is Needed," http://ncf.idallen.com/theobald_healing.html. Accessed October 2013. Theobald goes on to wonder if this is killing our ability to think deeply and fashion wisdom.

21. Randall Stross, *Planet Google: One Company's Audacious Plan to Organize Everything We Know* (New York: Free Press, 2008), 66–67.

22. Robert Darnton, *The Case for Books: Past, Present, and Future* (New York: Public Affairs, 2009), 29.

23. G. K. Chesterton, *The Everlasting Man* (New York: Dodd, Mead, 1925), 149. Chesterton's exact words are, "Perhaps there are no things out of which we get so little truth as the truisms; especially when they are really true."

24. Thomas Friedman, "Revolution Hits the Universities," *New York Times* (January 27, 2013), SR1. Also found at http://www.nytimes.com/2013/01/27/opinion/sunday/friedman-revolution-hits-the-universities.html?_r=1&, accessed February 8, 2013. Friedman is known for his provocations, as when he pleaded that the U.S. become more like totalitarian China in its decision-making, at least on some issues.

25. Steve Kolowich, "American Council on Education Recommends 5 MOOCs for Credit," *Chronicle of Higher Education* (February 7, 2013). http://chronicle.com/article/American-Council-on-Education/137155/. Accessed July 2013. But it may have been premature since Coursera is now combating widespread plagiarism.

26. Sherry Turkle, *Alone Together: Why We Expect More from Technology and Less from Each Other* (New York: Basic Books, 2011), 9–15, but also *passim*.

Chapter 2

1. I am fully aware that the words Internet, the web and the World Wide Web are not necessarily identical terms. For my purposes, however, I use them interchangeably and ask forbearance.

2. When Google came into being in March 1996, it was then called BackRub and was only a shell of what it was later to be. By 2000, Google had begun offering advertising but was still more or less a crying baby.

3. Vannevar Bush, "As We May Think," *The Atlantic* (July 1945), Vol. 176 (1), 101–108.

4. Bush, 101.

5. Bush, 108. Also quoted in Wayne Bivens-Tatum, *Libraries and the Enlightenment* (Los Angeles: Library Juice Press, 2011), 174ff. Emphasis added.

6. http://www.google.com/about/company/. Accessed February 2013.

7. Bryce Emley, "How Google Flushes Knowledge Down the Toilet," *Salon* (August 18, 2013), http://www.salon.com/2013/08/18/how_google_flushes_knowledge_down_the_toilet/. Accessed August 2013.

8. See, for example, the site http://justfuckinggoogleit.com/. The site isn't really a site, just something offensive you can send someone when you think they should be using Google more than anything else. The site reminds you that smart people use Google and you're an idiot for not using it. So next time, be sure and use it, though the site prefers the profane way of reminding you.

9. http://www.chmtl.indiana.edu/tme/16th/16th.html. Accessed February 2013.

10. http://www.chmtl.indiana.edu/tme/16th/16th.html. Accessed February 2013.

11. For more, see here: http://whatis.techtarget.com/definition/Internet2.

12. For more, see Laura Cohen, "The Deep Web," http://www.internettutorials.net/deepweb.asp. Accessed February 2013.

13. BrightPlanet, "Why You Should Tap into the Deep Web in 2013." http://www.brightplanet.com/2013/01/why-you-should-tap-into-the-deep-web-in-2013/. Accessed February 2013.

14. For a more detailed discussion, see Michael K. Bergman, "The Deep Web: Surfacing Hidden Value," http://quod.lib.umich.edu/cgi/t/text/text-idx?c=jep;view=text;rgn=main;idno=3336451.0007.104. Accessed February 2013.

15. Jane Devine and Francine Egger-Sider, *Going Beyond Google Again: Strategies for Using and Teaching the Invisible Web* (Chicago: American Library Association, 2014).

16. Serendipitously, I happened to be reading some months ago Thomas Penn's *Winter King: The Dawn of Tudor England* (London: Allen Lane, 2011), 162–165.

17. Robert Darnton, "Digitize, Democratize: Libraries and the Future of Books." Conference on "Open Access per la Comunicazione Scientifica: Diffusione Sostenible della Scienza e Mondo Digitale," Trieste (September 2012). www2.units.it/.../Darnton. Accessed February 2013.

18. Weinberger, 21.

19. Weinberger, 13–20. The next few paragraphs draw strongly from these pages.

20. The phrase is from Nate Silver, *The Signal and the Noise: Why So Many Predictions Fail—But Some Don't* (New York: Penguin, 2012).

21. David Weinberger, *Everything Is Miscellaneous: The Power of the New Digital Disorder* (New York: Henry Holt, 2007).

22. See, for example, David H. Freedman, *Wrong: Why the Experts Keep Failing Us—And How to Know When Not to Trust Them* (New York: Little, Brown, 2010).

23. And it isn't just students who do this, as Chinese and North Korean officials have proved on more than one occasion as they pulled things from *The Onion* as truth.

24. Aleks Krotoski, *Untangling the Web: What the Internet Is Doing to You* (London: Faber and Faber, 2013).

Chapter 3

1. For more about the nature of searching, see Peter Morville, *Ambient Findability* (Sebastopol, CA: O'Reilly, 2005).

2. Michael Miller, *Google-pedia: The Ultimate Google Resource* (Indianapolis: Pearson Education, 2009), 18–20.

3. Googlebots are "smart enough" to know to crawl some news sources daily. Miller, 19.

4. Google, "Knowledge Graph," http://www.google.com/insidesearch/features/search/knowledge.html. Accessed July 2013.

5. See, for example, an excellent overview from Pete Coco, "Leaves of Graph," *ACRLog* (August 23, 2012). http://acrlog.org/2012/08/23/leaves-of-graph/. Accessed July 2013.

6. Coco. http://acrlog.org/2012/08/23/leaves-of-graph/.

7. Cory Doctorow, "How an Algorithm Came Up with Amazon's KEEP CALM AND RAPE A LOT t-Shirts," *BoingBoing* (March 2, 2013). http://boingboing.net/2013/03/02/how-an-algorithm-came-up-with.html. Accessed July 2013.

8. Ricardo Bilton, "Things Not Strings: How Google's New Hummingbird Algorithm Sets the Stage for the Future of Mobile Search," *VentureBeat* (October 2, 2013). http://venturebeat.com/2013/10/02/things-not-strings-how-googles-new-humming bird-algorithm-sets-the-stage-for-the-future-of-mobile-search/. Accessed October 2013.

9. Katherine Q. Seelyle, "Snared in the Web of a Wikipedia Liar," *New York Times* (December 4, 2005). http://www.nytimes.com/2005/12/04/weekinreview/04seelye.html?pagewanted=all&_r=0. Accessed February 2013.

10. Miller, 20.

11. Miller, 94.

12. Yiang-Yi Li and Gwo-Dong Chen, "A Web Browser Interface to Manage the Searching and Organizing of Information on the Web by Learners," *Educational Technology & Society*, 13 (4) (2010), 86–97.

13. Miller, 116.

14. Eric Schonfeld, "Poor Google Knol Has Gone from a *Wikipedia* Killer to a Craigslist Wannabe," *TechCrunch* (August 11, 2009)." http://techcrunch.com/2009/08/11/poor-google-knol-has-gone-from-a-wikipedia-killer-to-a-craigslist-wannabe/. Accessed February 2013.

15. Hayley Tsukayama, "Google News Searches Turn Up Incomplete Results, Researcher Finds," *The Washington Post* (May

13, 2013). https://ssl1.washingtonpost.com/business/technology/google-news-searches-turn-up-incomplete-results-critic-finds/2013/05/15/cde426dc-b80d-11e2-b94c-b684dda07add_story.html. Accessed July 2013.

16. Yes and no. Libraries have federated search engines, and they do cut across databases, but we do not yet have one that will cut across everything we provide access to. A "front door" that allows users to search everything we own and everything we provide access to will make our users *want* to log into us and stay on our websites/portals. We know from various Pew Reports that not only do our users not log onto us, they don't even want to. We are essentially the last place they look. More on this in Part Three.

17. Randall Stross, *Planet Google: One Company's Audacious Plan to Organize Everything We Know* (New York: Free Press, 2008), 186.

18. In Part Three, I examine why this is so and why libraries may have brought it on themselves.

19. Bill Tancer, *Click: What Millions of People Are Doing Online and Why It Matters* (New York: Hyperion, 2008), 120–123.

20. Quoted in Tancer, 124.

21. See "Reading" in Part Two for a more detailed discussion of this point.

22. Erika Martinez Ramirez and Rene V. Mayorga, "A Rough Sets Approach for Relevant Internet/Web Online Searching," *International Journal of Mathematical, Physical and Engineering Sciences* 3:2 (2009), 86–95.

23. David Weinberger, *Everything Is Miscellaneous: The Power of the New Digital Disorder* (New York: Times Books/Henry Holt, 2007), 106.

24. Morville, 4–5.

25. Morville, 4–5.

26. Chia-Ching Lin and Chin-Chung Tsai, "A Navigation Flow Map Method of Representing Students' Searching Behaviors and Strategies on the Web, with Relation to Searching Outcomes," *Cyberpsychology & Behavior* 10 (5) (2007), 694.

Chapter 4

1. Reported numerous places, I chose this one: Wired Blogs, "Your Own Personal Internet" (June 6, 2006). http://www.wired.com/threatlevel/2006/06/your_own_person/. Accessed February 2012.

2. Adrian Sannier, "A New American University for Next-Gen Learners," Campus Technology 2008 Conference (July 29, 2008). http://campustechnology.com/articles/2008/08/video-spotlight-campus-technology-2008-keynote-address.aspx. Accessed February 2013.

3. Cory Doctorow, "Libraries, Hackspaces, and E-waste: How Libraries Can Be the Hub of a Young Maker Revolution," Raincoast Books (February 24, 2013). http://www.raincoast.com/blog/details/guest-post-cory-doctorow-for-freedom-to-read-week//. Accessed February 2013.

4. Clifford Stoll, *Silicon Snake Oil: Second Thoughts on the Information Highway* (New York: Doubleday, 1995), 4. Some may argue that Stoll is talking about an Internet that has been replaced by a new and improved one, but I would hold his point remains valid.

5. Cass Sunstein, *Infotopia: How Many Minds Produce Knowledge* (New York: Oxford University Press, 2008), 25. Sunstein has a very helpful discussion of the Condorcet Jury Theorem and I have followed it closely. I know this is not the end of the question, but his discussion of it sheds important light on why crowdsourcing alone is not the answer to all our problems.

6. David H. Freedman, *Wrong: Why Experts Keep Failing Us—And How to Know When Not to Trust Them* (New York: Little, Brown, 2010), 173.

7. Freedman, 176–177.

8. Sunstein, 33.

9. Quoted in Sunstein, 79.

10. Sunstein, 81.

11. For a good discussion of Internet porn and its psychological impact, see Patricia Wallace, *The Psychology of the Internet* (New York: Cambridge University Press, 1999), 157ff.

12. Leslie Horn, "The U.S. Has More Internet Porn Than Any Other Country," *Gizmodo*

(August 14, 2013). http://gizmodo.com/the-u-s-has-more-internet-porn-than-any-other-country-1135870485. Accessed August 2013.

13. CyTalk, "Pornography Industry Is More than the Revenues of the Top Technology" (January 1, 2010). http://blog.cytalk.com/2010/01/web-porn-revenue/. Accessed March 2013. Dan Miller, "Poll: Porn Revenues Exceed $5 Billion According to Industry Survey," XBIZ (July 25, 2012). http://camgirlnotes.fr.yuku.com/topic/3549. Accessed March 2013. I've taken an average of costs mentioned in more than half dozen places. Bill Tancer, *Click: What Millions of People Are Doing Online and Why It Matters* (New York: Hyperion, 2008), 16. Tancer cites $87 billion but admits it is a figure that is wildly decried. Worldwide figures estimate revenues at $100 billion, however. I've encountered amounts as "small" as $5 billion and as much as $113 billion. I think it's safe to say it's a lot of money, regardless.

14. Ashley Feinberg, "A State by State Map of America's Filthy Porn Searches," *Gizmodo* (August 27, 2013). http://gizmodo.com/heres-all-the-dirty-details-on-americas-thriving-porn-1208587525?utm_source=feedburner&utm_medium=feed&utm_campaign=Feed%3A+gizmodo%2Ffull+%28Gizmodo%29. Accessed August 2013.

15. Yes, I know, "brown paper wrapper" only resonates with the over 50 crowd.

16. Eric Larson, "It's Still Easy to Get Away with Revenge Porn," *Mashable* (October 21, 2013). http://mashable.com/2013/10/21/revenge-porn/. Accessed October 2013.

17. These are but a few of the many bills that have either made their way to Congress or been enacted: Child Pornography Prevention Act, Child Online Protection Act, and Children's Internet Protection Act. Sadly, the American Library Association has been at the forefront to help these bills remain impotent, so to say.

18. Yes, I am aware that the producers of the loathsome videos "Girls Gone Wild" has filed for bankruptcy and has recently been sent to jail. But such things as drunken women running about without their clothes on, or participating in various sex acts, live on beyond anyone's ability to delete them.

19. See Tancer, Chapter 1, "PPC–Porn, Pills, and Casinos."

20. Don Tapscott and Anthony Williams, *Macrowikinomics: Rebooting Business and the World* (New York: Penguin Group, 2010), Chapter 11. Most, but not all. James Taranto of the *Wall Street Journal Online* refers to it, pointedly, as Puffington Host.

21. Tapscott, et al., 204.

22. Eric Alterman, "Out of Print: The Life and Death of the American Newspaper," in Robert W. McChesney and Victor Pickard, *Will the Last Reporter Please Turn Out the Lights: The Collapse of Journalism and What Can Be Done to Fix It* (New York: New Press, 2011), 7.

23. Nate Silver, "The Economics of Blogging and the Huffington Post," Five-Thirty-Eight, *New York Times* (February 12, 2011). http://fivethirtyeight.blogs.nytimes.com/2011/02/12/the-economics-of-blogging-and-the-huffington-post/. Accessed March 2013.

24. Rebecca Greenfield, "Judge Upholds Huffington Post's Right Not to Pay Bloggers," *The Atlantic Wire* (March 30, 2012). http://www.theatlanticwire.com/business/2012/03/judge-upholds-huffington-posts-right-not-pay-bloggers/50577/. Accessed March 2013.

25. This is the point made in McChesney and Pickard, *Will the Last Reporter Please Turn Out the Lights*, 2011.

26. Robert W. McChesney and John Nichols, "Down the News Hole," in McChesney and Pickard, *Will the Last Reporter Please Turn Out the Lights*, 105.

27. I should point out that Tapscott and Williams see this problem but dismiss it as something not to worry too much about, pp. 218ff. In fact, their view is that when a business model is "turned upside down," one should "Get with the program and embrace wikinomics!" (p. 255).

28. Tapscott, et al., 254–255.

29. Eric Schmidt and Jared Cohen, *The New Digital Age: Reshaping the Future of People, Nations and Business* (New York: Knopf, 2013), 3. I think the author meant the sentence to be more optimistic than it sounds.

30. See, for example, Mark Potok, "Inter-

net Hate and the Law." http://www.splcen
ter.org/get-informed/intelligence-report/
browse-all-issues/2000/winter/internet-
hate-and-the-law. Accessed March 2013. See
also, Anti-Defamation League, "Poisoning
the Web: Hatred Online. The Internet as a
Hate Tool." http://archive.adl.org/poison
ing_web/net_hate_tool.asp. Accessed March
2013.

31. For a discussion of this, see Freedman,
174–176.

32. For a terrific discussion of the Yelp ex-
ample and much more, see Evgeny Morozov,
*To Save Everything, Click Here: The Folly of
Technological Solutionism* (New York: Public
Affairs, 2013), 170–180.

33. Andrew Keen, *The Cult of the Amateur: How Today's Internet Is Killing Our Culture* (New York: Doubleday/Currency, 2007),
148–150.

34. Freedman, 202.

35. "About." http://en.citizendium.org/
wiki/CZ:About. Accessed March 2013.

36. A search on "Citizendium" will reveal
as many stories regarding its failure as one
wishes to read.

37. Shirky, 136.

38. Tim Sampson, "Where Do Wikipedia's Donations Go? Outgoing Chief Warns
of Corruption," *Mashable* (October 18, 2013).
http://mashable.com/2013/10/17/wiki
pedia-donation-corruption/?utm_campaign
=Mash-Prod-RSS-Feedburner-All-Partial&
utm_cid=Mash-Prod-RSS-Feedburner-All-
Partial&utm_medium=feed&utm_source=
rss. Accessed October 2013.

39. David Weinberger. *Everything Is Miscellaneous: The Power of the New Digital Disorder* (New York: Times Books/Henry Holt,
2007), 139. The title is captivating with its
"digital disorder." Can anything that is dis-
ordered bring order into our lives? It seems,
at the very least, counterintuitive.

40. Jeff Jarvis, *What Would Google Do?*
(New York: HarperCollins), 84.

41. For more on the topic see Evgeny Morozov, *The Net Delusion: The Dark Side of
the Internet* (New York: Public Affairs, 2011),
57–58.

42. This is quoted several places, including Weinberger, p. 40, and "An American

Original," *Vanity Fair*, October 6, 2010. http:
//www.vanityfair.com/politics/features/
2010/11/moynihan-letters-201011. Accessed
March 2013. What is interesting is that I
could not confirm this quote, although I did
find it repeated in *Daniel Patrick Moynihan:
A Portrait in Letters of an American Vision-
ary*, Steven R. Weisman, editor (New York:
Public Affairs, 2010), p. 3. The trouble is that
the quip appears in various dress and there is
even one, somewhat altered, by an entirely
different individual, the American financier
Bernard M. Baruch. Ah, the joys of the Internet.

43. Morozov, 70.

44. Freedman, 175, note.

45. Henry David Thoreau, *Walden* (New
York: Thomas Y. Crowell, 1910), 67.

46. Weinberger, 104ff.

47. Christine L. Borgman, *Scholarship in
the Digital Age: Information, Infrastructure,
and the Internet* (Cambridge, MA: MIT
Press, 2007), 95ff.

48. Stoll, 214.

Chapter 5

1. For more on algorithms and what
they inadvertently do to us, see Evgeny Morozov, *To Save Everything, Click Here: The
Folly of Internet Solutionism* (New York:
Public Affairs, 2013), Chapter One.

2. Clifford Stoll, *Silicon Snake Oil: Second Thoughts on the Information Highway*
(New York: Doubleday, 1995), 4.

3. MIT Technology Review, "Internet
Archaeologists Reconstruct Lost Web Pages,"
MIT Technology Review (September 18, 2013).
http://www.technologyreview.com/view/
519391/internet-archaeologists-reconstruct-
lost-web-pages/. Accessed September 2013.

4. Scott McLemee, "In Search of the
Missing Link," *Inside Higher Ed* (July 24,
2013). http://www.insidehighered.com/
views/2013/07/24/essay-link-rot. Accessed
August 2013.

5. Adam Liptak, "In Supreme Court
Opinions, Web Links to Nowhere," *New
York Times* (September 23, 2013). http://
www.nytimes.com/2013/09/24/us/politics/
in-supreme-court-opinions-clicks-that-lead-

nowhere.html?_r=0. Accessed September 2013. The original report is here: Jonathan Zittrain, "Perma: Scoping and Addressing the Problem of 'Link Rot,'" *The Future of the Internet and How to Stop It* (September 22, 2013). http://blogs.law.harvard.edu/future oftheinternet/2013/09/22/perma/. Accessed September 2013.

6. Wikipedia, "Categories Needing Link Rot Cleanup from February 2013." http://en.wikipedia.org/wiki/Category:Articles_needing_link_rot_cleanup_from_February_2013. Accessed March 2013.

7. Jennifer Howard, "Hot Type: A Modern Scholar's Ailments: Link Rot and Footnote Flight," *Chronicle of Higher Education* (October 10, 2010). http://chronicle.com/article/Hot-Type-A-Modern-Scholars/124870/.

8. Jennifer Howard, "Hot Type: Publishers Find Ways to Fight 'Link Rot' in Electronic Texts," *Chronicle of Higher Education* (October 31, 2011). http://chronicle.com/article/Hot-Type-Publishers-Fight/125189/. Accessed October 2013.

9. Kurt Shiller, "301Works.org: Seeking an End to Link Rot," *Information Today* Vol. 27 (1) (January 2010), 1, 3.

10. John Markwell and David Brooks, "Evaluating Web-based Information: Access and Accuracy," *Journal of Chemical Information*, Vol. 85 (3) (March 2008), 458–459. Erick Ducut, Liu Fang, and Paul Fontello, "An Update on Uniform Resource Locator (URL) Decay in Medline Abstracts and Measures for its Mitigation," *BMC Medical Informatics & Decision Making*, Vol. 8 (1) (2008), special section 1–8.

11. Some of these issues and others are discussed in Thomas H.P. Gould, "Protocols and Challenges of the Creation of a Cross-Disciplinary Journal," *Journal of Scholarly Publishing* Vol. 42 (2) (January 2011), 105–141.

Chapter 6

1. I refer to Twain's famous quip, "Suppose you were an idiot, and suppose you were a member of Congress; but I repeat myself."

2. Jacob Kastrenakes, "Entire Vatican Library to Be Digitized Across 2.8 Petabytes

of Storage," *The Verge* (March 13, 2013). http://www.theverge.com/2013/3/13/4100508/entire-vatican-library-digitized-2-8-petabytes. Accessed March 2013.

3. The phrase is not mine but Whittaker Chambers who, it is said, would sit for hours waiting to give federal testimony by reading Dante.

4. Jacob Kastrenakes, "Entire Vatican Library to Be Digitized Across 2.8 Petabytes of Storage," *The Verge* (March 13, 2013). http://www.theverge.com/2013/3/13/4100508/entire-vatican-library-digitized-2-8-petabytes. Accessed March 2013.

5. Margaret Hedstrom, "Digital Preservation A Time Bomb for Digital Libraries," *Computers and the Humanities* (Vol. 31, 1998), 189–202. http://deepblue.lib.umich.edu/bitstream/handle/2027.42/42573/10579?sequence=1. Accessed July 2013.

6. For an interesting discussion of this problem, see Lucien X. Polastron, *The Great Digitization and the Quest to Know Everything* (Rochester, VT: Inner Traditions, 2009), first two chapters.

7. Nicholson Baker, *Double Fold: Libraries and the Assault on Paper* (New York: Random House, 2001).

8. Baker, vii.

9. Jennifer Howard, "Digitizing the Personal Library," *Chronicle of Higher Education* (September 28, 2010). http://chronicle.com/blogs/wiredcampus/digitizing-the-personal-library/27222. Accessed March 2013. Brewster Kahle, "Why Preserve Books? The New Physical Archive of the Internet Archive" (June 6, 2011). http://blog.archive.org/2011/06/06/why-preservebooks-the-new-physical-archive-of-the-internet-archive/. Accessed March 2013.

10. "UC Libraries Mass Digitization Project. Frequently Asked Questions," Questions 5 & 7. http://www.cdlib.org/services/collections/massdig/faq.html. Accessed March 2013.

11. Karen Coyle, "Mass Digitization of Books." http://www.kcoyle.net/jal-32-6.html. Accessed March 2013.

12. Hannibal Travis, "Estimating the Economic Impact of Mass Digitization Projects on Copyright Holders: Evidence from the Google Book Search Litigation," *Journal*

of the Copyright Society of the USA, Vol. 57 (July 1, 2010), Florida International University Legal Studies Research Paper No. 41–62. http://papers.ssrn.com/sol3/papers.cfm?abstract_id=1634126. Accessed March 2013.

13. Randall Stross, *Planet Google: One Company's Audacious Plan to Organize Everything We Know* (New York: Free Press, 2008), 95.

14. Stross, 106–107.

15. For an interesting take on Gallica, see Polastron, 10–15.

16. See Sun Microsystems' CEO Scott McNealy's infamous charge that "you have zero privacy anyway. Get over it?" Polly Sprenger, "Sun on Privacy: 'Get Over It,'" *Wired* (January 26, 1999). http://www.wired.com/politics/law/news/1999/01/17538. Accessed March 2013. This quote appears in various similar renditions in, literally, hundreds of places on the web.

17. But not for free: http://www.hathitrust.org/cost.

18. Scott McLemee, "Commentary on the Digital Public Library of America," *Inside Higher Ed* (April 24, 2013). http://www.insidehighered.com/views/2013/04/24/commentary-digital-public-library-america. Accessed July 2013.

19. Stef van Gompel and P. Bernt Hugenholtz, "The Orphan Works Problem: The Copyright Conundrum of Digitizing Large-Scale Audiovisual Archives, and How to Solve It," *Popular Communication* (January 1, 2010, Vol. 8), 61–71. http://www.ivir.nl/publications/vangompel/the_orphan_works_problem.pdf. Accessed February 2013.

20. Carnegie Mellon did a study in 2004–05 of orphan works and placed the number at 22 percent. See, for example, http://www.copyright.gov/orphan/comments/OW0537-CarnegieMellon.pdf. Accessed March 2013.

21. Graham Greene, *The Quiet American* (New York: Penguin Classics, 2004), 29.

22. Christine L. Borgman, *Scholarship in the Digital Age: Information, Infrastructure, and the Internet* (Cambridge, MA: MIT Press, 2007), 8.

23. Arik Hassedahl, "Mary Meeker's Legendary Internet Slide Deck: The D10 Highlights (video)" (May 30, 2012). http://all

thingsd.com/20120530/mary-meekers-legendary-internet-slide-deck-the-d10-highlights-video/. Accessed July 2013.

24. Heather Christenson, "Mass Digitization Projects Update" (February 9, 2009), *California Digital Library*. http://www.cdlib.org/cdlinfo/2009/02/09/mass-digitization-projects-update-2/. Accessed March 2013. Miguel Helft, "Microsoft Will Shut Down Book Search Program," *New York Times* (May 28, 2008). http://www.nytimes.com/2008/05/24/technology/24soft.html?ref=technology&_r=0. Accessed March 2013.

25. Camira Powell, "Don't Worry About a Thing," *AllThingsD* (March 18, 2013). http://allthingsd.com/20130318/dont-worry-about-a-thing/. Accessed March 2013.

26. There are many places to view just the video. Here's a brief analysis and the video: Amanda Wills, "What Would We Do Different If the Internet Crashed?" *Mashable* (March 18, 2013). http://mashable.com/2013/03/18/internet-crash-danny-hillis/. Accessed March 2013.

27. Wills, emphases added.

28. See http://www.internet2.edu/network/, "About." Accessed March 2013.

29. Carolyn Hawk, "Blogging Your Academic Self: The What, the Why, and the How Long?" in *Social Media for Academics: A Practical Guide* (Oxford, England: Chandos Publishing, 2012), 15.

30. Guillermo Contreras, "Library Visits Enter Future at BiblioTech," *MySA* (September 14, 2013). http://www.mysanantonio.com/news/local/article/Library-visits-enter-future-at-BiblioTech-4814924.php. Accessed September 2013.

Chapter 7

1. Mine has been Lolly Gassoway's very helpful chart, found here: Lolly Gassoway, "When Works Pass into Public Domain." http://www.unc.edu/~unclng/public-d.htm. Accessed March 2013.

2. Kevin Smith, "The Problem with Permission," *Scholarly Communications @ Duke* (July 18, 2013). http://blogs.library.duke.edu/scholcomm/2013/07/18/the-problem-with-permission/. Accessed August 2103.

3. Kevin Smith, "The Problem with Permission," *Scholarly Communications @ Duke* (July 18, 2013).

4. Paul Rubin, "More Money Into Bad Suits?" *New York Times* (November 16, 2010). http://www.nytimes.com/roomfordebate/2010/11/15/investing-in-someone-elses-lawsuit/more-money-into-bad-suits. Accessed March 2013.

5. http://www.copyright.gov/title17/92chap1.pdf, 8. Accessed March 2013.

6. Mary Cross, *Bloggerati, Twitterati: How Blogs and Twitter Are Transforming Popular Culture* (Santa Barbara, CA: Praeger, 2011), 113.

7. Tracy Mitrano, "A Letter to Parents About Copyright," *Inside Higher Ed* (June 21, 2013). http://www.insidehighered.com/blogs/law-policy-and-it/letter-parents-about-copyright. Accessed June 2013.

8. Steven Levy, *In the Plex: How Google Thinks, Works, and Shapes Our Lives* (New York: Simon & Schuster, 2011), 357.

9. Levy, 365.

10. Levy, 10.

11. Robert Levine, *Free Ride: How Digital Parasites Are Destroying the Culture of Business and How the Culture of Business Can Fight Back* (New York: Doubleday, 2011), 71, 79, 80–81.

12. Levine, 99–106

13. Harold Abelson, Peter A. Diamond, Andrew Grosso and Douglas W. Pfeifer (support), *Report to the President: MIT and the Prosecution of Aaron Swartz* (July 26, 2013). http://swartz-report.mit.edu/docs/report-to-the-president.pdf. Accessed August 2013. Some critics see this report as a "whitewashing" but it should be read first—and beyond the executive summary—before aspersions are thrown.

14. Quoted in Levine, 4.

15. The Digital Millennium Copyright Act of 1998. http://www.copyright.gov/legislation/dmca.pdf. Accessed March 2013.

16. Levine, chapter one, has a good discussion of the DMCA and the confusion subsequent to its passage.

17. David Kravets, "10 Years Later, Misunderstood DMCA Is the Law That Saved the Web," *Wired* (October 27, 2008). http://www.wired.com/threatlevel/2008/10/ten-years-later/. Accessed March 2013.

18. Timothy B. Lee, "Members of Congress Finally Introduce Serious DMCA Reform," *Ars Techinica* (May 9, 2013). http://arstechnica.com/tech-policy/2013/05/members-of-congress-finally-introduce-serious-dmca-reform/. Accessed May 2013.

19. For more on this see Barbara R. Jansy, "Realities of Data Sharing Using the Genome War Case Study—An Historical Perspective and Commentary," *EPJ Data Science* Vol. 2 (1) (2013). http://www.epjdatascience.com/content/2/1/1. Accessed October 2013. As the article puts it, "Information may be free in heaven, but it isn't so easy down here."

20. Section 107, Title 17, Copyright Act of 1976. http://www.copyright.gov/title17/92chap1.pdf. Accessed March 2013.

21. Jennifer Howard, "Long Awaited Ruling in Copyright Case Mostly Favors Georgia State U," *Chronicle of Higher Education* (May 13, 2012). http://chronicle.com/article/Long-Awaited-Ruling-in/131859/. Accessed March 2013, subscription required. The opinion may be found here: http://www.tc.umn.edu/~nasims/GSU-opinion.pdf. Accessed March 2013.

22. Doug Lederman, "Librarians and Colleges File Briefs Backing HathiTrust," *Inside Higher Ed* (June 5, 2013). http://www.insidehighered.com/quicktakes/2013/06/05/librarians-and-colleges-file-briefs-backing-hathitrust. Accessed June 2013.

23. The full text of the opinion is here: http://www.tc.umn.edu/~nasims/HathivAG10_10_12.pdf. Accessed March 2013.

24. John M. Budd, *The Changing Academic Library: Operations, Culture Environment* (Chicago: Association of College and Research Libraries, 2012), 34.

25. Creative Commons, "Education." http://creativecommons.org/education. Accessed March 2013. Also quoted in Budd, 346.

26. Creative Commons, "Frequently Asked Questions," "About CC," "2. Is CC Against Copyright?" http://wiki.creativecommons.org/FAQ. Accessed March 2013.

27. Scott Jaschik, "Not So Fast on Open

Access," *Inside Higher Ed* (September 27, 2012). http://www.insidehighered.com/news/2012/09/24/historians-organization-issues-statement-calling-caution-open-access. Accessed August 2013.

28. Peter Suber, "Open Access: Six Myths Put to Rest," *The Guardian: Higher Education Network* (October 21, 2013). http://www.theguardian.com/higher-education-network/blog/2013/oct/21/open-access-myths-peter-suber-harvard. Accessed October 2013.

29. Peter Suber, "Open Access Overview." http://legacy.earlham.edu/~peters/fos/overview.htm. Accessed March 2013.

30. John Bohannon, "Who's Afraid of Peer Review?" *Science* Vol. 342, no. 6154 (October 4, 2013), 60–65. http://www.sciencemag.org/content/342/6154/60.full. Accessed October 2013. For a good counterpoint, see Sal Robinson, "John Bohannon's Open Access Sting Paper Annoys Many, Scares the Easily Scared, and Accomplishes Relatively Little," *Melville House* (October 9, 2013). http://www.mhpbooks.com/john-bohannons-open-access-sting-paper-annoys-many-scares-the-easily-scared-accomplishes-relatively-little/. Accessed October 2013.

31. Editors, "How Science Goes Wrong," *The Economist* (October 19, 2013). http://www.economist.com/news/leaders/215880 69-scientific-research-has-changed-world-now-it-needs-change-itself-how-science-goes-wrong. Accessed October 2013.

32. "Copyright Clearance Center Launches Open Access Solutions." http://www.copyright.com/content/cc3/en/toolbar/about US/newsRoom/pressReleases/press_2012/press-release-12-10-11.html. Accessed July 2013.

33. Randall Stross, *Planet Google: One Company's Audacious Plan to Organize Everything We Know* (New York: Free Press, 2008), 88.

34. The sense of the phrase is that according to a reader's ability, books have their fate, or, in other words, books live as long as readers read them.

35. The quoted text is from Jeff Jarvis, *What Would Google Do?* (New York: Harper Collins, 2009), 136–7.

36. Thomas More, *Utopia*, Edward S. Surtz, editor (New Haven: Yale University Press, 1964), 24. A similar point is made in Andrew Keen, *The Cult of the Amateur: How Today's Internet Is Killing Our Culture* (New York: Doubleday, 2007), 131.

37. Keen, 141.

38. Tim Kreider, "Slaves of the Internet, Unite!" *New York Times* (October 26, 2013). http://www.nytimes.com/2013/10/27/opinion/sunday/slaves-of-the-internet-unite.html. Accessed October, 2013.

39. Tarleton Gillespie, *Wired Shut: Copyright and the Shape of Digital Culture* (Cambridge, MA: MIT Press, 2007), 4.

40. "The Wired Sh*tlist," *Wired*, n.d. http://www.wired.com/wired/archive/3.01/shitlist_pr.html. Accessed March 2013. Also quoted in Gillespie, 4.

41. Gillespie, 31.

42. Gillespie, 33.

43. "Google Starts Reporting False DMCA Takedown Notices," *TorrentFreak* (December 13, 2012). http://torrentfreak.com/google-starts-reporting-false-dmca-takedown-requests-121213/. Accessed March 2013.

Chapter 8

1. John Marenbon, *Medieval Philosophy: An Historical and Philosophy Introduction*, Routledge History of Philosophy, Vol. 3 (New York: Routledge, 2006), 49.

2. "Anne Lamott: By the Book," *New York Times Review* (November 21, 2012). http://www.nytimes.com/2012/11/25/books/review/anne-lamott-by-the-book.html?page wanted=all&_r=0. Accessed July 2013.

3. Quoted in Lucien X. Polastron, *The Great Digitization: The Quest to Know Everything* (Rochester, VT: Inner Traditions, 2009), 31.

4. Nicholas Carr, "Never Mind Ebooks. Why Print Books Are Here to Stay," *Wall Street Journal Online* (January 5, 2013). http://online.wsj.com/article/SB10001424 12788732387420457821956335369700 2. html. Accessed April 2013.

5. Shiv Malik, "Kindle Ebook Sales Have Overtaken Amazon Print Sales, Says Book Seller," *The Guardian* (August 5, 2012). http://www.guardian.co.uk/books/2012/

aug/06/amazon-kindle-ebook-sales-over take-print. Accessed April 2013.

6. Nicholas Carr, "Never Mind Ebooks."

7. http://libraries.pewinternet.org/ 2013/06/25/younger-americans-library-services/. Accessed July 2013.

8. Lauren Indvik, "Nation's First Bookless Public Library Could Be in Texas," *Mashable* (January 14, 2013). http://mashable. com/2013/01/14/bookless-library-bexar-county/. Accessed April 2013.

9. John Budd, *The Changing Academic Library: Operations, Culture, Environment* (Chicago: Association of College & Research Libraries, 2012), 254.

10. Budd, 254.

11. Much of what I have written here is also discussed by Clifford A. Lynch, "Ebooks in 2013: Promises Broken, Promises Kept, and Faustian Bargains," *American Libraries* (June 2013). http://www.americanlibrariesmaga zine.org/article/ebooks-2013. Accessed June 2013.

12. David Weinberger, *Too Big to Know— Rethinking Knowledge, Now That the Facts Aren't the Facts, Experts Are Everywhere, and the Smartest Person in the Room Is the Room* (New York: Basic Books, 2011), 96–98.

13. Jill Harness. "Finally Your eBooks Can Smell Like a Book Again," *Neatorama* (June 25, 2012). http://www.neatorama. com/2012/06/25/finally-your-ebooks-can-smell-like-a-book-again/II!qAIrQ. Accessed December 2013.

14. See Clifford Lynch, "Ebooks in 2013."

15. The extended discussion for this argument may be found in Nicholas Carr, *The Shallows: What the Internet Is Doing to Our Brains* (New York: Norton, 2010).

16. Andrew Piper, "Out of Touch. E-Reading Isn't Reading," *Slate* (November 15, 2012). http://www.slate.com/articles/arts/ culturebox/2012/11/reading_on_a_kindle_ is_not_the_same_as_reading_a_book. single.html. Accessed July 2013.

17. James Bridle, "E-readers: The Best Way to Get the World's Children Reading," *The Guardian* (September 8, 2013). http:// www.theguardian.com/technology/2013/ sep/08/ebooks-ereaders-worldreader-kade ghana. Accessed September 2103.

18. Weinberger makes these and other points, 107–109.

19. Suzanne Bowness, "The Latest Academic Book (Hopefully) One Click Away," *UA/AU University Affairs* (September 10, 2012). http://www.universityaffairs.ca/the-latest-academic-book-hopefully-one-click-away.aspx. Accessed July 2013.

20. www.dropbox.com; http://calibre-ebook.com; http://evernote.com; http:// www.zotero.org/.

21. Damien Walter, "Who Owns the Networked Future of Reading?" *The Guardian* (August 23, 2013). http://www.theguardian. com/books/2013/aug/23/reading-net worked-future-readmill-app. Accessed September 2013.

22. See, for example, Barbara Fister, "The Revolution Will Not Be Subscription Based," *Inside Higher Ed* (October 13, 2011). http:// www.insidehighered.com/blogs/library_ babel_fish/the_revolution_will_not_be_ subscription_based. Accessed May 2013.

23. Audry Watters, "Will Your Local Library Lend Ebooks (Or Can They)?" *Readwrite* (November 10, 2010). http://readwrite. com/2010/11/10/will_your_local_library_ lend_e-books_or_can_they. Accessed April 2013.

24. K. T. Bradford, "Why Borrowing an Ebook from the Library Is So Difficult," *Digital Trends* (June 15, 2013). http://www. digitaltrends.com/mobile/e-book-library-lending-broken-difficult/. Accessed June 2013.

25. Josh Constine, "Google Framed as Book Stealer Bent on Data Domination in New Documentary," *TechCrunch* (May 8, 2013). http://techcrunch.com/2013/05/08/ google-book-search-and-the-world-brain-book/. Accessed July 2013.

26. Jeff John Roberts, "Google Wins Book-Scanning Case: Judge Finds 'Fair Use' Cites Many Benefits," *Gigaom* (November 14, 2013). http://gigaom.com/2013/11/14/goo gle-wins-book-scanning-case-judge-finds-fair-use-cites-many-benefits/. Accessed November 2013.

27. Martin Bryant, "Can Ownshelf, the 'Dropbox for ebooks,' Sail Clear of Controversy?" *The Next Web* (January 11, 2013). http://thenextweb.com/media/2013/01/11/

can-ownshelf-the-dropbox-for-ebooks-sail-clear-of-lending-controversy. Accessed April 2013.

28. When I accessed this site several times in April 2013, Google warned "this site may be compromised."

29. Quoted in James Galbraith, "E-book on the Internet," in Sue Polanka, *No Shelf Required* (Chicago: American Library Association, 2011), 1.

30. Wahba, Phil, "Barnes & Noble Sells Fewer Nooks, Retail Sales Fall," *Reuters* (January 3, 2013). http://www.reuters.com/article/2013/01/03/us-barnesandnoble-results-idUSBRE9020BD20130103. Accessed April 2013.

31. "Barnes & Noble Reports Fiscal 2013 Third Quarter Results" (February 28, 2013). http://www.barnesandnobleinc.com/press_releases/2_28_13_fy_2013_3Q_financial_results.html. Accessed April 2013.

32. http://phx.corporate-ir.net/phoenix.zhtml?c=97664&p=irol-newsArticle&ID=1779040&highlight=. Accessed April 2013. Joan Engebretson, "Amazon May Be Subsidizing Price of New Kindle Fire" (September 12, 2012). http://www.telecompetitor.com/amazon-may-be-subsidizing-price-of-new-kindle-fire/. Accessed 2013.

33. Romain Dillet, "E-Ink Reports 46 percent Sales Drop, Expects E-Reader Shipments to Be Flat This Year," *TechCrunch* (August 16, 2013). http://techcrunch.com/2013/08/16/e-ink-reports-46-sales-drop-expects-e-reader-shipments-to-be-flat-this-year/. Accessed August 2013.

34. John Paczkowski, "Apple's Chances on an Ebook Ruling Appeal Are Lousy, Say Legal Scholars," *AllThingsD* (July 10, 2013). http://allthingsd.com/20130710/apples-chances-on-an-e-book-ruling-appeal-are-lousy-say-legal-scholars/. Accessed July, 2103. See also Sam Gustin, "Apple Found Guilty in Ebook Price Fixing Conspiracy Trial," *Time* (June 10, 2013). http://business.time.com/2013/07/10/apple-found-guilty-in-e-book-price-fixing-conspiracy-trial/. Accessed July 2013.

35. Andrew Albanese, "Publishers Have Paid $166 Million to Settle Ebook Claims," *Publishers Weekly* (July 24, 2013). http://www.publishersweekly.com/pw/by-topic/digital/content-and-e-books/article/58412-publishers-have-paid-166-million-to-settle-e-book-claims.html. Accessed August 2013.

36. Art Brodsky, "The Other Ebook Pricing Problem," *Huffington Post* (July 17, 2013). http://www.huffingtonpost.com/art-brodsky/the-other-e-book-pricing_b_3611087.html. Accessed August 2013.

37. Art Brodsky, "The Abomination of Ebooks: They Price People Out of Reading," *Wired* (October 2, 2013). http://www.wired.com/opinion/2013/10/how-ebook-pricing-hurts-us-in-more-ways-than-you-think/. Accessed October 2013.

38. It really depends on where you look. The University of California Irvine Medical Center claims a 23 percent increase in medical scores of the first class to use iPads: "UCI Med School's iPad Program Showing Results," *eCampus News*, Vol. 6 (4) (April 2013), 20. But problems still arise with their use: Michael Silgadaze, "5 Problems with iPads in Education," *BetaNews* (October 24, 2012). http://betanews.com/2012/10/24/5-problems-with-ipads-in-education/. Accessed April 2013. My guess is that many programs offering iPads do so without training, preparation or anything else. In a school district where my wife once worked, the superintendent promised iPads to all the teachers. When questioned about training, the superintendent suggested they just ask their students since they'd be more familiar with them.

39. Ben Wieder, "iPads Could Hinder Teaching, Professors Say," *Chronicle of Higher Education* (March 13, 2011). http://chronicle.com/article/iPads-for-College-Class rooms-/126681/. Accessed April 2013.

40. A good discussion of all these issues can be found in Polanka, *No Shelf Required*, 76–79. Polanka is a great deal more sanguine than am I.

41. Some will complain that you cannot, or certainly should not, annotate *any* print library book, but with post-it notes, it isn't difficult at all.

42. Alice Crosetto, "The Use and Preservation of Ebook," in Polanka, *No Shelf Required*, 125ff.

43. Porter Anderson, "Extra Ether: Ebooks Gone in 5 Years?" *Jane Friedman* (July 3, 2012). http://janefriedman.com/2012/07/03/extra-ether-ebooks-gone-in-5-years/. Accessed May 2013.

44. www.lockss.org.

45. http://www.portico.org/digital-preservation/about-us.

46. http://www.clockss.org/clockss/Home.

47. See http://www.clockss.org/clocksswiki/files/LOCKSSCLOCKSSChart.pdf for a good thumbnail description of the differences between the two services.

48. "75 percent Prefer Traditional Book to Electronic Reading Device," *Rasmussen-Reports* (July 18, 2013). http://www.rasmussenreports.com/public_content/lifestyle/general_lifestyle/july_2013/75_prefer_traditional_book_to_electronic_reading_device. Accessed August 2013.

Chapter 9

1. Greg Kumparak, "Google Recently Made a Silent Shift to a New Search Algorithm, 'Hummingbird,'" *TechCrunch* (September 26, 2013). http://techcrunch.com/2013/09/26/google-recently-made-a-silent-shift-to-a-new-search-algorithm-hummingbird/. Accessed September 2013.

2. Nick Bilton, "Researcher Controls Another Person's Brain Over the Internet," *New York Times* (August 27, 2013). http://bits.blogs.nytimes.com/2013/08/27/researcher-controls-another-persons-brain-over-the-internet/?_r=0. Accessed August 2013.

3. Arik Hesseldahl, "Talking Brain and Immortality with Ray Kurzweil and Jaun Enriquez (Video)," *All Things D* (December 4, 2012). http://allthingsd.com/20121204/talking-brains-and-immortality-with-ray-kurzweil-and-juan-enriquez-video/. Accessed April 2013. The talk is a little over an hour.

4. Jane O'Brien, "Learn English Online: How the Internet Is Changing the Language," *BBC News Magazine* (December 13, 2012). http://www.bbc.co.uk/news/magazine-20332763. Accessed April 2013.

5. Arik Hesseldahl, "IBM's Game Show Winning Computer Goes to Work on Cancer," *All Things D* (February 9, 2013). http://allthingsd.com/20130209/ibms-game-show-winning-watson-computer-goes-to-work-treating-cancer/. Accessed April 2013.

6. Time Editors, "Exclusive: Time Talks to Google CEO Larry Page About Its Venture to Extend Human Life," *Time* (September 18, 2013). http://business.time.com/2013/09/18/google-extend-human-life/. Accessed September 2013. Apparently, Mr. Page wants to solve death instead.

7. I'll not mention the fact that Watson, after answering 91 percent of all questions right, bit the dust in Final Jeopardy. When asked to name a U.S. city, the two largest airports of which are named for a World War II hero and battle, Watson replied with ... Toronto? [sic]. Let's hope it never replies with "Take arsenic and call me in the morning."

8. Maggie Koerth-Baker, "Dr. Google Proves Himself Somewhat Useful," *BoingBoing* (March 7, 2013). http://boingboing.net/2013/03/07/dr-google-proves-himself-some.html?utm_source=feedburner&utm_medium=feed&utm_campaign=Feed%3A+boingboing%2FiBag+%28Boing+Boing%29. Accessed April 2013.

9. "75 percent Prefer Traditional Book to Electronic Reading Device," *Rasmussen Report* (July 18, 2013). http://www.rasmussenreports.com/public_content/lifestyle/general_lifestyle/july_2013/75_prefer_traditional_book_to_electronic_reading_device. Accessed July 2013.

10. Gautam Naik, "Storing Digital Data in DNA," *The Wall Street Journal* (January 24, 2013). http://online.wsj.com/article/SB10001424127887324539304578259883507543150.html. Accessed April 2013.

11. I am indebted to Robert Franklin for this interesting detail (roughly: 400 to 450 words per page at 7 or 8 characters each = ca. 3300 characters, one-thousandth of which is 3.3 wrong characters, or typos).

12. Patrick Lo, "Closing the Internet Divide," *All Things D* (October 17, 2012). http://allthingsd.com/20121017/closing-the-internet-divide/. Accessed April 2013.

13. Kathryn Zickuhr and Aaron Smith,

"Home Broadband 2013," *Pew Internet & American Life Project* (August 26, 2013). http://pewinternet.org/Reports/2013/Broadband.aspx. Accessed September 2013.

14. Kathryn Zickuhr, "Who's Not Online and Why," *Pew Internet & American Life Project* (September 25, 2013). http://pewinternet.org/Reports/2013/Non-internet-users/Summary-of-Findings.aspx. Accessed September 2013.

15. John Paczkowski, "Auto-Ban: German Court Orders Google to Delete Offensive Search Suggestions," *All Things D* (May 14, 2013). http://allthingsd.com/20130514/auto-ban-german-court-orders-google-to-delete-offensive-search-suggestions/. Accessed May 2013.

16. "Online Pornography to Be Blocked by Default, PM Announces," *BBC News* (July 22, 2013). http://www.bbc.co.uk/news/uk-23401076. See also ReadWrite Editors, "UK Declares War on Internet Pornography," *Read Write* (July 22, 2013). http://readwrite.com/2013/07/22/uk-internet-child-pornography-block-cameron-announcement#awesm=~odnK9cSvfMgv8T. Accessed August 2013.

17. Ryan Tate, "Bribery, Porn, and Spam Are the Path to Riches in the App World," *Wired* (July 6, 2012). http://www.wired.com/business/2012/07/app-dirty-tricks/all/. Accessed June 2013.

18. Gina Kolata, "Scientific Articles Accepted. (Personal Checks, Too.)," *New York Times* (April 13, 2013). http://www.nytimes.com/2013/04/08/health/for-scientists-an-exploding-world-of-pseudo-academia.html?smid=tw-nytimesscience&seid=auto&_r=1&pagewanted=all&. Accessed April 2013.

19. Gina Kolata, "Scientific Articles Accepted. (Personal Checks, Too.)," *New York Times* (April 13, 2013). http://www.nytimes.com/2013/04/08/health/for-scientists-an-exploding-world-of-pseudo-academia.html?smid=tw-nytimesscience&seid=auto&_r=1&pagewanted=all&. Accessed April 2013.

20. Alexis C. Madrigal, "If You Can't Beat Them, Subvert 'Em. Countering Misinformation on the Viral Web," *The Atlantic* (October 31, 2012). http://www.theatlantic.com/technology/archive/2012/10/if-you-cant-beat-em-subvert-em-countering-misinformation-on-the-viral-web/264366/. Accessed April 2013.

21. "Stem Cell Fraud: A 60 Minutes Investigation," *60 Minutes* (August 12, 2012). http://www.cbsnews.com/8301-18560_162-57497588/stem-cell-fraud-a-60-minutes-investigation/. Accessed April 2013.

22. Carl Eliot, "The Scambuster: An Interview with Doug Sipp of Stem Cell Treatment Monitor," *Chronicle of Higher Education* (March 28, 2012). http://chronicle.com/blogs/brainstorm/the-scambuster-an-interview-with-doug-sipp-of-stem-cell-treatment-monitor/45187. Accessed April 2013.

23. Virginia Heffernan, "A Prescription of Fear," *New York Times* (February 4, 2011). http://www.nytimes.com/2011/02/06/magazine/06FOB-Medium-t.html. Accessed April 2013.

24. Decan Butler, "When Google Got Flu Wrong," *Nature*, Vol. 494 (7436) (February 13, 2103). http://www.nature.com/news/when-google-got-flu-wrong-1.12413. Accessed April 2013.

25. "A Suicide Goes Viral on the Web," *teknoids* (September 20, 2012). http://www.teknoids.net/content/suicide-goes-viral-internet. Accessed April 2013.

26. Paul Wright, "Teen-ager Commits Suicide After Photograph of Her 'Being Gang Raped' Goes Viral," *The Telegraph* (April 11, 2013). http://www.telegraph.co.uk/news/worldnews/northamerica/canada/9985196/Teenager-commits-suicide-after-photograph-of-her-being-gang-raped-goes-viral.html. Accessed April 2013.

27. Thomas J. Sheeran, "Ohio Teen Sentenced to Life Over Craigslist Plot," *USA Today* (November 9, 2012). http://www.usatoday.com/story/news/nation/2012/11/09/ohio-teen-craigslist-scheme-sentence/1695795/. Accessed April 2013.

28. Sam Laird, "Reddit Apologizes for Boston Marathon 'Witch Hunt,'" *Mashable* (April 22, 2013). http://mashable.com/2013/04/22/reddit-apologizes-boston-marathon/. Accessed May 2013.

29. Hunter Stuart, "Facebook Deletes

Two Graphic Videos, Will Evaluate Policy on Explicit Content," *Huffington Post* (July 24, 2013). http://www.huffingtonpost.com/2013/05/02/facebook-deletes-decapitation-videos_n_3202945.html. Accessed July 2013.

30. The reinstitution is here: Ashley Feinberg, "Facebook Is Lifting Its Ban on Decapitation Videos (Updated)," *Gizmodo* (October 21, 2013). http://gizmodo.com/facebook-is-lifting-its-ban-on-decapitation-videos-1449606221. Accessed October 2013. The second rescission is here: Casey Chan, "Facebook Changes Its Mind Again: It Is Now Re-Banning Decapitation Videos," *Gizmodo* (October 22, 2013). http://gizmodo.com/facebook-changes-its-mind-again-its-now-re-banning-de-1450384342?utm_source=feedburner&utm_medium=feed&utm_campaign=Feed%3A+gizmodo%2Ffull+%28Gizmodo%29. Accessed October 2013.

31. Marcus Tullius Cicero, *Pro Sexto Roscio Americo*, Vol. LIII, Loeb Classic Edition, p. 263.

32. Geoffrey A. Fowler, "When the Most Personal Secrets Get Outed on Facebook," *Wall Street Journal Online* (October 13, 2012). http://online.wsj.com/article/SB10000872396390444416580457800874057820 0224.html. Accessed July 2013.

33. Gregory Ferenstein, "88 Percent of Teens' Sexual Pics Reposted by 'Parasite Websites,'" *TechCrunch* (October 22, 2012). http://techcrunch.com/2012/10/22/88-of-teens-sexual-pics-reposted-by-parasite-web sites/. Accessed July 2013.

34. Ina Fried, "EWW! Nearly Half of Business Travelers Would Skip Brushing Teeth Before Giving Up iPad," *All Things D* (September 17, 2012). http://allthingsd.com/20120917/eww-nearly-half-of-business-travelers-would-skip-brushing-teeth-before-giving-up-ipad/. Accessed April 2013.

35. Matt Enis, "Patrons Expect More Mobile Services," *Library Journal* (August 16, 2012). http://www.thedigitalshift.com/2012/08/mobile/patrons-expect-more-mob ile-services-handheld-librarian-conference/. Accessed April 2013.

Part Two

1. Quoted in William H. Davidow, *Over-Connected: The Promise and Threat of the Internet* (New York: Delphinium Press, 2011), 20.

2. Jeremy Kirk, "ID Theft May Cost the IRS $21B Over the Next Five Years," *Computerworld* (August 3, 2012). http://www.computerworld.com/s/article/9229939/ID_theft_may_cost_IRS_21B_over_next_five_years. Accessed April 2013.

3. "Identity Theft Cost Americans $1.52 Billion in 2011, FTC Says," *Huffington Post* (February 28, 2012). http://www.huffington post.com/2012/02/28/identity-theft-cost-americans-152-billion-2011-ftc_n_1307485.html. Accessed April 2013.

4. Polly Sprenger, "Sun on Privacy: 'Get Over It,'" *Wired* (October 26, 1999). http://www.wired.com/politics/law/news/1999/01/17538. Accessed April 2013.

Chapter 10

1. Sven Birkerts, *The Gutenberg Elegies: The Fate of Reading in an Electronic Age* (Boston: Faber and Faber, 1994).

2. Z. Liu, "Print vs. Electronic Resources: A Study of Their Perceptions, Preferences, and Use," *Information Processing and Management* Vol. 42 (2) (2006), 583–592; Gunther Kres, *Literacy in the New Media Age* (New York: Routledge, 2003); Margaret Mackey, *Literacies Across Media: Playing the Text* (New York: Routledge, 2007).

3. Friedrich Nietzsche, *On the Genealogy of Morals and Ecce Homo*, translated by Walter Kaufmann and R.J. Hollindale, edited and with a commentary by Walter Kauffman (New York: Vintage Books, 1989), 23.

4. "Teachers: Internet's Effect on Writing Not All for the Worse," *Inside Higher Ed* (July 16, 2013). http://www.insidehighered.com/quicktakes/2013/07/16/teachers-internets-effect-writing-not-all-worse. Accessed August 2013.

5. Nicholas Carr, "Is Google Making Us Stupid? What The Internet Is Doing to Our Brains," *The Atlantic* (July/August 2008). http://www.theatlantic.com/magazine/arch

ive/2008/07/is-google-making-us-stupid/
306868/. Accessed April 2013.

6. Carr, "Is Google Making Us Stupid?"

7. Mary Cross, *Bloggerati, Twitterati: How Blogs and Twitter Are Transforming Popular Culture* (Santa Barbara, CA: Praeger: ABC-CLIO, 2011), 74. I understand that Cross is not in the same camp as Carr, but I found her assertion interesting.

8. Pew Research Center, Pew Internet and American Life Project, *Social Media and Young Adults* (February 3, 2010). http://pewinternet.org/Reports/2010/Social-Media-and-Young-Adults.aspx. Accessed April 2013.

9. Michael Gorman, "Revenge of the Blog People!" *Library Journal* (February 15, 2005). http://lj.libraryjournal.com/2005/02/ljarchives/backtalk-revenge-of-the-blog-people/. Accessed April 2013.

10. Dan Fagin, "Alive and Tweeting," *Slate Magazine* (July 10, 2013). http://www.slate.com/articles/health_and_science/medical_examiner/2013/07/social_media_communication_facebook_twitter_linkedin_thought_i_was_dying.html. Accessed July 2013.

11. Mokoto Rich, "Literacy Debate: Online, RU Really Reading," *New York Times* (July 27, 2008). http://www.nytimes.com/2008/07/27/books/27reading.html?pagewanted=all&_r=0. Accessed April 2013.

12. Rich, "Literacy Debate: Online, RU Really Reading."

13. National Assessment of Educational Progress, *The Nation's Report Card*, "Reading" (2011). http://nationsreportcard.gov/reading_2011/summary.asp. Accessed April 2013.

14. The Wing Institute, "Have NAEP Reading Scores Improved Over the Last 40 Years of School Reform?" http://winginstitute.org/Graphs/Student/NAEP-reading-scores/. Accessed April 2013. See also National Literacy Trust, *Children's and Young People's Reading Today* (London: National Literacy Trust, 2012), 9–10. The report indicates a decline in daily reading since 2005. It's too early to say why this is, however.

15. See for example the work the Elgin foundation has done in this regard: Helen McCoy, "Turning Kids into Readers." http://education-consumers.org/Elgin_Case Study.pdf. (I am an unpaid board member of the Education Consumers Foundation, an entity wholly separate from the Elgin Foundation, but both foundations work together from time to time to improve reading.)

16. Andrew Piper, "Out of Touch: E-Reading Isn't Reading," *Slate Magazine* (November 15, 2012). http://www.slate.com/articles/arts/culturebox/2012/11/reading_on_a_kindle_is_not_the_same_as_reading_a_book.html. Accessed April 2013.

17. Nick Bilton, "Disruptions: Your Brain on Ebooks and Smartphone Apps," *New York Times* (September 30, 2012). http://bits.blogs.nytimes.com/2012/09/30/your-brain-on-e-books-and-smartphone-apps/. Accessed April 2013.

18. For more on this, see Joshua Foer, *Moonwalking with Einstein: The Art and Science of Remembering Everything* (New York: Penguin Press, 2011).

19. Anne Mangen, "Hypertext Fiction Reading: Haptics and Immersion," *Journal of Research and Reading*, Vol. 31 (4) (November 1, 2008), 404.

20. "Students Want More Class Assignments Available on Mobile Devices," *ECampus News,* Vol. 6 (8) (September 2013), 12.

21. Stephen Abram, "P-Books Versus Ebooks: Are There Education Issues?" *Multimedia & Internet@Schools*, Vol. 17 (6) (November/December 2010) 13–16."

22. Steve Krug, *Don't Make Me Think: A Common Sense Approach to Web Usability* (Berkeley, CA: Riders Publishing, 2006), 22–23.

23. Robert Darnton, *The Case for Books: Past, Present, and Future* (New York: Public Affairs, 2009), 68.

24. Darnton, 69.

25. David Bonagura, "What's 12 × 11? Um, Let Me Google That," *Wall Street Journal* (October 30, 2013). http://online.wsj.com/news/articles/SB10001424052702303471004579165310256329006. Accessed October 2013.

26. Farhad Manjoo, "You Won't Finish This Article," *Slate Magazine* (June 6, 2013). http://www.slate.com/articles/technology/technology/2013/06/how_people_read_

online_why_you_won_t_finish_this_article.html. Accessed June 2013.

27. Eve LaPlante, *Marmee & Louisa: The Untold Story of Louisa May Alcott and Her Mother* (New York: Free Press, 2012), 26.

28. Quoted in Nicholas Carr, *The Shallows* (New York: W.W. Norton, 2010), 7.

29. Melanie Eversley, "Neil Armstrong IS Dead, But It Happened a Year Ago," *USA Today* (August 28, 2013). http://www.usatoday.com/story/news/nation/2013/08/27/neil-armstrong-twitter-internet-death-rumor/2711419/?utm_source=feedburner&utm_medium=feed&utm_campaign=Feed%3A+UsatodaycomNation-TopStories+%28USATODAY+-+Nation+Top+Stories%29. Accessed September 2013.

30. The phrase is from Daniel Patrick Moynihan's famous article by the same name, "Defining Deviancy Down," *American Scholar* (Winter 1993). Moynihan argued that things were not getting better, we had just lowered the bar.

31. Page Jaeger, "Transliteracy—New Library Lingo and What It Means for Instruction," *Library Media Connection*, Vol. 30 (2) (October 2011), 44–47.

32. Mangen, 404.

33. Mangen, 405.

34. Kathryn Zickuhr, et al., "Younger Americans' Reading and Library Habits," *Pew Internet & American Life Project* (October 23, 2012). http://libraries.pewinternet.org/2012/10/23/younger-americans-reading-and-library-habits/. Accessed April 2013.

35. Lee Raine and Maeve Duggan, "E-book Reading Jumps; Print Books Reading Declines," *Pew Internet & American Life Project*, http://libraries.pewinternet.org/2012/12/27/e-book-reading-jumps-print-book-reading-declines/. Accessed April 2013.

Chapter 11

1. See, for example, Nicholas Carr, *The Shallows* (New York: W. W. Norton, 2010), 6.

2. One, among the very many places it can be found, is here: http://www.justice.gov/opcl/privstat.htm. Accessed April 2013.

3. Alexandra Alter, "Your Ebook Is Reading You," *Huffington Post* (July 19, 2012).

http://online.wsj.com/article/SB10001424052702304870304577490950051438304.html?mod=WSJ_Tech_RIGHTTopCarousel_1. Accessed April 2013.

4. David Pogue, "Why Google Glass Is Creepy," *Scientific American* (May 21, 1013). http://www.scientificamerican.com/article.cfm?id=why-google-glass-is-creepy. Accessed August 2013.

5. John Hall, "Vatican Pornography: Transsexual Adult Films Downloaded on Computers Within Catholic Church Headquarters," *The Independent* (April 9, 2013). http://www.independent.co.uk/news/world/europe/vatican-pornography-transsexual-adult-films-downloaded-on-computers-within-catholic-church-headquarters-8566432.html. Accessed April 2013.

6. Lee Rainie, Sara Kiesler, Ruogu Kang, and Mary Madden, "Anonymity, Privacy, and Security Online," *Pew Internet & American Life Project* (September 5, 2013). http://www.pewinternet.org/Reports/2013/Anonymity-online.aspx. Accessed September 2013.

7. Nicole Perlroth, Jeff Larson, and Scott Shane, "N.S.A. Able to Foil Basic Safeguards of Privacy on Web," *New York Times* (September 5, 2013). http://www.nytimes.com/2013/09/06/us/nsa-foils-much-internet-encryption.html?pagewanted=all&_r=0. Accessed September 2013.

8. Mike Isaac, "Facebook Hooks Up with Attorneys General for Teen Profile Privacy Awareness," *All Things D* (April 15, 2013). http://allthingsd.com/20130415/facebook-hooks-up-with-attorneys-general-for-teen-profile-privacy-awareness/. Accessed April 2013.

9. Nicholas Carlson, "Chatroulette's Penis Problem," *Business Insider* (April 8, 2010). http://www.businessinsider.com/chatroulette-penis-problem-solved-2010-04?op=1. Accessed August 2013.

10. David Von Drehle, "The Surveillance Society," *Time* (August 1, 2013). http://nation.time.com/2013/08/01/the-surveillance-society/. Accessed August 2013.

11. Angela Moscaritolo, "Google's Schmidt Concerned by Lack of Internet 'Delete Button,'" *PC Magazine* (May 6, 2013). http://www.pcmag.com/article2/0,2817,2418601,00.asp. Accessed August 2013.

12. Eric Schmidt and Jared Cohen, *The New Digital Age: Reshaping the Future of People, Nations and Business* (New York: Knopf, 2013), 54.

13. Ed Bayley, "The Clicks That Bind: Ways That Users "Agree" to Online Terms of Service," *Electronic Frontier Foundation* (November 16, 2009). https://www.eff.org/wp/clicks-bind-ways-users-agree-online-terms-service. Accessed April 2013.

14. Klint Finley, "Putting an End to the Biggest Lie on the Internet," *TechCrunch* (August 13, 2012). http://techcrunch.com/2012/08/13/putting-an-end-to-the-biggest-lie-on-the-internet/. Accessed April 2013.

15. Mike Isaac, "Facebook Hooks Up with Attorneys General for Teen Profile Privacy Awareness," *All Things D* (April 15, 2013). http://allthingsd.com/20130415/facebook-hooks-up-with-attorneys-general-for-teen-profile-privacy-awareness/. Accessed April 2013.

16. David Meyer, "This Man Thinks Big Data and Privacy Can Co-Exist, and Here's His Plan," *GigaOM* (August 27, 2013). http://gigaom.com/2013/08/27/this-man-thinks-big-data-and-privacy-can-co-exist-and-heres-his-plan/. Accessed October 2013.

17. John Paczkowski, "German Court Slams Apple on Privacy," *All Things D* (May 7, 2013). http://allthingsd.com/20130507/german-court-slams-apple-on-privacy/. Accessed August 2013. The United Kingdom is doing the same with Google and its privacy policies, or lack thereof: Mike Isaac, "European Watchdogs Order Google to Rewrite Privacy Policy," *All Things D* (July 5, 2103). http://allthingsd.com/20130705/european-watchdogs-order-google-to-rewrite-privacy-policy/. Accessed August 2013.

18. Elizabeth Dwoskin, "Facebook Reminds Users: All Your Data Is Fair Game," *Wall Street Journal* (August 29, 2013). http://blogs.wsj.com/digits/2013/08/29/facebook-reminds-users-all-your-data-is-fair-game.

19. But apparently not forever. See William Saletan, "I'll Be His Weiner Wife," *Slate Magazine* (April 10, 2013). http://www.slate.com/articles/news_and_politics/frame_game/2013/04/anthony_weiner_s_new_york_times_magazine_confession_if_you_don_t_want_to.html. Accessed April 2013.

20. See Finley, note 14 TOS;DR (http://tosdr.org/) Attempt to categorize TOS at various levels of comprehensibility and meaningfulness. Accessed April 2013.

21. CBS News, "Did the Internet Kill Privacy?" *Sunday Morning* (February 6, 2011). http://www.cbsnews.com/8301-3445_162-7323148.html. Accessed April 2013.

22. Stephen Levy, *In the Plex: How Google Thinks, Works, and Shapes Our Lives* (New York: Simon & Schuster, 2011), 173–175.

23. Levy, 174.

24. Levy, 177.

25. Tom Cochran, "Personal Information Is the Currency of the 21st Century," *All Things D* (May 7, 2013). http://allthingsd.com/20130507/personal-information-is-the-currency-of-the-21st-century/. Accessed August 2013.

26. Eric Limer, "Google Never Actually Deleted That Street View Data Breach," *Gizmodo* (July 27, 2012). http://gizmodo.com/5929636/google-never-actually-deleted-street-view-breach-data. Accessed April 2013.

27. Matthew Ingram, "The Google Now Dilemma: Yes, It's Kind of Creepy—But It's Incredibly Useful," *GigaOM* (May 3, 2013). http://gigaom.com/2013/05/03/the-google-now-dilemma-yes-its-kind-of-creepy-but-its-also-incredibly-useful/. Ingram admits the "creepy" factor but decides the privacy invasion is worth it. Accessed August 2013.

28. Jeff John Roberts, "Look-Out Google: Disconnect Says Its No-Track Search Tool Is Taking Off," *GigaOM* (October 9, 2013). http://gigaom.com/2013/10/09/look-out-google-disconnect-says-its-no-track-search-tool-is-taking-off/?utm_source=feedburner&utm_medium=feed&utm_campaign=Feed%3A+OmMalik+%28GigaOM%3A+Tech%29. Accessed October 2013.

29. Robert O'Harrow, Jr., *No Place to Hide* (New York: Free Press, 2005), 4.

30. "Sentencing Set for 17-Year-Old in Ohio's Craigslist Killings of 3 Men, Wounding a Fourth," *Yahoo News* (November 9, 2012). http://news.yahoo.com/sentencing-set-17-old-ohios-craigslist-killings-3-073109893.html. Accessed April 2013.

31. O'Harrow, 70.

32. David Meyer, "Without the Option of Privacy, We Are Lost," *GigaOM* (July 10, 2013). http://gigaom.com/2013/07/10/with out-the-option-of-privacy-we-are-lost/. Accessed August 2013.

33. See O'Harrow, 125–130, for just one of those harrowing tales of mistaken identity.

34. O'Harrow, 139, italics added.

35. Randall, 151.

36. Tracy Mitrano, "Abortion and Information Management," *Inside Higher Ed* (November 26, 2012). http://www.insidehigher ed.com/blogs/law-policy-and-it/abortion-and-information-management. Accessed April 2013.

37. See Patricia Wallace, *The Psychology of the Internet* (New York: Cambridge Press, 1999), xiv–xxix.

38. Simson Garfinkel, *Database Nation: The Death of Privacy in the 21st Century* (Sebastopol, CA: O'Reilly Media, 2000), 1–3, 11.

39. It's no secret that as a professional organization, the American Library Association has no love lost for the G.W. Bush administration in particular or Republicans in general.

Chapter 12

1. Tracy Mitrano, "International Intellectual Property Enforcement—III," *Inside Higher Ed* (October 10, 2012). http://www. insidehighered.com/blogs/law-policy-and-it/international-intellectual-property-enforcement-iii. Accessed May 2013.

2. One of the best new books is by Adrian Johns: *Piracy: The Intellectual Property Wars from Gutenberg to Gates* (Chicago: University of Chicago Press), 2009.

3. John Briggs, "We Can All Go Home Now, Piracy Is Mostly Dead," *TechCrunch* (July 16, 2013). http://techcrunch.com/ 2013/07/16/we-can-all-go-home-now-pir acy-is-mostly-dead/. Accessed August 2013. See also Janko Roettgers, "Charts: How Spotify IS Killing Music Piracy" (July 18, 2013). http://paidcontent.org/2013/07/18/charts-how-spotify-is-killing-music-piracy/. Accessed August 2013.

4. Jeff Tyson, "How the Old Napster Worked," *HowStuffWorks* (n.d.). http://www.howstuffworks.com/napster.htm. Accessed May 2013.

5. Felix Oberholzer-Gee and Koleman Strumpf, "The Effect of File Sharing on Record Sales: An Empirical Analysis" (March 2004). http://www.unc.edu/~cigar/papers/FileSharing_March2004.pdf. Accessed April 2013.

6. Oberholzer-Gee and Strumpf, 24–25.

7. This is the contention of Robert Levine in *Free Ride: How Digital Parasites Are Destroying the Culture of Business and How the Culture of Business Can Fight Back* (New York: Doubleday, 2011), 63–65.

8. Felix Oberholzer-Gee and Koleman Strumpf, "File-Sharing and Copyright." http://www.hbs.edu/faculty/Publication%20 Files/09–132.pdf. Accessed April 2013, p. 24.

9. Andrew Orlowski, "Apple, Tesco 'Most to Blame' for Music Biz Crisis," *The Register* (October 19, 2007). http://www. theregister.co.uk/2007/10/19/vrs_value_ gap_report/. Accessed April 2013.

10. Levine, 67–68.

11. Motion Picture Association of America, *The Cost of Movie Piracy*, n.d. http://austg.com/include/downloads/PiratePro file.pdf. Accessed May 2013. The "average pirate" is said to be a young male, 16–24, living in an urban area.

12. Levine, 206.

13. Brad Plumer, "SOPA: How Much Does Online Piracy Really Cost the Economy?" *The Washington Post: Wonkblog* (January 5, 2012). http://www.washingtonpost. com/blogs/wonkblog/post/how-much-does-online-piracy-really-cost-the-economy/ 2012/01/05/gIQAXknNdP_blog.html. Accessed May 2013.

14. Carl Bialik, "Putting a Price Tag on Film Piracy," *The Wall Street Journal* (May 1, 2013). http://blogs.wsj.com/numbersguy/ putting-a-price-tag-on-film-piracy-1228/. Accessed May 2013.

15. This figure appears preposterous and has been well ventilated in the following: Julian Sanchez, "How Copyright Industries Con Congress," Cato Institute (January 3, 2012), http://www.cato.org/blog/how-copy right-industries-con-congress; Kal Raustiala

and Chris Sprigman, "How Much Do Music and Movie Piracy Really Hurt the U.S. Economy?" *Freakanomics* (January 12, 2012), http://www.freakonomics.com/2012/01/12/how-much-do-music-and-movie-piracy-really-hurt-the-u-s-economy/. Accessed May 2013. As preposterous as this figure is, it is equally preposterous to argue that piracy has no effect on the economy at all.

16. Bialik.

17. Levine, 185.

18. Thomas Friedman, *The World Is Flat: A Brief History of the Twenty-First Century* (New York: Farrar, Strauss, and Giroux, 2005).

19. Johns, 2–4.

20. Johns, 463–462.

21. IDC, *The Dangerous World of Counterfeit and Pirated Software: How Pirated Software Can Compromise the Cybersecuirity of Consumers, Enterprises, and Nations ... and the Resultant Costs in Time and Money* (March 2013). http://www.microsoft.com/en-us/news/download/presskits/antipiracy/docs/IDC030513.pdf. Accessed May 2013.

22. Grant Gross, "Chinese Residents Charged with Selling $100M Worth of Pirated Software," *PCWorld* (April 18, 2012). http://www.pcworld.com/article/254050/chinese_residents_charged_with_selling_100m_worth_of_pirated_software.html. Accessed August 2013.

23. Richard Pérez-Peña, "Universities Face a Rising Barrage of Cyberattacks," *New York Times* (July 16, 2103). http://www.nytimes.com/2013/07/17/education/barrage-of-cyberattacks-challenges-campus-culture.html?pagewanted=all&_r=0. Accessed August 2013.

24. See, for example, how Stuxnet, a series of cyber worms, may have helped make Iran's enrichment of uranium stronger: Alex Hesseldahl, "Did Stuxnet Actually Improve Iran's Nuclear Capabilities?" *All Things D* (May 15, 2013). http://allthingsd.com/20130515/did-stuxnet-actually-improve-irans-nuclear-capabilities/. Accessed August 2013.

25. Robert J. Samuelson, "Beware the Internet and the Dangers of Cyberattacks," *Washington Post* (June 30, 2013). http://articles.washingtonpost.com/2013-06-30/opinions/40292503_1_internet-richard-bejtlich-hackers. Accessed August 2013.

26. Matthias Schepp and Thomas Tuma, "Anti-Virus Pioneer Evgeny Kaspersky: 'I Fear the Net Will Soon Become a War Zone,'" *Der Spiegel Online International* (June 24, 2011). http://www.spiegel.de/international/world/anti-virus-pioneer-evgeny-kaspersky-i-fear-the-net-will-soon-become-a-war-zone-a-770191.html. Accessed May 2013.

27. Johns, 474–475.

28. Tony Bradley, "Microsoft Plagued by Software Piracy," *PC World* (May 25, 2012). http://www.pcworld.com/article/256318/microsoft_plagued_by_software_piracy.html. Accessed May 2013.

29. Benji Edwards, "Why History Needs Software Piracy," *Technologizer* (January 23, 2012). http://technologizer.com/2012/01/23/why-history-needs-software-piracy/. Accessed May 2013.

30. Greenfield, Jeremy, "Does Piracy Hurt Digital Content Sales? Yes," *Digital Book Wire* (January 16, 2013). http://www.digitalbookworld.com/2013/does-piracy-hurt-digital-content-sales-yes/. Accessed May 2013.

31. "Simon & Schuster Brings Attributor Anti-Piracy Data to Authors," *Digital Book Wire* (March 21 2013). http://www.digitalbookworld.com/2013/simon-schuster-brings-attributor-anti-piracy-data-to-authors/. Accessed May 2013.

32. Suw Charman-Anderson, "Piracy, Savior of the Book Industry," *Forbes* (February 13, 2013). http://www.forbes.com/sites/suwcharmananderson/2013/02/13/piracy-saviour-of-the-book-industry/. Accessed May 2013.

33. http://thomas.loc.gov/cgi-bin/query/z?c112:H.R.3261. Accessed May 2013.

34. See Steven Kolowich, "A Legal Sweep," *Inside Higher Ed* (October 12, 2012), http://www.insidehighered.com/news/2012/10/12/hathitrust-ruling-universities-fair-use-winning-streak. Accessed May 2013; Kevin Smith, "The GSU Decision—Not an Easy Road for Anyone," *Scholarly Communications @ Duke* (May 12, 2012), http://blogs.library.duke.edu/scholcomm/2012/05/12/the-gsu-decision-not-an-easy-road-for-anyone/. Accessed May 2013.

35. Rebecca Greenfield, "The Internet Is Not Freaking Out About SOPA Sequel," *The*

Atlantic Wire (April 22, 2013). http://www. theatlanticwire.com/technology/2013/04/ internet-not-freaking-out-about-sopa-se quel/64428/. Accessed May 2013.

36. See, for example, Mathew Ingram, "Should You Be Worried About the New 'Six Strikes' Anti-Piracy Rules? Yes and No," *GigaOM* (February 26, 2013). http://gigaom. com/2013/02/26/should-you-be-worried-about-the-new-six-strikes-anti-piracy-rules-yes-and-no/. Accessed May 2013. Ingram is less sanguine about the laws than I am.

37. Nicole E. Ruedy, Celia Moore, Francesca Gino and Maurice E. Schweitzer, "The Cheater's High: The Unexpected Affective Benefits of Unethical Behavior," *Journal of Personality and Social Psychology* Vol. 105 (4) (2013), 531–548. http://www.apa.org/pubs/ journals/releases/psp-a0034231.pdf. Accessed October 2013.

38. Igor Stravinsky, *Poetics of Music: In the Form of Six Lessons*, translated by Arthur Knodel and Ingolf Dahl (Cambridge: Harvard University Press, 1947), 64–65, 63. Emphases added.

Part Three

1. John Chrastka, "Libraries in Crisis," *Everylibrary* (September 4, 2013). http:// everylibrary.org/library-crisis/. Accessed September 2013.

2. M. G. Seigler, "The End of the Library," *TechCrunch* (October 13, 2013). http: //techcrunch.com/2013/10/13/the-end-of-the-library/. Accessed October 2013. See also Eli Neiburger, "The End of the Public Library (As We Knew It)?" *Book: A Futurist's Manifesto*, edited by Hugh McGuire and Brian O'Leary. #26. http://book.pressbooks. com/chapter/ann-arbour-district-library-eli-neiburger. Accessed October 2103.

3. Quentin Hardy, "Information Technology Spending to Hit $3.6 Trillion in 2012, Report Says," *New York Times. Bits* (July 9, 2012). http://bits.blogs.nytimes. com/2012/07/09/information-technology-spending-to-hit-3-6-trillion-in-2012-report-says/. Accessed May 2013.

4. America Library Association, *State of America's Libraries Report 201*, "Academic Libraries" (Chicago: ALA, 2013). According to the report, "[M]ost students in higher education don't consider the campus library website a must for success." http://www.ala. org/news/state-americas-libraries-report-2013/academic-libraries. Accessed August 2013.

5. David Nasaw, *The Patriarch: The Remarkable Life and Turbulent Times of Joseph P. Kennedy* (New York: Penguin, 2012), 789.

6. "Neil Gaiman Talks About His Love of Libraries," *BookPage* (April 14, 2010). http: //www.bookpage.com/the-book-case/2010/ 04/14/neil-gaiman-talks-about-his-love-of-libraries/. Accessed August 2013. Cory Doctorow has made similar statements, one of which, worth reading, is here: http://www. natesbroadcast.com/journal/cory-doctorow-answers-those-blowhards-who-ask-why-we-still-need-libraries. Accessed August 2013.

7. Association of College and Research Libraries, "2012 Top Ten Trends in Academic Libraries," *College and Research Library News* Vol. 73 (6) (June 2012), 311–320.

8. See Robert J. Bliwise, "Books by Design," *The Chronicle of Higher Education* (September 6, 2013), B12–B14.

9. Wayne Smutz, "MOOCs Are No Education Panacea, but Here's What Can Make Them Work," *Forbes* (April 8, 2013). http:// www.forbes.com/sites/forbesleadership forum/2013/04/08/moocs-are-no-educa tion-panacea-but-heres-what-can-make-them-work/. Accessed May 2013.

Chapter 13

1. Quoted in Robert Darnton, *The Case for Books: Past, Present, and Future* (New York: Public Affairs, 2009), xiv–xv.

2. William Shakespeare, *Julius Caesar*, Act 1, Scene II, lines 140–142.

3. Bureau of Labor Statistics, *Occupation Outlook Handbook 2012–2013 Edition*, "Librarians." http://www.bls.gov/ooh/Educa tion-Training-and-Library/Librarians.htm. Accessed October 2013.

4. Jacquelyn Smith, "The Best and Worst Master's Degrees for Jobs," *Forbes* (June 6, 2011). http://www.forbes.com/sites/jacque

lynsmith/2011/06/06/the-best-and-worst-masters-degrees-for-jobs/. Accessed May 2013. And yes, I've read all the counterpoints to this article, including Mia Breitkopf's "61 Non-Librarian Jobs for LIS Graduates" (http://infospace.ischool.syr.edu/2011/12/23/61-non-librarian-jobs-for-librarians/). But isn't that the point of Smith's assertion: all of those 61 jobs could be done *without* the LIS, making the library degree superfluous?

5. See the least hysterical of the posts regarding these comments at "A Library Without Librarians? The Opinion of a PhD-Librarian on the Jeff Trzeciak Controversy," *Lakia MedLibLo* (April 20, 2011). http://laikaspoetnik.wordpress.com/2011/04/20/a-library-without-librarians-the-opinion-of-a-phd-librarian-on-the-jeffrey-trzeciak-controversy/; and Steven Mandeville-Gamble, *Outloud Librarian* (May 22, 2011). http://outloudlibrarian.blogspot.com/2011/05/fear-and-loathing-in-academic-libraries.html. Accessed May 2013. Only about 15 seconds of the notorious presentation is available here: http://www.youtube.com/watch?v=hplDHVCk85E. All other links have ended up with link rot, so to say. The medical librarian blog provides a good view of the "offending" slide 56.

6. Joan C. Durrance, "Reference Success: Does the 55 Percent Rule Tell the Whole Story?" *Library Journal* (April 15, 1987). http://durrance.people.si.umich.edu/CPLScholar2004/JCDLibraryJournal_1989.pdf. Accessed June 2013.

7. Marie L. Radford and Lynn Silipigni Connaway, "Not Dead Yet! A Longitudinal Study of Query Type and Ready Reference Accuracy in Live Chat and IM Reference" (2012). http://www.oclc.org/resources/research/publications/library/2012/radford-connaway-lisr.pdf. Accessed June 2013.

8. Karl Albrecht, *At America's Service: How Corporations Can Revolutionize the Way They Treat Their Customers* (Homewood, IL: Dow Jones–Irwin, 1988), 14–16.

9. Jordan Novet, "The Future According to Google," *Gigaom* (May 17, 2013). http://gigaom.com/2013/05/17/the-future-according-to-google/. Accessed May 2013.

10. John Budd, *The Changing Academic Library: Operations, Culture, Environment* (Chicago: The Association of College & Research Libraries, 2012), 119.

11. Charles Martell, *The Client-Centered Academic Library: An Organizational Model.* (Westport, CT: Greenwood, 1983), 22. Also quoted in part in Budd, p.119.

12. I say eager for print because recall that a recent Rasmussen poll indicates that even young people like printed materials. See Kathryn Zickuhr, Lee Rainie and Kristen Purcell, *Young Americans Library Habits and Expectations*, Pew Internet & American Life Project (June 25, 2013). http://libraries.pewinternet.org/2013/06/25/younger-americans-library-services/. Accessed August 2013.

13. For more, see Charles D. Wrege and Ronald G. Greenwood, *Frederick W. Taylor: The Father of Scientific Management: Myth and Reality* (Homewood, IL: Business One Irwin, 1991). Taylor held, more or less, that each job had one best way of doing it, and only through scientific analyzing could one ascertain that "one best way" of doing every job. He didn't necessarily advocate a one-size-fits-all approach but inevitably his theory devolved into that.

14. See Budd, 338.

15. Miriam Hospitals Centers for Behavioral and preventive Medicine, "Texting, Social Networking and Other Media Use Linked to Poor Academic Performance," *Science News* (April 11, 2013). http://www.sciencedaily.com/releases/2013/04/130411131755.htm. Accessed June 2013.

16. Eric Topol, *The Creative Destruction of Medicine: How the Digital Revolution Will Create Better Health Care* (New York: Basic Books, 2012), 3–5.

17. Juliette Garside, "Facebook Loses Millions of Users as Biggest Markets Peak," *The Guardian* (April 28, 2013). http://www.guardian.co.uk/technology/2013/apr/28/facebook-loses-users-biggest-markets. Accessed May 2013.

18. But don't put any money on that. And this serves to underscore what I said at the beginning of this chapter. Scryers are beaten or shot for a reason: we are nearly always wrong.

19. Kristen Domonell, "The Rights Question," *University Business* (May 2013), 44–46.

20. Roy Wood, "Understanding Technological Hype Cycles," *Wired* (August 30, 2012). http://www.wired.com/geekdad/2012/08/understanding-technological-hype-cycles/. Accessed May 2013.

21. Mark Hachman, "Gartner May Be Too Scared to Say It, but the PC Is Dead," *ReadWrite* (April 5, 2103). http://readwrite.com/2013/04/05/gartner-may-be-too-scared-to-say-it-but-the-pc-is-dead. Accessed May 2013.

22. Topol, 181.

23. Kel Fidler, "Why the Internet Will Never Replace Universities," *The Telegraph* (May 28, 2013). http://www.telegraph.co.uk/education/universityeducation/10059088/Why-the-internet-will-never-replace-universities.html. Accessed May 2013.

24. American Library Association, *The State of America's Libraries, 2013*. http://www.ala.org/news/state-americas-libraries-report-2013/academic-libraries. Accessed May 2013.

25. Lisa Fleisher, "City Schools Are Quietly Using Fewer Librarians," *Wall Street Journal* (August 11, 2013). http://online.wsj.com/article/SB10001424127887324769704579006604137520932.html. Accessed August 2013.

26. Liz Bury, "Library Campaigners Predict 1,000 Closures by 2016," *The Guardian* (July 12, 2013). http://www.theguardian.com/books/2013/jul/12/library-campaigners-1000-closures-2016. Accessed August 2013.

27. See, for example, Richard DeMillio, "Traditional Institutions Will Close, Number of Colleges and Universities Will Rise," *The Evolllution* [*sic*]. (March 20, 2013). http://c21u.gatech.edu/sites/default/files/buzz/Traditional%20Institutions%20Will%20Close,%20Number%20of%20Colleges%20and%20Universities%20Will%20Rise%20-%20Richard%20DeMillo.pdf. Accessed June 2013. And see Jeffrey J. Selingo, "Colleges Struggling to Stay Afloat," *New York Times* (April 12, 2013). http://www.nytimes.com/2013/04/14/education/edlife/many-colleges-and-universities-face-financial-problems.html?pagewanted=all. Accessed June 2013. And Nathan Harden, "The End of the University as We Know It," *American Interest* (January/February 2013). http://www.the-american-interest.com/article.cfm?piece=1352. Accessed June 2013.

28. Harden, "The End of the University as We Know It."

29. Jeff Gamet, "Apple Ebook Price Fixing Trail: Amazon Had the Same Deal," *The Mac Observer* (June 6, 2013). http://www.macobserver.com/tmo/article/apple-ebook-price-fixing-trial-amazon-had-the-same-deal. Accessed June 2013. Also, Sam Gustin, "Apple Says It's Not an Ebook Crook as Price Fixing Trial Begins," *Time* (June 4, 2013). http://business.time.com/2013/06/04/apple-says-its-not-an-e-book-crook-as-price-fixing-trial-begins/. Accessed June 2013.

30. It has been tried but found politically inexpedient.

31. Tim Vanson, "Super-Libraries Herald a New Age in the Life of a Humble Institution," *The Guardian* (October 10, 2013). http://www.theguardian.com/public-leaders-network/2013/oct/10/super-libraries-birmingham-public-resources. Accessed October 2013.

32. ALA, *The State of America's Libraries: 2013*. http://www.ala.org/news/state-americas-libraries-report-2013/academic-libraries. Accessed May 2013.

33. John Regazzi, "Comparing Academic Library Spending with Public Libraries, Public K–12 Schools, Higher Education Institutions, and Public Hospitals, 1998–2008," *Journal of Academic Libraries* Vol. 38 (4) (July 2012), 205–216.

34. Susie Allen, "Mansueto Library Creates New Space for Thought," The University of Chicago. http://www.uchicago.edu/features/20110520_mansueto/. Accessed May 2013.

35. See, for example, Lucien X. Polastron, *The Great Digitization and the Quest to Know Everything* (Rochester, VT: Inner Traditions, 2009).

36. For more on this (and it's really quite interesting), see Lane Wilkinson, "Creation, Consumption, and the Library," *Sense and Reference: A Philosophical Library Blog* (May 21, 2013). http://senseandreference.wordpress.com/2013/05/21/creation-consumption-and-the-library/. Accessed May 2013. A

short blog appears here: "The Library as a Makerspace," *Between the Lines: The Washington State Library Blog* (December 11, 2012). http://blogs.sos.wa.gov/library/index.php/2012/12/the-library-as-a-makerspace//. Accessed May 2013.

37. Justin Davidson, "All the Panic Over the New York Public Library's Renovation Plans Is Overwrought," *New York Magazine* (December 19, 2012). http://nymag.com/daily/intelligencer/2012/12/panic-over-nypls-renovation-is-overwrought.html. Accessed May 2013.

38. "Opponents Sue Over NYC Renovation Plan," *USA Today* (July 5, 2013). http://www.usatoday.com/story/news/nation/2013/07/05/nyc-library-renovation-lawsuit/2491687/. Accessed August 2013.

39. Jennifer Maloney, "New York Public Library Rethinks Design," *Wall Street Journal* (August 27, 2013). http://online.wsj.com/article/SB1000142412788732340710457903930291137452.html. Accessed September 2013.

40. Corydon Ireland, "Library in Transition," *Harvard Gazette* (October 4, 2012). http://news.harvard.edu/gazette/story/2012/10/library-in-transition/. Accessed May 2012.

41. Many such stories exist. See, for example, Samuel Y. Weinstock, Justin C. Worland, and Crimson Staff Writers, "The Sun Sets on the Traditional Library," *The Harvard Crimson* (May 24, 2012). http://www.thecrimson.com/article/2012/5/24/libraries-digitize-centralize-staff/?page=single#. Accessed May 2013.

42. Matthew Reisz, "Librarians or Baristas?" *Inside Higher Education* (November 26, 2012). http://www.insidehighered.com/news/2012/11/26/oxford-debates-role-its-librarians-and-libraries. Accessed May 2013.

43. David Streitfeld, "One on One: Jason Merkoski and the View of Ebooks from the Inside," *New York Times* (April 8, 2013). http://bits.blogs.nytimes.com/2013/04/08/one-on-one-jason-merkoski-and-the-view-of-e-books-from-the-inside/?smid=tw-share. Accessed May 2013.

44. Anna-Lilja Dawson, "1.1 Million Books to Be Removed from University of Saskatchewan Libraries," *The Ubyssey* (January 6, 2013). http://ubyssey.ca/news/libraries-912/. Accessed May 2013.

45. Ralph Blumenthal, "College Libraries Set Aside Books in a Digital Age," *New York Times* (May 14, 2005). http://www.nytimes.com/2005/05/14/education/14library.html?pagewanted=all&_r=0. Accessed May 2013.

46. K. C. Scharnberg, "Nation's First Bookless Library on University Campus Is Thriving at UTSA," *USA Today*, (Friday, May 13, 2013). http://utsa.edu/today/2013/03/aetlibrary.html. Accessed May 2013.

47. Joanna Stern, "The First Bookless Public Library: Texas to Have BibliTech," *ABC News* (January 13, 2013). http://abcnews.go.com/Technology/bookless-public-library-texas-home-bibliotech/story?id=18213091#.UZ-8K5w5P9p. Accessed May 2013.

48. Tim Newcomb, "Is a Bookless Library Still a Library?" *Time* (July 11, 2011). http://www.time.com/time/nation/article/0,8599,2079800,00.html. Accessed May 2013.

49. "Libraries Without Books? Not Here. Not Yet," *Library Stuff* (October 7, 2013). http://www.librarystuff.net/2013/10/07/libraries-without-books-not-here-not-yet/. Accessed October 2013.

50. Marc Bodnick, "Will Public Libraries Become Extinct?" *Forbes* (October 2, 2012). http://www.forbes.com/sites/quora/2012/10/02/will-public-libraries-become-extinct/. Accessed May 2013.

51. See Barbara Fister, "The Library as a Free Enterprise," *Inside Higher Ed* (December 13, 2012), http://www.insidehighered.com/blogs/library-babel-fish/library-free-enterprise; and Karen Schneider, "How OPACS Suck, Part 1, Relevance Ranking (or the Lack of It)," *ALA Tech Source* (March 13, 2006), http://www.alatechsource.org/blog/2006/03/how-opacs-suck-part-1-relevance-rank-or-the-lack-of-it.html. Accessed May 2013.

Chapter 14

1. E. H. Warmington (ed.), *Remains of Old Latin, Vol. VI Archaic Inscriptions* (Cambridge, MA: Harvard University Press, 1959), 247.

2. I am hardly the first to think in this

manner. See *Reflecting on the Future of Academic and Public Libraries*, edited by Peter Hernon and Joseph R. Matthews (Chicago: American Library Association, 2013), especially Chapter 3.

3. A story is told about the famous preacher, Dwight L. Moody. Moody was said to have been walking along a Chicago sidewalk with friends when a well-known saloon-keeper flashed a hundred dollar bill before him and asked if he would take it. Moody snatched it up and pocketed it. His friends were horrified. He looked at them and said, "The devil has had that money long enough."

4. See for example, Chris Bourg, "Agendas: Everyone Has One," *Feral Librarian* (August 25, 2013). http://chrisbourg.word press.com/2013/08/25/agendas-everyone-has-one/. Accessed September 2013. I don't dispute her contention, just her conclusion. It's fine to have an agenda but it's best that it not show obtrusively to those controlling the purse strings.

5. Randall Stross, *Planet Google: One Company's Audacious Plan to Organize Everything We Know* (New York: Free Press, 2008), 200.

6. John M. Budd, *The Changing Academic Library: Operations, Culture, Environment* (Chicago: Association of Colleges and Research Libraries, 2012), 258–259.

7. Budd, 208–209.

8. Brian T. Sullivan, "Academic Library Autopsy Report, 2050," *The Chronicle of Higher Education* (January 2, 2011). http://chronicle.com/article/article-content/125767/. Accessed June 2013.

9. For an interesting overview of this, see Nancy Kranich, "Libraries the Information Commons of Civil Society," in *Shaping the Network Society: The New Role of Civil Society in Cyberspace*, edited by Douglas Schuler and Peter Day (Cambridge, MA: MIT Press, 2004), 282–285.

10. Reuben Fischer-Baum, "Infographic: Is Your State's Highest-Paid Employee a Coach? (Probably.)," *Deadspin* (May 9, 2013). http://deadspin.com/infographic-is-your-states-highest-paid-employee-a-co-4896352 28. Accessed June 2013. Even if you account for the revenue coaches bring in, you have to

understand that that money isn't going elsewhere. See also Allie Grasgreen, "Disproportionate Paychecks," *Inside Higher Ed* (May 8, 2013). http://www.insidehighered.com/news/2013/05/08/coaching-salaries-rising-10-times-faster-instructional-salaries. Accessed June 2013. The NCAA released a report in 2010 that showed only 14 of the 120 football subdivisions made money, down from the year before: Associated Press Reports, "NCAA Report: Economy Cuts into Sports," *ESPN* (August 23, 2010). http://sports.espn.go.com/ncf/news/story?id=549 0686. Accessed June 2013. Sean Gregory, "College Sports Spending: The Real March Madness?" *Time* (March 21, 2013). http://keepingscore.blogs.time.com/2013/03/21/college-sports-spending-the-real-march-madness/. Accessed June 2013.

11. Chad Perrin, "Why Strict Copyright Enforcement Is Becoming Obsolete," *TechRepublic* (June 13, 2011). http://www.techre public.com/blog/security/why-strict-copyright-enforcement-is-becoming-obso lete/5616.

12. David H. Freedman, *Why the Experts Keep Failing Us—and How to Know When to Trust Them* (New York: Little, Brown, 2010), 112, note 2.

13. Alison Fairbrother, "U.S. Scientists Top Research-Fraud List—How Concerned Should We Be?" *Huffington Post* (December 25, 2010). http://www.politicsdaily.com/2010/12/25/u-s-scientists-top-research-fraud-list-how-concerned-should/. Accessed June 2013. See also Elizabeth Gibney, "Tangled Webs Unwoven Online," *Times Higher Education* (June 13, 2013). http://www.timeshighereducation.co.uk/news/tangled-webs-unwoven-online/2004690.article. Accessed June 2013.

14. Eric Schmidt and Jared Cohen, *The New Digital Age: Reshaping the Future of People, Nations, and Business* (New York: Knopf, 2013), 253.

15. Tina Brown, "A Turn of the Page for Newsweek," *The Daily Beast* (October 18, 2012). http://www.thedailybeast.com/art icles/2012/10/18/a-turn-of-the-page-for-newsweek.html. Accessed June 2013.

16. Susanna Kim, "Magazines May Fol-

low Newsweek's Lead in Shuttering Print Version," *ABC News* (October 18, 2012). http://abcnews.go.com/Business/maga zines-follow-newsweeks-lead-shuttering-print-version/story?id=17508305#.Ubtwjpz NmRs. Accessed June 2013.

17. Jean-Louis Gassée, "Jeff Bezos and the Washington Post—A Culture War," *The Guardian* (August 12, 2013). http://www. theguardian.com/technology/2013/aug/12/ jeff-bezos-washington-post. Accessed August 2013.

18. Jon Gertner, *The Idea Factory: Bell Labs and the Great Age of American Innovation* (New York: Penguin, 2012), 342–343. I think this might well be the idea behind the recent movie *Elysium*.

19. Andrius Plepys, "The Grey Side of ITC," *Environmental and Assessment Impact Review* Vol. 22 (5) (October 2002), 509–523.

20. Plepys, 510.

21. Clifford Lynch, "Ebooks in 2013: Promises Broken, Promises Kept, and Faustian Bargains," *American Libraries* (June 2013). http://www.amercianlibrariesmagazine.org/ article/ebooks-2013. Accessed June 2013.

22. *Ernst Cassirer on Form and Technology*, edited by Aud Sissel Hoel and Ingvild Folkvord (New York: Palgrave Macmillan, 2012), 15–16.

23. Arik Hesseldahl, "Cyberwar in Iran Comes Home to U.S. Banks. Is Anyone Surprised?" *All Things D* (January 9, 2013). http://allthingsd.com/20130109/cyberwar-in-iran-comes-home-to-u-s-banks-is-any one-surprised/. Accessed June 2013.

24. Arik Hesseldahl, "Denials of Service Attacks Are Getting Bigger and Badder," *All Things D* (April 17, 2013). http://allthingsd. com/20130417/denial-of-service-attacks-are-getting-bigger-and-badder/. Accessed June 2013.

25. Lorenzo Franceschi-Bicchierai, "16-Year-Old Arrested After 'Biggest Cyberat-tack Ever,'" *Mashable* (September 9, 2013). http://mashable.com/2013/09/26/teen ager-cyberattack-spamhaus/?utm_campaign =Feed%3A+Mashable+%28Mashable%29 &utm_cid=Mash-Prod-RSS-Feedburner-All-Partial&utm_medium=feed&utm_ source=feedburner. Accessed October 2013.

26. Carl Franzen, "Largest Public Denial of Service Attack in Internet History Linked to European Spam Dispute," *The Verge* (March 27, 2013). http://www.theverge.com/2013/ 3/27/4152540/largest-ddos-attack-spam haus-linked-to-cyberbunker-spam. Accessed June 2013.

27. Adam Clark Estes, "The Future of Hack Sounds Pretty Ridiculous," *The Atlantic* (February 21, 2012). http://www.theat lanticwire.com/technology/2012/02/future-hacking-sounds-pretty-ridiculous/48962/. Accessed July 2013.

28. Peggy Noonan, "What We Lose If We Give Up Privacy," *Wall Street Journal* (August 15, 2013). http://online.wsj.com/art icle/SB10001424127887323639704579015 101857760922.html. Accessed August 2013.

29. Lawrence Lessig, "It's Time to Rewrite the Internet to Give Us Better Privacy, and Security," *The Daily Beast*. (June 12, 2013). http://www.thedailybeast.com/art icles/2013/06/12/it-s-time-to-rewrite-the-internet-to-give-us-better-privacy-and-secur ity.html. Accessed July 2013.

30. Christopher Shea, "Watch What You Think. Others Can," *The Chronicle Review* Vol. LX (No. 3) (September 20, 2013), 6–9.

31. Tom Gara, "Are Facebook Users Peaking? Beware of the Missing Mobiles," *Wall Street Journal Online* (May 2, 2013). http:// blogs.wsj.com/corporate-intelligence/2013/ 05/02/are-facebook-users-peaking-beware-of-the-missing-mobiles/. Accessed July 2013.

32. *Trends in College Spending, 1998– 2008: Where Does the Money Come From? Where Does It Go? What Does It Buy?* Delta Cost Project (Lumina Foundation, 2010). http://www.deltacostproject.org/resources/ pdf/Trends-in-College-Spending-98-08.pdf. Accessed July 2013,

33. Jennifer Medina, "California Cuts Threaten the Status of Universities," *New York Times* (June 1, 2012). http://www.ny times.com/2012/06/02/us/california-cuts-threaten-the-status-of-universities.html? pagewanted=all&_r=0. Accessed July 2013.

34. Kathryn Zickuhr, Lee Rainie and Kristen Purcell, *Younger Americans' Library Habits and Expectations*, Pew Internet & American Life Project (June 25, 2013). http:

//libraries.pewinternet.org/2013/06/25/ younger-americans-library-services/. Accessed July 2013.

35. A good summary of states' economy ranking appears here: http://truecostblog. com/2012/01/01/us-state-economic-rank ings/. Accessed July 2013.

36. Although this relates mainly to public library funding, similar graphics could be made for academic libraries: http://www.ala. org/research/plftas/2011_2012/plftasgraph ics. Accessed July 2013.

37. David Schenk, *Data Smog: Surviving the Information Glut, Revised and Updated* (New York: HarperOne, 1998).

38. Nicholas Carr, *The Shallows: What the Internet Is Doing to Our Brains* (New York: W. W. Norton, 2011).

39. U. Nitzan, E. Shoshan, S. Lev-Ran, S. Fennig, "Internet-Related Psychosis—A Sign of the Times," *Israel Journal of Psychiatry and Related Sciences* Vol. 48 (3) (2011), 207–211.

40. Patricia Cohen, "Internet Use Affects Memory, Study Finds," *New York Times* (July 14, 2011). http://www.nytimes.com/2011/ 07/15/health/15memory.html?_r=0. Accessed July 2013.

41. Carr, 134–135.

42. Farhad Manjoo, "You Won't Finish This Article," *Slate Magazine* (June 6, 2013). http://www.slate.com/articles/technology/ technology/2013/06/how_people_read_ online_why_you_won_t_finish_this_art icle.html. Accessed June 2013.

43. Suzanne LeBarre, "Why We're Shut-ting Off Our Comments," *Popular Science* (September 24, 2013). http://www.popsci. com/science/article/2013-09/why-were-shutting-our-comments?. Accessed October 2013.

44. Maria Konnikova, "The Psychology of Online Comments," *New Yorker* (October 24, 2013). http://www.newyorker.com/on line/blogs/elements/2013/10/the-psychol ogy-of-online-comments.html. Accessed Oc-tober 2013.

45. This is, of course, Morozov's argu-ment in *To Save Everything, Click Here: The Folly of Technological Solutionism* (New York: Public Affairs, 2013).

46. See Carr, 120–122.

47. Danny Carter, "College Students: We're 'Digitally Distracted,'" *ECampusNews* (October 24, 2013). http://www.ecampus news.com/research/college-students-digit ally-222/. Accessed October 2013.

48. See also Neil Gaiman, "Neil Gaiman: Why Our Future Depends on Libraries, Reading, and Daydreaming," *The Guardian* (October 15, 2013). http://www.theguard ian.com/books/2013/oct/15/neil-gaiman-future-libraries-reading-daydreaming. Ac-cessed October 2013.

Selected Bibliography

Books

Agger, Ben. *The Virtual Shelf: A Contemporary Sociology.* Oxford: Blackwell Publishing, 2004.

Albrecht, Karl. *At America's Service: How Corporations Can Revolutionize the Way They Treat Their Customers.* Homewood, Illinois: Dow Jones–Irwin, 1988.

Anderson, Chris. *Free. The Future of a Radical Price.* New York: Hyperion, 2009.

Au, Wagner James. *The Making of Second Life: Notes from the New World.* New York: Collins, 2008.

Baker, Nicholson. *Double Fold: Libraries and the Assault on Paper.* New York: Random House, 2001.

Bauerlein, Mark. *Dumbest Generation: How the Digital Age Stupefies Young Americans and Jeopardizes Our Future (Or Don't Trust Anyone Under 30).* New York: Jeremy P. Tarcher/Penguin, 2008.

Becerra-Fernandez, Irma, and Dorothy Leidner, eds. *Knowledge Management: An Evolutionary View.* Armonk, New York: M.E. Sharpe, 2008.

Birkerts, Sven. *The Gutenberg Elegies: The Fate of Reading in the Electronic Age.* London: Faber and Faber, 1994.

Bivens-Tatum, Wayne. *Libraries and the Enlightenment.* Los Angeles: Library Juice Press, 2011.

Boellstorff, Tom. *Coming of Age in Second Life: An Anthropologist Explores the Virtually Human.* Princeton, New Jersey: Princeton University Press, 2008.

Borgman, Christine L. *Scholarship in the Digital Age: Information, Infrastructure, and the Internet.* Cambridge, Massachusetts: MIT Press, 2007.

Budd, John M. *The Changing Academic Library: Operations, Culture, Environments.* Chicago: Association of College and Research Libraries, 2012.

Carr, Nicholas. *The Shallows: What the Internet Is Doing to Our Brains.* New York: W.W. Norton, 2010.

Cross, Mary. *Bloggerati, Twitterati: How Blogs and Twitter Are Transforming Popular Culture.* Santa Barbara, California: Praeger–ABC-CLIO, 2011.

Crystal, David. *Txtng: The Gr8 Db8.* Oxford: Oxford University Press, 2008.

Darnton, Robert. *The Case for Books: Past, Present, and Future.* New York: Public Affairs, 2009.

Davidow, William H. *Overconnected: The Promise and Threat of the Internet.* Harrison, New York: Delphinium Books, 2011.

Deibert, Ronald, John Palfrey, Rafal Rohozinski, and Jonathan Zittrain. *Access Denied: The Practice and Policy of Global Internet Filtering*. Cambridge, Massachusetts: MIT Press, 2008.

Drake, William J., and Ernest J. Wilson III, eds. *The Information Revolution and Global Politics*. Cambridge, Massachusetts: MIT Press, 2008.

Eden, Bradford Lee, ed. *Innovative Redesign and Reorganization of Library Technical Services: Paths for the Future and Case Studies*. Westport, Connecticut: Libraries Unlimited, 2004. Print.

_____, ed. *More Innovative Redesign and Reorganization of Library Technical Services*. Westport, Connecticut: Libraries Unlimited, 2009.

Edwards, Douglas. *I'm Feeling Lucky: The Confessions of Google Employee Number 59*. Boston: Houghton Mifflin Harcourt, 2011.

Eisenberg, Michael B., Carrie A. Lowe, and Kathleen L. Spitzer. *Information Literacy: Essential Skills for the Information Age*. 2nd edition. Westport, Connecticut: Libraries Unlimited, 2004.

Freedman, David H. *Wrong: Why Experts* Keep Failing Us—And How to Know When Not to Trust Them*. New York: Little, Brown, 2010.

Friedman, Thomas. *The World Is Flat: A Brief History of the Twenty-First Century*. New York: Farrar, Straus, and Giroux, 2005.

Garfinkel, Simson. *Database Nation: The Death of Privacy in the 21st Century*. Sebastopol, California: O'Reilly Media, 2000.

Gertner, Jon. *The Idea Factory: Bell Labs and the Great Age of American Innovation*. New York: Penguin Press, 2012.

Gillespie, Tarleton. *Wired Shut: Copyright and the Shape of Digital Culture*. Cambridge, Massachusetts: MIT Press, 2007.

Gorman, Michael. *The Enduring Library: Technology, Tradition, and the Quest for Balance*. Chicago: American Library Association, 2003.

Graff, Garrett M. *The First Campaign: Globalization, the Web, and the Race for the White House*. New York: Farrar, Straus, and Giroux, 2007.

Gregory, Gwen Meyer, ed. *The Successful Academic Librarian: Winning Strategies from Library Leaders*. Medford, New Jersey: Information Today, 2005.

Hernon, Peter, and Joseph R. Matthews, eds. *Reflecting on the Future of Academic and Public Libraries*. Chicago: American Library Association, 2013.

Hoel, Aud Sissel, and Ingvild Folkvord, eds. *Ernst Cassirer on Form and Technology*. New York: Palgrave Macmillan, 2012.

Jarvis, Jeff. *What Would Google Do?* New York: Collins, 2009.

Johns, Adrian. *Piracy: The Intellectual Property Wars from Gutenberg to Gates*. Chicago: University of Chicago Press, 2009.

Keen, Andrew. *The Cult of the Amateur: How Today's Internet Is Killing Our Culture*. New York: Doubleday, 2007.

Kimball, Roger. *The Fortunes of Permanence: Culture and Anarchy in an Age of Amnesia*. South Bend, Indiana: St. Augustine's Press, 2012.

Kres, Gunther. *Literacy in the New Media Age*. New York: Routledge, 2003.

Krotoski, Aleks. *Untangling the Web: What the Internet Is Doing to You*. London: Faber and Faber, 2013.

Krug, Steve. *Don't Make Me Think! A Common Sense Approach to Web Usability*. 2nd edition. Berkeley, California: New Riders Publishing, 2006.

Lankes, R. David. *The Atlas of New Librarianship*. Cambridge, Massachusetts: MIT Press, 2011.

Levine, Rick, Christopher Locke, Doc Searls, and David Weinberger. *The Cluetrain Manifesto:*

The End of Business as Usual. Cambridge, Massachusetts: Perseus Books, 2000 (reprint 2009).

Levine, Robert. *Free Ride: How Digital Parasites Are Destroying the Culture Business, and How the Culture Business Can Fight Back.* New York: Doubleday, 2011.

Levy, Steven. *In the Plex: How Google Thinks, Works, and Shapes Our Lives.* New York: Simon & Schuster, 2011.

Mackey, Margaret. *Literacies Across Media: Playing the Text.* New York: Routledge, 2007.

Mash, S. David. *Decision-Making in the Absence of Certainty: A Study in the Context of Technology and the Construction of 21st Century Libraries.* Chicago: Association of College and Research Libraries, 2011.

McChesney, Robert W., and Victor Pickard, eds. *Will the Last Reporter Please Turn Out the Lights: The Collapse of Journalism and What Can Be Done to Fix It.* New York: New Press, 2011.

Miller, Michael. *Googlepedia: The Ultimate Google Resource.* Indianapolis: Que, 2008.

Miller, William, and Rita M. Pellen, eds. *Googlization of Libraries.* New York: Routledge, 2009.

Montanelli, Dale S., and Patricia F. Stenstrom, eds. *People Come First: User-Centered Academic Library Service.* Chicago: Association of College and Research Libraries, 1999.

Morozov, Evgeny. *The Net Delusion: The Dark Side of Internet Freedom.* New York: Public Affairs, 2011.

_____. *To Save Everything, Click Here: The Folly of Technological Solutionism.* New York: Public Affairs, 2013.

Morville, Peter. *Ambient Findability.* Cambridge, Massachusetts: O'Reilly, 2005.

Neal, Diane Rasmussen, ed. *Social Media for Academics: A Practical Guide.* Oxford, England: Chandos Publishing, 2012.

O'Harrow, Robert, Jr. *No Place to Hide.* New York: Free Press, 2005.

Polanka, Sue, ed. *No Shelf Required: E-Books in Libraries.* Chicago: American Library Association, 2011.

Polastron, Lucien X. *The Great Digitization and the Quest to Know Everything.* Translated by Jon E. Graham. Rochester, Vermont: Inner Traditions, 2009.

Putnam, Robert. *Bowling Alone: The Collapse and Revival of the American Community.* New York: Simon & Schuster, 2000.

Rosen, Larry D., Ph.D. *Me, My Space, and I: Parenting the Net Generation.* New York: Macmillan, 2007.

Schmidt, Eric, and Jared Cohen. *The New Digital Age: Reshaping the Future of People, Nations and Business.* New York: Knopf, 2013.

Schuler, Douglas and Peter Day, eds. *Shaping the Network Society: The New Role of Civil Society in Cyberspace.* Cambridge, Massachusetts: MIT Press, 2004.

Shirky, Clay. *Here Comes Everybody. The Power of Organizing Without Organizations.* New York: Penguin Press, 2008.

Silver, Nate. *The Signal and the Noise: Why So Many Predictions Fail—But Some Don't.* New York: Penguin Press, 2012.

Stoll, Clifford. *Silicon Snake Oil: Second Thoughts on the Information Highway.* New York: Doubleday, 1995.

Stross, Randall. *Planet Google: One Company's Audacious Plan to Organize Everything We Know.* New York: Free Press, 2008.

Sunstein, Cass R. *Infotopia: How Many Minds Produce Knowledge.* New York: Oxford University Press, 2006.

Tancer, Bill. *Click: What Millions of People Are Doing Online and Why It Matters.* New York: Hyperion, 2008.

Tapscott, Don. *Grown Up Digital: How the Net Generation Is Changing Your World*. New York: McGraw-Hill, 2009.

_____, and Anthony D. Williams. *Macrowikinomics: Rebooting Business and the World*. New York: Penguin Group, 2010.

Thompson, Clive. *Smarter Than You Think: How Technology Is Changing Our Minds for the Better*. New York: Penguin Press, 2013.

Turkle, Sherry. *Alone Together: Why We Expect More from Technology and Less from Each Other*. New York: Basic Books, 2011.

_____, ed. *The Inner History of Devices*. Cambridge, Massachusetts: MIT Press, 2008.

Wallace, Patricia. *The Psychology of the Internet*. Cambridge, England: Cambridge University Press, 1999.

Weinberger, David. *Everything Is Miscellaneous: The Power of the New Digital Disorder*. New York: Times Books, 2007.

_____. *Too Big to Know: Rethinking Knowledge Now That the Facts Aren't the Facts, Experts Are Everywhere, and the Smartest Person in the Room Is the Room*. New York: Basic Books, 2011.

Yellin, Emily. *Your Call Is (Not That) Important to Us: Customer Service and What It Reveals About Our World and Our Lives*. New York: Free Press, 2009.

Articles

(N.B.: Web articles show the month in which they were accessed at least three different times.)

Abelson, Harold, et al. *Report to the President: MIT and the Prosecution of Aaron Swartz* (July 26, 2013), http://swartz-report.mit.edu/docs/report-to-the-president.pdf. Accessed August 2013.

Alter, Alexandra. "Your Ebook Is Reading You." *Huffington Post* (July 19, 2012), http://on line.wsj.com/article/SB10001424052702304870304577490950051438304.html?mo d=WSJ_Tech_RIGHTTopCarousel_1. Accessed April 2013.

"Anne Lamott: By the Book." *New York Times Review* (November 21, 2012), http://www. nytimes.com/2012/11/25/books/review/anne-lamott-by-the-book.html?pagewanted =all&_r=0. Accessed July 2013.

Anti-Defamation League. "Poisoning the Web: Hatred Online. The Internet as a Hate Tool." http://archive.adl.org/poisoning_web/net_hate_tool.asp. Accessed March 2013.

Bergman, Michael K. "The Deep Web: Surfacing Hidden Value." (August 2001). http://quod.lib.umich.edu/cgi/t/text/text-idx?c=jep;view=text;rgn=main;idno=33 36451.0007.104. Accessed February 2013.

Bilton, Ricardo. "Things Not Strings: How Google's New Hummingbird Algorithm Sets the Stage for the Future of Mobile Search." *VentureBeat* (October 2, 2013). http://ven turebeat.com/2013/10/02/things-not-strings-how-googles-new-hummingbird-algo rithm-sets-the-stage-for-the-future-of-mobile-search/. Accessed October 2013.

Bradford, K.T. "Why Borrowing an Ebook from the Library Is So Difficult." *Digital Trends* (June 15, 2013), http://www.digitaltrends.com/mobile/e-book-library-lending-bro ken-difficult/. Accessed June 2013.

Bridle, James. "E-readers: The Best Way to Get the World's Children Reading." *The Guardian* (September 8, 2013), http://www.theguardian.com/technology/2013/sep/08/ebooks- ereaders-worldreader-kade-ghana. Accessed September 2013.

Carr, Nicholas. "Is the Google Making Us Stupid?" *The Atlantic*. (July/August 2008). http://www.theatlantic.com/magazine/archive/2008/07/is-google-making-us-stu pid/306868/. Accessed March 2013.

_____. "Never Mind Ebooks. Why Print Books Are Here to Stay." *Wall Street Journal Online*

(January 5, 2013). http://online.wsj.com/article/SB1000142412788732387420457821956335369702.html. Accessed April 2013.

Christenson, Heather. "Mass Digitization Projects Update." (February 9, 2009), http://www.cdlib.org/cdlinfo/2009/02/09/mass-digitization-projects-update-2/. Accessed March 2013.

Coco, Pete. "Leaves of Graph." *ACRLog* (August 23, 2012). http://acrlog.org/2012/08/23/leaves-of-graph/. Accessed July 2013.

Cohen, Patricia. "Internet Use Affects Memory, Study Finds." *New York Times* (July 14, 2011), http://www.nytimes.com/2011/07/15/health/15memory.html?_r=0. Accessed July 2013.

Constine, Josh. "Google Framed as Book Stealer Bent on Data Domination in New Documentary." *TechCrunch* (Wednesday May 8, 2013), http://techcrunch.com/2013/05/08/google-book-search-and-the-world-brain-book/. Accessed July 2013.

Doctorow, Cory. "Libraries, Hackspaces, and E-waste: How Libraries Can Be the Hub of a Young Maker Revolution." *Raincoast* Books (February 24, 2013). http://www.raincoast.com/blog/details/guest-post-cory-doctorow-for-freedom-to-read-week// Accessed February 2013.

Ducut, Erick, Liu Fang, and Paul Fontello. "An Update on Uniform Resource Locator (URL) Decay in Medline Abstracts and Measures for its Mitigation." *BMC Medical Informatics & Decision making*. Vol. 8 (1) (2008), Special section 1–8.

Emley, Bryce. "How Google Flushes Knowledge Down the Toilet." *Salon*. (August 18, 2013), http://www.salon.com/2013/08/18/how_google_flushes_knowledge_down_the_toilet/. Accessed August 2013.

Fagin, Dan. "Alive and Tweeting." *Slate Magazine* (July 10, 2013), http://www.slate.com/articles/health_and_science/medical_examiner/2013/07/social_media_communication_facebook_twitter_linkedin_thought_i_was_dying.html. Accessed July 2013.

Friedman, Thomas. "Revolution Hits the Universities." *New York Times*. January 27, 2013. http://www.nytimes.com/2013/01/27/opinion/sunday/friedman-revolution-hits-the-universities.html?_r=1&, Accessed February 2013.

Gaiman, Neil. "Neil Gaiman: Why Our Future Depends on Libraries, Reading, and Daydreaming." *The Guardian* (October 15, 2013), http://www.theguardian.com/books/2013/oct/15/neil-gaiman-future-libraries-reading-daydreaming. Accessed October 2013.

Gompel, Stef van, and P. Bernt Hugenholtz. "The Orphan Works Problem: The Copyright Conundrum of Digitizing Large-Scale Audiovisual Archives, and How to Solve It." *Popular Communication* (January 1, 2010, Vol. 8), 61-71. http://www.ivir.nl/publications/vangompel/the_orphan_works_problem.pdf. Accessed February 2013.

Greenfield, Rebecca. "Judge Upholds Huffington Post's Right Not to Pay Bloggers." *The Atlantic Wire* (March 30, 2012). http://www.theatlanticwire.com/business/2012/03/judge-upholds-huffington-posts-right-not-pay-bloggers/50577/. Accessed March 2013.

Grimmelmann, James. "Eight Years Later, Google Books Fight Lumbers On." *Publishers Weekly* (September 5, 2013), http://www.publishersweekly.com/pw/by-topic/digital/content-and-e-books/article/58953-eight-years-later-the-google-books-fight-lumbers-on.html. Accessed September 2013.

Gustin, Sam. "Apple Found Guilty in Ebook Price Fixing Conspiracy Trial." *Time* (June 10, 2013), http://business.time.com/2013/07/10/apple-found-guilty-in-e-book-price-fixing-conspiracy-trial/. Accessed July 2013.

Hedstrom, Margaret. "Digital Preservation: A Time Bomb for Digital Libraries." *Computers and the Humanities* (vol. 31, 1998), 189-202. http://deepblue.lib.umich.edu/bitstream/handle/2027.42/42573/10579?sequence=1. Accessed July 2013.

Helft, Miguel. "Microsoft Will Shut Down Book Search Program." *New York Times* (May 28, 2008), http://www.nytimes.com/2008/05/24/technology/24soft.html?ref=tech nology&_r=0. Accessed March 2013.

Howard, Jennifer. "Digitizing the Personal Library." *Chronicle of Higher Education* (September 28, 2010), http://chronicle.com/blogs/wiredcampus/digitizing-the-personal-library/27222. Subscription may be required. Accessed March 2013.

_____. "Long Awaited Ruling in Copyright Case Mostly Favors Georgia State U." *Chronicle of Higher Education* (May 13, 2012), http://chronicle.com/article/Long-Awaited-Rul ing-in/131859/. Accessed March 2013.

_____. "Publishers Find Ways to Fight 'Link Rot' in Electronic Texts." *Chronicle of Higher Education*. Vol. 57 (11) (November 5, 2011).

_____. "Vanishing Act: A Modern Scholar's Ailments: Link Rot and Footnote Flight." *Chronicle of Higher Education* Vol. 57 (8), (October 10, 2010), A10–A11.

Kahle, Brewster. "Why Preserve Books? The New Physical Archive of the Internet Archive." (June 6, 2011) http://blog.archive.org/2011/06/06/why-preservebooks-the-new-phys ical-archive-of-the-internet-archive/. Accessed March 2013.

Kolata, Gina. "Scientific Articles Accepted. (Personal Checks, Too.)." *New York Times* (April 13, 2013), http://www.nytimes.com/2013/04/08/health/for-scientists-an-exploding-world-of-pseudo-academia.html?smid=tw-nytimesscience&seid=auto&_r=1&page wanted=all&. Accessed April 2013.

Lessig, Lawrence. "It's Time to Rewrite the Internet to Give Us Better Privacy and Security." *The Daily Beast*. (June 12, 2013), http://www.thedailybeast.com/articles/2013/06/12/it-s-time-to-rewrite-the-internet-to-give-us-better-privacy-and-security.html. Accessed July 2013.

Lin, Chia-Ching, and Chin-Chung Tsai. "A Navigation Flow Map Method of Representing Students' Searching Behaviors and Strategies on the Web, with Relation to Searching Outcomes." *Cyberpsychology & Behavior* 10 (5), (2007).

Liptak, Adam. "In Supreme Court Opinions, Web Links to Nowhere." *New York Times* (September 23, 2013), http://www.nytimes.com/2013/09/24/us/politics/in-supreme-court-opinions-clicks-that-lead-nowhere.html?_r=0. Accessed September 2013.

Liu, Z. "Print vs. Electronic Resources: A Study of Their Perceptions, Preferences, and Use. *Information Processing and Management* 42 (2) (2006). 583–592.

Lynch, Clifford. "Ebooks in 2013: Promises Broken, Promises Kept, and Faustian Bargains." *American Libraries* (June 2013), http://www.cni.org/wp-content/uploads/2013/05/ALA-Ebooks-Paper.pdf. Accessed June 2013.

Madrigal, Alexis C. "If You Can't Beat Them, Subvert 'Em. Countering Misinformation on the Viral Web." *The Atlantic* (October 31, 2012), http://www.theatlantic.com/tech nology/archive/2012/10/if-you-cant-beat-em-subvert-em-countering-misinformation-on-the-viral-web/264366/. Accessed April 2013.

Markwell, John, and David Brooks. "Evaluating Web-based Information: Access and Accuracy." *Journal of Chemical Information*. Vol. 85 (3) (March 2008), 458–459.

McLemee, Scott. "Commentary on the Digital Public Library of America." *Inside Higher Ed* (April 24, 2013), http://www.insidehighered.com/views/2013/04/24/commen tary-digital-public-library-america. Accessed July 2013.

_____. "In Search of the Missing Link." *Inside Higher Ed* (July 24, 2013). http://www.inside highered.com/views/2013/07/24/essay-link-rot. Accessed August 2013.

Mitrano, Tracy. "International Intellectual Property Enforcement—III." *Inside Higher Ed* (October 10, 2012), http://www.insidehighered.com/blogs/law-policy-and-it/inter national-intellectual-property-enforcement-iii. Accessed May 2013.

Naik, Gautam. "Storing Digital Data in DNA." *The Wall Street Journal* (January 24, 2013), http://online.wsj.com/article/SB10001424127887324539304578259883507543150.html. Accessed April 2013.

Nitzan, U., E. Shoshan, S. Lev-Ran, and S. Fennig. "Internet-Related Psychosis—A Sign of the Times." *Israel Journal of Psychiatry and Related Sciences* Vol. 48 (3) (2011), 207– 211.

Oberholzer-Gee, Felix, and Koleman Strumpf. "The Effect of File Sharing on Record Sales: An Empirical Analysis." (March 2004), http://www.unc.edu/~cigar/papers/FileSharing_March2004.pdf. Accessed April 2013.

Paczkowski, John. "Apple's Chances on an Ebook Ruling Appeal Are Lousy, Say Legal Scholars." *AllThingsD* (July 10, 2013), http://allthingsd.com/20130710/apples-chances-on-an-e-book-ruling-appeal-are-lousy-say-legal-scholars/. Accessed July, 2013.

_____. "Auto-Ban: German Court Orders Google to Delete Offensive Search Suggestions." *All Things D*, (May 14, 2013), http://allthingsd.com/20130514/auto-ban-german-court-orders-google-to-delete-offensive-search-suggestions/. Accessed May 2013.

Perlroth, Nicole, Jeff Larson, and Scott Shane. "N.S.A. Able to Foil Basic Safeguards of Privacy on Web." *New York Times* (September 5, 2013), http://www.nytimes.com/2013/09/06/us/nsa-foils-much-internet-encryption.html?pagewanted=all&_r=0. Accessed September 2013.

Piper, Andrew. "Out of Touch. E-Reading Isn't Reading." *Slate* (November 15, 2012), http://www.slate.com/articles/arts/culturebox/2012/11/reading_on_a_kindle_is_not_the_same_as_reading_a_book.single.html. Accessed July 2013.

Pogue, David. "Why Google Glass Is Creepy." *Scientific American* (May 21, 2013), http://www.scientificamerican.com/article.cfm?id=why-google-glass-is-creepy. Accessed August 2013.

Potok, Mark. "The Internet Hate and the Law." http://www.splcenter.org/get-informed/intelligence-report/browse-all-issues/2000/winter/internet-hate-and-the-law. (Winter 2000). Accessed March 2013.

Powell, Camira. "Don't Worry About a Thing." *AllThingsD* (March 18, 2013). http://allthingsd.com/20130318/dont-worry-about-a-thing/. Accessed March 2013.

Rainie, Lee, Sara Kiesler, Ruogu Kang, and Mary Madden. "Anonymity, Privacy, and Security Online." *Pew Internet & American Life Project* (September 5, 2013), http://www.pewinternet.org/Reports/2013/Anonymity-online.aspx. Accessed September 2013.

Rich, Mokoto. "Literacy Debate: Online, RU Really Reading." *New York Times* (July 27, 2008), http://www.nytimes.com/2008/07/27/books/27reading.html?pagewanted=all&_r=0. Accessed April 2013.

Ruedy, Nicole E., Francesca Gino, Celia Moore, and Maurice E. Schweitzer. "The Cheater's High: The Unexpected Affective Benefits of Unethical Behavior." *Journal of Personality and Social Psychology* Vol. 105 (4) (2013), 531–548, http://www.apa.org/pubs/journals/releases/psp-a0034231.pdf. Accessed October 2013.

Seelyle, Katherine Q. "Snared in the Web of a Wikipedia Liar." *New York Times* (December 4, 2005). http://www.nytimes.com/2005/12/04/weekinreview/04seelye.html?pagewanted=all&_r=0. Accessed February 2013.

Smith, Kevin. "The Problem with Permission." *Scholarly Communications @ Duke* (July 18, 2013), http://blogs.library.duke.edu/scholcomm/2013/07/18/the-problem-with-permission/. Accessed August 2013.

Tsukayama, Hayley. "Google News Searches Turn Up Incomplete Results, Researcher Finds." *The Washington Post* (May 13, 2013). https://ssl1.washingtonpost.com/business/technology/google-news-searches-turn-up-incomplete-results-critic-finds/2013/05/15/cde426dc-b80d-11e2-b94c-b684dda07add_story.html. Accessed July 2013.

Wieder, Ben. "iPads Could Hinder Teaching, Professors Say." *Chronicle of Higher Education*

(March 13, 2011), http://chronicle.com/article/iPads-for-College-Classrooms-/1266 81/. Accessed April 2013.

Zickuhr, Kathryn. "Who's Not Online and Why." *Pew Internet & American Life Project.* (September 25, 2013), http://pewinternet.org/Reports/2013/Non-internet-users/ Summary-of-Findings.aspx. Accessed September 2013.

Zickuhr, Kathryn and Aaron Smith. "Home Broadband 2013." *Pew Internet & American Life Project.* (August 26, 2013), http://pewinternet.org/Reports/2013/Broadband. aspx. Accessed September 2013.

Zickuhr, Kathryn, Lee Rainie and Kristen Purcell. *Young Americans' Library Habits and Expectations.* Pew Internet & American Life Project (June 25, 2013), http://libraries. pewinternet.org/2013/06/25/younger-americans-library-services/. Accessed July 2013.

Zickuhr, Kathryn, et al. "Younger Americans' Reading and Library Habits." *Pew Internet & American Life Project* (October 23, 2012), http://libraries.pewinternet.org/2012/ 10/23/younger-americans-reading-and-library-habits/. Accessed April 2013.

Zittrain, Jonathan. "Perma: Scoping and Addressing the Problem of 'Link Rot.'" *The Future of the Internet and How to Stop It* (September 22, 2013), http://blogs.law.harvard.edu/ futureoftheinternet/2013/09/22/perma/. Accessed September 2013.

Index